LYDIA

Seller of Purple

Also by Robert W. Faid:
A Scientific Approach to Christianity

LYDIA

Seller of Purple

ROBERT W. FAID
author of *A Scientific Approach to Christianity*

Bridge Publishing, Inc
Publishers of:
LOGOS • HAVEN • OPEN SCROLL

Lydia: Seller of Purple
Copyright © 1984 by Bridge Publishing, Inc.
All rights reserved
Printed in the United States of America
Library of Congress Catalog Card Number:
International Standard Book Number: 0-88270-569-5
Bridge Publishing, Inc., South Plainfield, New Jersey 07080

— Chapter One —

THYATIRA, A.D. 46

Lydia caught herself singing again and giggled as she saw Euodia smiling at her. She dumped the dough for the day's bread on the board and began twirling it into thin, round loaves. Euodia took them from the board, set them on racks in the open, glowing brick oven in the wall and shook her head at Lydia.

"From the look on your face, one would think you were already betrothed," she said.

Lydia put her hands on her hips. "Well, it's as good as done. Father has gone to see Mercatus to discuss it. And Father always gets what he goes after." She sat down and a frown crossed her face. "Well, almost always."

The older woman put her arm around Lydia. "He will," she said. "And I'm happy for you. If you think that's what you really want."

Lydia looked up at her sharply. "What do you mean by that? Why shouldn't I want to get married? I'm over twenty, Euodia. Most girls my age have been married for years."

The older woman stirred a pot on the hearth. "But you're different, Lydia. You always have been. You're special."

Lydia laughed and hugged the stout slave. "You're just prejudiced. But thanks anyway."

Although Euodia was a slave, owned by Lydia's family since birth, Lydia never thought of her as one. In fact, none of the slaves who worked either in the house or in the family-run business of dyeing cloth were thought of that way. They were, well, a part of the family and had always been treated as such. Euodia, Epaphroditus, Clement; all had been children of slaves owned by Lydia's grandfather years before.

"I wonder what they're saying," Lydia thought to herself. "I wonder what Nadius's father is demanding as a dowry." She stared out the door at the many shades of green of the trees and grass, the rows of vines in the vineyard stretching as far as her eyes could see. Spring had brought out the new, tender leaves in a rush, and the gentle rains had nurtured them, filling the air with spring smells and the music of the birds.

She really did not know Nadius very well. Of course everyone in Thyatira knew everyone else, for it was a small town. But she only knew him to be tall and handsome with a beautiful smile and a hearty laugh. He was several years older, at least twenty-four, she guessed. How fortunate for her that he had not been taken long ago by some other girl. But then, he had been busy in his father's business of making large clay jars that were sold to store everything from water to olive oil.

The gods have willed Nadius to be mine, she smiled to herself. And today, perhaps it will be official. Lydia could hardly wait for her father to return and tell her it had been arranged.

Licentor sipped his wine and nodded to the man at the table across from him. "As you know, my good friend, my daughter means very much to me. Since my dear wife died five years ago, Lydia has run the house and has done an excellent job of it."

The man nodded in agreement. "Lydia is a very capable girl,"

Mercatus said, "even if she does have a mind of her own, and at times a tongue to match."

Licentor put down his cup. "She has her mother's spirit. I tell you, Mercatus, no man wants a wife who has no spirit. It makes for a dull marriage."

"You realize, my dear Licentor, that my son, Nadius, is quite a catch. He is by far the most handsome young man in the city. And he excels in athletics. But for an unfortunate accident last year, he would have represented Thyatira at the Olympiad."

"I am aware of that," acknowledged Licentor. "It was very unfortunate that his foot slipped as he was about to throw the discus on his last try. But my daughter is quite a catch as well. I could have made arrangements many times in the past with well-placed families, even with a Roman one. Lydia will make a fine wife, strong, a hard worker, big-boned to bear many children. And she is a charming girl. Your Nadius could do much worse."

Mercatus placed his cup of wine on the table and faced Licentor. "We have known each other for a long time. May I speak very bluntly about something? I mean, I have no wish to hurt your feelings."

Licentor frowned. "Of course. Say what you will. My feelings are never hurt by honesty."

Mercatus cleared his throat. "Well, it is Lydia. It is just that, well, I mean to say she is rather—plain."

Licentor half raised himself from his chair and glared at the other man. "Plain! What do you mean, plain?"

Mercatus put out his hand toward the upset man. "I do not mean to detract from anything you have said about her. She is indeed charming. A hard worker. A bit headstrong perhaps, but not too much so. But she is not, how should I put it, not too—attractive."

Licentor sat down hard. He stared at the man across the table, his eyes burning, his mouth firm. "Mercatus, I must also speak with honesty. We both know what is truth. No, my daughter is not a raving beauty. She is twenty years of age, several years beyond the time when most girls are married. But listen to me and listen well. I know that your older sons have joined your business, both married and with children. I also know your business cannot afford another son in it. There are just so many mouths it can support."

"Well, now . . ." interrupted Mercatus. "I don't know—"

"Hear me out. I am giving half my business as Lydia's dowry. That and a promise of the other half at my death. That, my dear Mercatus, should make my daughter quite attractive, don't you think?"

Mercatus sat back. He pursed his lips and whistled. "Half your business?"

"Half my business. Do we have an agreement? I cannot waste any more time in foolish discussion. What do you say?"

Mercatus extended his hand. "It will be a pleasure," he said. "to welcome your . . . very attractive daughter into my family. Nadius will be very pleased." If he is not, Mercatus thought, I will soon make him so.

The men shook hands and finished their wine. "I shall make the announcement," Licentor told him. "But first I must return home and speak to my . . . very attractive daughter."

He left the inn and walked back toward his house. What foolish things we men say and do, he thought. Nadius is a weak and worthless scoundrel! But I must see to Lydia's future after I am gone. And the pains which he had been having in his heart left him quite doubtful as to how long that would be.

As Licentor entered the courtyard of his home, the dogs barked a welcome, announcing to those inside that he had arrived. Lydia looked out of the doorway at her father and her heart stood still. Licentor walked slowly toward her, his face wreathed with a frown.

"Father!" she said. Her emotions, which had been soaring just a moment before, now plummeted as she read the expression on his face. "What has happened?"

Licentor placed his long arms on the shoulders of his daughter, his face still sober. Then, no longer able to put on the false front, his face softened and his eyes twinkled, his lips arching into a boyish grin.

"It is settled, my dear. You are betrothed."

Her arms were about his neck. "Oh, Father! Why do you do things like that to me? From your face, I thought Mercatus had refused!"

He kissed her on the cheek and held her, looking down into her now laughing face. "My kitten, I hope that you are always as happy as you are this instant. Life can sometimes be cruel. Very cruel."

He held her close to him. She knew nothing about the pains in his chest, nothing about his worries, his concern about the time he might have left. It would be soon enough that she would know sadness and he would not hasten it. "I shall make the formal announcement tomorrow," he told her. "In perhaps a month you and Nadius will be married." Then his face took on the make-believe stern expression again. "That is, if that is what you want."

"Oh, Father. Yes. It is what I want. But why have you now agreed to choose a husband for me? You have put it off for years!"

He hugged her tightly and looked into her deep eyes, hoping to be able to conceal the truth in his lie. "Well, kitten, perhaps it is because I would like to bounce some grandchildren on my knee. All my friends have them and I am jealous. Is that reason enough for you?"

"That is the best of reasons, Father," she laughed. "I shall give you grandchildren to bounce upon your knee. But do not spoil them too much, as you have spoiled me. Oh, Father, I love you! And I am so happy!"

So it was that the next day in the town square Licentor announced the betrothal of his daughter to Nadius. There were cheers and backslapping and wine after the announcement to celebrate.

"And perhaps soon," he told his best friends, "I too, will have a fine grandson to boast about instead of having to listen to you all brag about yours."

It was a happy day, but as he returned home his mind was on other matters. Soon after the wedding he must teach Nadius all about the business of dyeing cloth. He must take him to meet the best customers across the Aegean in Achaia and Macedonia. He must train the young man quickly in the process of mixing the powdered dye produced from the sea snails and mixing it in the proper proportions in the vats. He must teach him the exact time the cloth must be left in the dye, the proper rinsing and drying. But then he thought about the secret, kept by his family for generations. Could he trust this irresponsible young man with such a treasured secret?

Anyone could dye wool. But the art of dyeing silk was different. And it was the secret ingredient and process that enabled his family alone to produce the brilliant and durable purples with silk. Lydia knew it, for he had been fearful that something might happen to him quickly and the secret would be forever lost. But could he entrust this newcomer to his family with the precious method, handed down from generation to generation? At that moment, he did not know.

The family business had prospered on the beautiful purples so coveted by the rich and royal Romans. In fact, Licentor could not wear his own cloth, for the Roman law forbade any but royalty from wearing purple. The silken cloths he produced were worth their weight in gold in the marketplaces to the wealthy and royal Roman ladies and gentlemen.

As a Greek, Licentor despised them, these conquerors of his land. Despite the Roman claim of equality of all under their rule, the Greeks could never accept their subservient state, for the roots of freedom ran deep.

But for Licentor and the rest of the Greek people, there was nothing they could do about the Romans. So he, as many of his compatriots like him, cursed the Romans in secret while contenting themselves with making an excellent living from the extravagant life styles of the rich Romans.

As Lydia looked back upon them, the weeks that followed passed both quickly and slowly. She had been counting the days and they had seemed to last forever; but now that the day had arrived, she wondered where the time had gone.

Now her father had taken her by the arm and they had walked to the temple of Diana in the center of Thyatira. Mercatus was waiting for them along with the other guests. Inside was Nadius standing beside the altar with the priest. The ox had been slain, and its bones and fat were upon the altar, waiting for the torch to light the sacrificial fire beneath it. The rest of the ox was now roasting on a spit for the wedding feast.

Lydia was dressed in a gown that Euodia had made for this occasion. Her dark hair was set in curls and flowers bound in it. In her hand she carried a small statue of Diana, who was next to Apollo as most sacred to the Thyatirans. Weddings held in her temple assured the fertility of the bride and the fruitfulness of the union.

Licentor looked at his daughter as she waited to enter the temple. Yes, he thought, today she is the loveliest of women, her cheeks pink and her skin radiant with happiness. None could tell him today that she was plain, for in his eyes she was beautiful indeed.

And as Licentor led her down the aisle and they walked slowly toward the groom, Nadius also saw her with different eyes. She was to him a most lovely and desirable bride. Inside his chest his heart beat faster. How could he have thought her plain, he asked himself? Has the caterpillar emerged from her cocoon as a beautiful butterfly? He held out his hand eagerly to her as she approached and felt the smoothness of her touch for the first time as she took it in her own.

The priest began the brief ceremony. The groom's father was asked whether he would receive this girl into his family and Mercatus replied he would. Then the bride's father was asked whether he gave his daughter to be part of this family and Licentor agreed. The bride and groom had no real part in this. The fathers gave permission and it was done. Then the priest took the burning torch from the stand and lit the sacrificial fire.

It was over. Lydia and Nadius were man and wife. The wedding party returned to Mercatus's house where the feast had been prepared. After the feast the happiness of the couple was toasted by the groom's father. Then it was toasted by the bride's father, then by friends of the groom, then friends of the bride. When this round of toasting was over, it began again. Long after the roasted ox had been consumed, the wine flowed freely.

It was late in the evening when Lydia and Nadius at last found themselves alone in a room of Mercatus's house. Nadius, who had responded heartily to each toast, weaved uncertainly to the bed. He fell face first across it, fast asleep. Lydia removed his sandals and lifted his heavy legs to the bed. Then she undressed and pulled the covers over herself. She reached out and patted her new husband on the head. "Goodnight, my drunken lover. Sweet dreams."

The next day the couple returned to Licentor's house where they would live. Licentor had moved into Lydia's former room, insisting that the newlyweds have his much larger bedroom. When they were alone in the room, Nadius took Lydia's hand. "I'm sorry about last night. I must have had too much wine."

Lydia kissed him. "That's all right. We have the rest of our lives, my husband."

His arms folded about her, his lips eagerly seeking hers. She gave herself willingly to him.

Although Licentor felt a pressing urgency to get on with Nadius's education and training in his business, he did not insist on this for the next two weeks. He had seen the radiance in his daughter's face and, not wishing to take her new husband from her too soon, he waited impatiently for the proper time. But after the two weeks had passed, he broached the subject at breakfast one morning.

"Well, Nadius, I am sure you are anxious to take your place in our business."

"Oh, Father, already?" Lydia had protested.

Nadius saw the look on the old man's face. "I am ready whenever you say," he replied, hoping Licentor would tell him they would wait a few more weeks.

"Good," Licentor replied. "We shall start today."

For Nadius, the next weeks were filled with days in the hot and humid rooms behind the house where the vats were located. The cloth to be dyed had to be thoroughly washed and dried in the sun. The vats had to be filled with clean water from the well and just the right amount of the proper dye added and stirred in. Since they were now dyeing wool, there was no reason for Licentor to show his son-in-law the family secret used to dye silk. But the old man insisted that Nadius actually perform each step himself, including the labor of filling the vats with water. Clement and Epaphroditus usually did this, but Licentor had told him, "The best way to learn is to do it yourself. This way you will never forget."

Nadius was surprised at how complicated the process was. He had assumed the dyeing of cloth to be a simple thing, just soaking the cloth in the dyeing vats and drying it. But he learned that it took much practice to tell just the moment when the fibers had absorbed the proper amount of dye to give the exact color desired. Timing was all important and it took much practice and skill to learn this.

Licentor talked to him constantly, explaining the details, correcting his mistakes, encouraging him. Nadius thought his head would burst from the constant instruction. But more than that, he resented having to do the physical work while the slaves stood by and watched. Work was what slaves were for, he indignantly told himself. But he had to put up with it, telling himself that when he had learned this business he would never again lift the heavy vats or carry water from the well as Licentor now made him do.

He smelled his hands and grimaced. They smelled like fish, as did the hands of all dyers of cloth. "Why did I get myself into this? I hate this dirty, smelly business," he cried.

Not even in the evenings would Licentor give him rest. After supper the old man would sit him down and for hours explain the hundreds of details of the business of dyeing cloth, the catching of the shellfish from which the dye was obtained, how to choose the best quality cloth in wool and silk. Would the man never stop, Nadius wondered?

But on the night when Licentor opened the ledgers of the business and showed Nadius how much profit was in the dyeing and selling of the cloth, Nadius's eyes opened wide with wonder. His father's business of making clay jars and pots dealt in staters and drachmas. But this business, and half of it now belonged to him, was calculated in minas and talents. The silken cloth obtained from the islands of Cos and Amorgos, when dyed to the rich, bright purple that only royalty could wear, sold for its weight in gold.

Perhaps, he thought, all this work will be worth it. Especially after the old man had passed on and the entire thing belonged to him. Then he would no longer have to turn his hand, to touch the cloth or the dye. He would certainly see that the slaves did the actual work of the business. That, after all, was what slaves were for.

Three months later Lydia was able to tell her delighted father and her somewhat disinterested husband that she was expecting a child. Licentor made her stop all work immediately and insisted she lie down every day to rest, despite her protests that she felt fine. Nadius celebrated the occasion by going out with his friends and getting drunk.

Euodia fussed about her as much as her father did. "It's about time there was a child in this house," she said. "It has been a long time since there was a baby here."

"I can't wait," Lydia laughed. "Oh, Euodia, my life has been so happy. The gods have blessed me. I have a wonderful family, a fine father, good friends such as you and Clement and Epaphroditus. And now I have a handsome husband and a baby coming. It will be a boy. I know it will be a boy. Don't you think so, Euodia?"

The older woman smiled. "Well, there is an even chance. It has to be one or the other, you know. Now stop running around and get back to bed. Your father will be angry if he finds you up and stirring about the kitchen."

"But I don't feel tired." Lydia danced about the older woman. "A baby," she sang. "I'm going to have a baby!"

Two weeks later Licentor announced that he must take Nadius and travel to Macedonia to visit customers. The storerooms were piled high with dyed cloth. The woolens and silks gleamed in bright colors, for beside the purples were shades of crimson, bright blues, saffrons and violets. These would be loaded aboard a ship on the dock on the Hyllus River and sailed down to where the river joined the Aegean Sea. Transferred to a larger ship, they would then sail on, hopping from island to island to the western side of the sea. They would stop at Neapolis, the port which served Philippi, where Licentor's best customer was located.

Nadius was glad to leave. He was tired of the hard work and getting somewhat bored with his new wife. All she ever talked about now was the baby coming. The change of scene would be good, he thought. And he had never been to the places they would be going.

Then the day came, and both husband and father said goodbye to Lydia. Standing at the dock, Lydia watched the small ship disappear around the bend of the river toward the sea. From the ship, Nadius watched the shoreline as they sailed down the river. The breeze was cool in his face and he was relieved that they were finally on their way. But his joy was short-lived as Licentor approached him at the rail.

"At Mytilene you will have the chance to see a dye factory. I want you to know all about this business, my son, for you will need all of this information when the business is all yours after I am gone."

Nadius nodded his head. "I am anxious to learn," he said without enthusiasm.

"There's a young girl outside who wants to see Nadius," Euodia told Lydia on the morning after they had left. "I think you should talk with her."

Lydia looked up, puzzled by the expression on the older woman's face.

"What is the matter?" she asked. "Why do you look at me like that?"

Euodia indicated the open window. "Look for yourself. Then you will know why."

Lydia went to the window. Outside stood a thin girl, perhaps sixteen years old. As Lydia's eyes moved over her, she knew what Euodia had meant.

"Yes," she said. "I believe I should talk with her. Bring her in."

Euodia brought the young girl in. Her eyes were wide as she examined every detail of the fine furniture, the large, airy rooms, the expensive wall hangings. Lydia met her in the atrium. "You wished to see my husband?" Lydia asked.

"I want to see Nadius," the girl replied. "I didn't know he was your husband."

"He is away," Lydia told her. "On a business trip. Is there something I can do for you?"

The girl's face was solemn as she answered. "There's nothing you can do for me. He's done enough." She looked at an inlaid table and picked up a silver pitcher that was on it. "Is this real silver?"

"Yes, it is real silver. Now tell me what you want of my husband."

The girl's eyes met hers and Lydia knew in her heart what the girl would say. "I'm going to have his child," she said in a low voice, her hand dropping to the prominent bulge in her stomach. "Now what is it that you can do for me?"

Lydia sat down, fighting to control herself as the room

suddenly began to whirl and a sensation of sinking came over her. Euodia, who had been standing in the doorway, rushed to her side. "No, I'm all right," Lydia told her. Then she faced the girl. "You had better sit down too," she said. "We have much to talk about."

— Chapter Two —

Nadius stood at the dye factory at Mytilene and gazed at the mountain of shells, some of them a hundred feet high.

"There are four kinds of shellfish that contain the purple dye," Licentor told him. "We must know what kind and in which order the dyes are used in order to achieve the particular shade of purple desired for each type of cloth."

"I had no idea so many shellfish were needed to dye just one bolt of cloth," Nadius said. "No wonder it is so expensive."

"And within each shellfish there is but a tiny gland that contains the dye," Licentor told him. "With the two smaller shellfish, the whole mussel is ground and crushed and the dye extracted by hot water and steam. But the two larger types are opened individually and the gland cut out. It takes much time and is exacting work. The dye must be extracted from fresh mussels. They cannot be more than three days out of the water before the dye is extracted, or the colors will not be right."

Nadius looked at the idle plant. "Why isn't the factory working now?"

"It is summer. The shellfish cannot be obtained during the summer months. They can be caught during fall and winter only. In the spring and summer the gland contains no dye."

Nadius stroked his chin. "Wouldn't it save you money if you produced your own dye? Then you would not have to pay the outrageous prices the dye makers demand."

Licentor put his hand on Nadius's shoulder. "Yes, it would save money. But I have an agreement with Busteles who owns the factory here. He will not dye cloth and I will not catch shellfish. It works well for both of us."

Nadius looked at the factory with the high mountains of shells and then at the sea. When I own this business outright, he said to himself, that will have to change.

The men boarded the ship which would take them to Troas and continue their journey. Licentor grasped the railing hard. The pains in his chest were sharp. He held his breath and in a few moments the pain subsided.

If only I can teach him what he must know before my time comes, he thought. Nothing matters but that. I must see that Lydia and my grandchild are taken care of. He prayed to the gods to give him the time he needed.

Lydia gazed at the young girl seated opposite her in the atrium.

"And just when did this . . . this thing . . . happen that you say my husband is responsible for?"

The girl's lusterless eyes met hers. "Five months ago. He came to my town, Pergamum, to compete in the games. We met at the stadium. He . . . he told me I was pretty. We walked in the moonlight and stopped at the grove of Daphne. Then we lay in the grass beneath the trees. He was so handsome and I . . . well, I could not help myself and he . . . we . . . ."

Lydia was thankful that at least it had happened before they had been married. But that changed nothing. What was she to do about this girl?

Lydia faced her again. "What did you expect by coming here? Did you expect him to marry you?"

"I don't know what I expected. But I had no where else to go. My father has thrown me out of the house. I had no place else to

go, nothing else to do but come and find Nadius. I . . . I . . . ."
The girl was in tears, and Lydia arose and put her arm around the small shoulders of the girl as she sobbed.

"You did the right thing," Lydia told her. "Now dry your eyes. Let us go and see what we can find you to eat. You must be hungry after so long a walk."

The girl ate hungrily what Euodia placed before her. Lydia watched her, thinking. What would she do with her? Certainly she could not stay here. It was not Nadius Lydia worried about but her father. If he learned of this, Lydia had no idea of what his reaction would be. Over and above the hurt she felt deep inside her, Lydia was concerned about Licentor. The shock of this might kill him, she thought. He must never, never know!

Then into Lydia's mind came a name. Melisus! Yes, Melisus. She would take the girl to Melisus. She would take her in. And Melisus, the midwife, would take care of her when her time came.

"When you have finished eating," Lydia told her, "we will go and see about a place for you to stay."

Half an hour later they stood outside a small cottage at the edge of the woods outside of town. "Wait here," Lydia told her. "I will go in and speak to the woman who owns this place." She knocked on the door and it was opened by a very stout woman.

"Lydia! Come in, child. It is good to see you!"

When she entered the cottage and was seated before the stout woman, Lydia explained the purpose of her visit. "There is a young girl outside who has no place to stay. She is expecting a child. I will pay her board and keep if you will let her stay here with you."

Melisus peered out the door. "Why, she is but a child herself! And she looks so downcast. Of course she can stay with me. Besides, I have been lonesome. It will do me good to have some company."

Lydia beckoned for the girl to come in. "This is Sybil, Melisus."

The stout woman hugged the thin figure, then held her at arm's length to look at her. "You will be staying here with me, dear," she told the girl. "And you are not to worry about a thing. I know how to handle situations like this. I've been doing it for years."

Sybil smiled for the first time at the warm greeting. "I don't eat much," she said. "And I will be as little trouble as I can to you."

"Trouble? Why, child, I am glad to have you here with me. Come, let me show you around. Let's see, in that corner of the room is the kitchen, and over here is where we eat, and in the corner is my bed. Over there is where you will sleep. My house is not large, but it is cozy," she said. "And by being small, it is little trouble to keep."

Lydia left them and walked home. She ignored the look Euodia gave her as she entered her own home and went straight to her room. Once inside she threw herself on her bed and buried her face in her pillow. For an hour she cried softly, her heart breaking with sadness and frustration.

Then she dried her eyes. "That was before we were married," she told herself. "He would do nothing like that now! He is all mine now!"

The ship left Mytilene on the island of Lesbos and skirted the coast between the island and the mainland until it had reached Troas. There the ship docked and Licentor took Nadius to meet the first of his customers.

Two bearers were hired at the dock to carry the bolts of cloth through the crowded streets, pushing their way through the throngs of people, past the stalls of the sellers in the market until they came to a small side street. Here was the shop of Pietrius who dealt in fine dyed goods.

They entered the shop and the proprietor saw Licentor. His face broke into a wide grin. "Licentor, my friend!" The men embraced. "It is good to see my old friend again. I hope you have brought me much of your fine purples. I have sold out everything you brought me on your last trip."

Licentor extracted himself from the big man's embrace. "Yes, I have brought you a fine quantity this time. And I have also brought with me my new son-in-law who is now my partner in business. This is Nadius, Lydia's husband. And this is my dear friend, Pietrius."

The shopkeeper shook Nadius's hand warmly. "Welcome. So you have married my dear, sweet Lydia. You are a fortunate man, Nadius. A most fortunate man, indeed."

"And," said Licentor, "I am to be a grandfather."

"Aha," exclaimed Pietrius, "this calls for a double celebration. Let us have some wine and toast both the new husband and the new grandfather-to-be. Here, bring out the best wine for my friends."

After the toasts and some small talk which bored Nadius, the men settled down to business. This took but little time. Nadius was surprised at how low the price was for the purple woolens and silks which Licentor agreed upon with the shopkeeper.

As they walked back to the ship, Nadius questioned his father-in-law about this. "That man told you he was completely out of purple cloth yet you sold him more at the standard price. You could have easily received much more and he would have been happy to pay it. Why didn't you increase the price?"

Licentor turned to Nadius. "That would be taking advantage of an old friend," he said, astonished at his son-in-law's words. "I do not do such things! Pietrius would have bought all that I had whether he needed it or not. We have done business together for over twenty-five years. This is a business with honor, Nadius.

I shall conduct it as such."

They boarded the ship again and the winds were favorable. Swiftly they passed the island of Tenedos and again followed the coastline up to the island of Imbros. Then the ship turned out into the open sea, passing to the east of Samothrace and sighting the island of Thasos. They put into the harbor of Neapolis, the port city of Philippi, and spent the night. The next morning they began the short, overland trip to Philippi, their cloth loaded onto the backs of mules which they had hired at the dock.

As they left Neapolis, Licentor pointed out a range of hills to the east. "See there, Nadius. On this plain, about a hundred years ago, the armies of Octavian and Marc Antony met those of Brutus and Cassius. It was right here that the fate of Rome was decided."

"Oh, yes," Nadius replied. "This was the site of the battle of Philippi, wasn't it?"

"That's right. To the east near the coast Cassius' army faced that of Antony. Farther inland Brutus's legions faced those of Octavian. On the first day of the battle, Brutus pushed Octavian's troops back, while Antony was defeating Cassius. When Cassius saw his men turn and flee, he stabbed himself. Some say it was with the same dagger he used to kill Julius Caesar two years before.

"But the battle was not yet over. Brutus rallied most of Cassius' troops and regrouped to fight again. Twenty days later the armies met again. This time Brutus was soundly beaten and committed suicide rather than be captured.

"After this battle, the world was divided between Antony and Octavian. An uneasy peace was established in the empire, but it was not to last. Two strong men such as Marc Antony and Octavian could not get along forever. Ten years later, they met at the battle of Actium where Antony and his Egyptian allies under Cleopatra were beaten. Then it was only Octavian who ruled the world. His name was changed to Augustus Caesar and he, alone, ruled the Roman empire for many years."

"That was a long time ago," Nadius observed. "How can you recall such things out of the past?"

Licentor smiled at the young man. "There is no past. The present and the future are but reenactments of what has happened before. But men do not learn from history, Nadius. They must repeat the same foolish errors again and again. This world is but a stage where the same play is presented over and over. It is only the cast of actors who are different."

They were now approaching Philippi. "Did you know that this city was once called Krenides? The name was changed to Philippi after Philip of Macedon captured it from Thrace and enlarged it. That was over three hundred years ago. Philip was the father of Alexander, our greatest hero, who spread the fame of Greece throughout the world."

Nadius shrugged off the history lesson. It is a shame, Licentor, he thought to himself, that you know so much about the ancient world and so little about modern business. But he kept this comment to himself as they entered the city and engaged rooms at a modest but clean and comfortable inn where Licentor always stayed while in Philippi.

"What are you going to do?" Euodia asked her.

Lydia clenched her eyes tightly shut and shook her head. "I don't know. I just don't know yet what to do."

"I'll tell you what you ought to do. You should send that little tramp packing. Back to her father in Pergamum, that's what. It's only her word that Nadius is the child's father."

Lydia looked up at her. "It's his child. I know it is. And she is so young to have this kind of trouble."

"She should have thought of that then. It's too late now."

Euodia got up and put her arms around Lydia. "I just don't want to see you hurt. You don't deserve this, honey. That tramp and your . . . husband started this, and you wind up getting hurt by it. It just isn't fair!"

Lydia smiled wanly. "There are very few fair things in this life, Euodia. Life doesn't let you get by without your share of unfair things. That's the way this world is and there's not much we can do about it."

"Well, that may be true, but I don't have to like it."

Lydia's gaze went to the expanse of green fields and hills that led to the river. This house was the only home she had ever known. In it were all of the reminders, all of the little things that brought back memories, thoughts of her life here. They were happy thoughts for the most part. The only clouds were those things that reminded Lydia of her mother. She still missed her mother. But her life had been filled to overflowing with her family, her father, her loving friends such as Euodia, Clement and Papie.

And now, Lydia thought, she had a handsome husband and would bear his first child. No, she remembered sadly. It would not be his first child. Sybil carried that. But the first by her, her own baby, which would delight her father. She would have to do something to prevent Nadius's mistake from ruining all this. She had to think of something.

As for now, Sybil would be cared for by Melisus, safely out of sight and away from her father and family. Melisus would be discreet. In time the child would be born and no one would be the wiser. Then she would have to think of some way to send Sybil and the child away, away to some place where they would be out of her life forever. There was certainly enough money from her father's business to take good care of both of them.

The next morning in Philippi Licentor took Nadius to meet his largest customer. Stetius sold cloth to the royal Roman families who lived in the provincial capital of Philippi. They were more than willing to pay the prices for the fine double-dyed purple woolens and silks that Licentor produced. Nadius was very impressed by Stetius' place of business, which made the small shop he had just visited in Troas look drab by comparison.

They learned at the shop that Stetius was at home, so they called on him there. A servant answered the door and immediately recognized Licentor. She showed them into a magnificent atrium to await Stetius. Nadius looked with envy at the fine furnishings and the exquisite wall hangings. "This is the type of home I would like to own someday," he said to Licentor.

The older man shrugged his shoulders. "It is indeed a fine house," he said, "but one needs to meet only his comfort. Of what use are more rooms than a man finds necessary? A man can sleep in but one bed at a time, and eat in but one dining room. Happiness, Nadius, comes from within, not from the possession of mere things, even those as fine as these."

Nadius pursed his lips. "That may be true, but I could find myself happier in these surroundings than in a hovel. Why live in hovel?"

Licentor grew tired of his son-in-law's constant carping on material things and irritated by his tone of voice. "Are you saying that my home is a hovel?"

Nadius knew he had gone too far. "Oh, no. Not so at all. You have a fine house. A magnificent home. But you have to admit, Licentor, that it certainly lacks much in comparison with this."

Licentor grunted. He was about to reply when a small, thin man entered the atrium. "Welcome, Licentor. It is good to see you again."

"I know how busy you are, Stetius. It is good of you to see us."

The short man grinned. "May the gods strike me dead if I am ever too busy to see an old friend."

"And this," Licentor said, indicating Nadius, "is Lydia's new husband, Nadius."

"So? I did not know she had an old one," Stetius joked. He shook Nadius by the hand and motioned for both of them to be seated. "If Lydia did have an old one, I should like to have been that fortunate man," he laughed.

Licentor smiled. "What I meant is that they have not been married very long. Nadius has joined me in the business. I am getting on in years, my friend. Perhaps it will be Nadius who calls on you in the years to come."

"Old!" Stetius guffawed. "Why, you look no different now than when we first met. How long ago was that? Twenty, twenty-five years?"

"I have stopped counting. But it is true. I am feeling the effects of time. My legs grow weary and my body calls for rest. I think I have earned the right to take it a bit easier."

"Indeed," Stetius' face grew serious. "I jest about the years but I know what you say is true. But old warriors such as you and I do not usually admit it." He turned to Nadius. "Now, young man, tell me, what do you think of this business of dyeing cloth? Are you learning much? Licentor is the master in this art. You could not have a better teacher."

Nadius forced a smile. "I am fascinated by it. And I have indeed learned much from my father-in-law."

"Good. Now, Licentor, let us see what fine goods you have brought me on this trip. Have your bearers bring it in so that I may observe what the fashionable Roman ladies shall be wearing this season."

The cloth was brought into the atrium and displayed. Bolts of deep purple, of crimson, of violet, all dyed evenly and to perfection. In the bright sunlight that shone down through the open roof of the atrium, the fabrics were turned into a spectrum of sparkling rainbows. Stetius felt the silks between his fingers and rubbed the woolens against his face.

"Your usual perfection," he told Licentor. "Of course, from you I would expect nothing less."

Stetius bought all of the cloth Licentor had brought for him, filling the order he had given him on the last trip. He then gave the order for his next requirements for each color and fabric. He left the room and returned with a purse, which he gave to Licentor. Nadius noted that Licentor did not bother to count the money.

They left to return to the inn. Nadius turned to the old man. "That man makes a fortune on your cloth. It is not fair that we do not receive higher profits for all the work which goes into it. Can't you see that the price could—should—be increased by half again. He would gladly pay more."

Licentor shook his head. "I will hear no more of that talk. I am satisfied with the profits as they now are. If I were to increase the price, many customers would simply find another source. There are many in the business of dyeing cloth. I have no monopoly on this business."

"But he said himself that you are the master of the art. Your goods are far superior. They deserve more in exchange for them."

For the first time, Licentor's temper flared. "Now listen to me, Nadius. You have been in this business for only three months. I have spent my lifetime. When you have been in it for thirty years, then you can tell me how to conduct it. But until then, shut up. I will hear nothing more about raising prices. Do you understand?"

Nadius held his tongue but his thoughts were livid. I shall hold my tongue now, old man, he thought to himself, but as soon as I have the say, I shall not let these people take advantage of me the way they do you.

They returned to the inn in silence. Licentor had felt the pains return to his chest when he became angry with his son-in-law. He lay on his bed at the inn and rested. When it was time to eat supper, he told Nadius he was not hungry and bade the younger man to go on without him.

Nadius was just as well pleased to be away from Licentor. He went to the dining room of the inn and ordered his meal. He noticed that most of the patrons were very well dressed, and he looked at his own clothing, which suffered by comparison. But there would come a time, he promised himself, when he would not feel ashamed of his clothing. He determined to become wealthy and enjoy the fine things of life despite what Licentor said.

He had finished his meal and was enjoying his wine when a splendidly dressed young man entered the room. As the tables were all full, the servant seated the man at the table which Nadius occupied, asking him first if he would mind.

"Not at all," Nadius replied and the man was seated across the table from him.

"My name is Herteles," the man said by way of introduction.

"And I am Nadius, the son of Mercatus."

"Mercatus? Is that the Mercatus from Corinth who deals in fine leather?"

"No. I am from Thyatira. I . . . I am in the dyed cloth business. Purples."

The man's eyes widened. "Purples," he exclaimed. "Then you must be very wealthy."

Nadius, flattered, replied with affected modesty, "It is a good living."

"Good! You are overly modest, my friend. Purple cloth is worth its weight in gold."

"And what is your business, if I may ask?"

The man laughed. "I used to be engaged in selling grain. My father and his before him were in this. But I have sold out my interests. I have bought property here near Philippi. A mine."

The waiter arrived to take the man's order. Nadius saw that Herteles ordered only the best food and wine, and the waiter obviously knew him. And Nadius noted from the respect the waiter showed him that the man was indeed very rich.

When the waiter had gone, Nadius leaned across the table. "A mine, you say? What sort of mine?"

The man smiled at him. "Obviously you know little about Philippi," he said. "What kind of mine, indeed? There is but one kind of mine here, my friend. A gold mine."

Nadius choked on his wine. "A gold mine? There is gold here?"

The young man reached into his robe and produced a small pouch. He dumped the contents on the table before Nadius. "And what does this appear to be?" he asked.

On the table were nuggets, most of them small, but one was about the size of the tip of Nadius's thumb. The light of the oil lamp caught them and returned a glimmering yellow in the flickering light. "Yes," Herteles smiled, "gold. And this is but a small sample. In six months the mine has produced sufficient gold to make me fabulously wealthy. I shall never have to work or worry again. I have enough money to last a dozen lifetimes."

After the meal, Herteles arose. "I am sorry to have to go," he said. "I have enjoyed your company. But I have been invited to a party at the proconsul's mansion. It is not good to keep these Romans waiting, you know. They are disgustingly punctual people."

Nadius sat at the table after the rich young man had left. In his mind's eye he could still see the glimmer of gold. Enough to last a dozen lifetimes, he murmured to himself. Oh, if I could somehow do the same!

He thought of ordering more wine but thought better of it. He would not like Licentor to find him drunk. No, he could wait. He paid his bill and returned to his room, first checking on his father-in-law, whom he found fast asleep. He undressed and lay down on his bed. As hard as he tried he could not fall asleep, for in his mind's eye still danced those glittering, yellow nuggets, and that was all he could think of until the morning came.

The knock came on the door of Melisus's cottage well after midnight. When she did not answer immediately, the man pounded his fist against the door and shouted. "Melisus! You must come right away! My wife needs you! The baby's coming!"

She turned up the lamp and went to the door. "I hear you. Don't scream. I'm coming." She opened the door and the man gestured wildly.

"Hurry! Come with me quickly!"

Melisus wagged her finger at him. "Calm down. I haven't missed a birthing yet. I have to get my things. You men are all alike! Always so impatient." She turned and went back inside. Sybil, awakened by the noise, sat upright on her pallet on the floor.

"What's happening? Why all the shouting?"

"I've got to go out," Melisus told her. "There's a mother and a baby on the way that needs me." She picked up her bag and turned again to Sybil. "Say, would you want to come with me? Bet you never have seen a baby born, have you?"

Sybil's eyes widened. "No, I never have. Can I really come and watch?"

"Watch nothing, you can help. Now get your clothes on quick. Hurry or we'll have to treat the father-to-be for nervous exhaustion before we go. He's ready to have a fit." She turned to the door and spoke to the man who was pacing up and down outside. "Bet this is your first, isn't it?"

He nodded his head. "Yes, but hurry. It's coming fast."

"Fast," Melisus laughed as she and Sybil came out the door. "They all say the same thing. But we'll wait for hours before that baby decides it's time to be born. Never fails."

Despite her large bulk, Melisus was able to move along at a rapid pace, and it was Sybil who lagged behind. They reached the man's cottage and Melisus opened the door. As the man tried to enter, her body blocked the door. "No, you don't," she said emphatically. "This is women's work. Men just get in the way."

She and Sybil moved inside and stood beside the crude bed where the woman lay moaning. "Now, honey, you just tell old Melisus when you have each pain and we'll take it from there."

Sybil, not knowing what to do, just stood back and watched. In a few moments the woman screamed, "Now! It hurts now!" Melisus rubbed her stomach and held her hand.

"It just seems bad, child. After it's all over you won't even remember the pain. Now just relax and tell me when the next one comes."

Melisus was right, of course. The birth did not take place for many hours. The stout woman checked frequently on the position of the baby. Then when the time was right, she went to work. Sybil's eyes grew wide as Melisus held the tiny thing up by the ankles and whacked it on the bottom. With a shrill cry, the child announced to his father that he was there.

Half an hour later, when the mother and child had been bathed, the father was allowed in. He peered at the tiny form that lay nestled beside his wife, cuddled in her arm.

"There," Melisus told him, "everything's over. Now don't ask me if your wife and son are all right or anything like that. Old Melisus always delivers healthy babies."

The sun was just rising over the mountains as Melisus and Sybil returned to the cottage. The stout midwife sat down and removed her sandals. "Roughest thing about this work is the feet. Mine always hurt bad after it's all over."

Sybil suddenly put her arm around the stout woman and kissed her on the cheek. "I think you are just great, Melisus. That was the most beautiful thing I've ever seen. Thank you for letting me go."

Melisus frowned. "Nothing spectacular about being born," she said. "Everybody does it. Never met anybody yet who came into this world any other way."

She lay on her bed and closed her eyes. "I think I'll just rest awhile, child. Not that I'm going to sleep or anything. Just have to rest my eyes." And in a moment, she was snoring.

Licentor awoke the next morning feeling much better. The pains had gone from his chest and his head no longer rang like a bell. There was business he must take care of in Thessalonica, and he instructed the men to pack the remainder of his cloth and wrap them in skins to protect them against the weather. When the mules were loaded, he and Nadius started off again, down the Egnation Way, the paved road connecting the eastern provinces of Macedonia with Achaia. Along the way was an inn spaced a day's journey apart for the convenience of travelers. They reached Thessalonica in four days' travel.

Licentor sold the rest of his cloth to his customer there, a dour man who said little and was the first customer to haggle over the price. As they left, Licentor told Nadius, "He will buy cloth from anyone with the cheapest price. He cares little for quality. Do not trust him. He tells everyone that their price is too high, that he can buy cheaper elsewhere. Just tell him to take it or leave it and he will always take our goods. But never trust him."

Now they could start for home. They had been away for almost a month when they boarded a ship in the harbor of Thessalonica bound for Troas. The next morning found them on the clear, blue waters of the Aegean under a cloudless sky. The breeze swiftly carried the ship along, skirting the myriad small and large Greek islands. Three days later they reached Troas. From there they boarded a smaller vessel and sailed back to Mytilene and the mouth of the Hyllus River.

"There is one thing I shall teach you when we get back home," Licentor told Nadius. "There is a secret which has been in my family for generations. Many can dye wool with the purple, but only with this secret can silk be successfully dyed. This is the greatest asset our business has. You must guard this secret with your life."

The small boat had just begun to cross the channel between the island of Lesbos and the mainland when a cry came, "Waterspout!"

Nadius saw it coming, a horrifying sight, water swirling about like a funnel standing on end across the sea. "Catch hold of the boat," Licentor shouted to him, "and hold on."

On it came, careening wildly, stopping in one spot for a moment, then proceeding on, leaving havoc and wreckage in its wake. He saw it smash a small boat only a hundred yards from them, splintering it to bits. On it came, directly toward them, its hungry lips devouring everything in its path.

Then the thing stopped, as if it were eyeing them up before consuming them. Once more it moved—closer and closer to their ship. At the last moment the waterspout veered, passing a few scant yards away from the small ship. Nadius felt the ship lurch as the spout turned the water into a boiling cauldron beneath them.

He felt the salt spray as it closed over his head. His lungs suddenly choked with the taste of the briny water. Over and over he tumbled, feeling himself pulled downward.

Then the motion was reversed, and he crashed through the surface of the water into brilliant sunlight. His tortured lungs gasped eagerly for air. Nadius was an excellent swimmer and his strong arms took over, pulling him back toward the ship. He pulled himself aboard and fell exhausted to the deck.

For a moment he lay still, his chest heaving from the exertion. Then he saw the form on the deck beside him and recognized it as Licentor's. He crawled quickly to the prostrate man and rolled him over. "Are you all right?" he demanded, but no answer came from the inert form. The eyes were open and Nadius could see the pain in them as Licentor gasped for breath.

Nadius saw his father-in-law's lips move, trying to form words. But the iron grip had seized the old man's heart and was squeezing the very life from it.

"Licentor!" Nadius screamed. "You must not die!" The old man, with superhuman effort, pulled Nadius's head down close to his mouth, trying to speak into his ear. Licentor strained to make the sounds, but they would not come. Then he felt himself falling, falling, deeply into oblivion and he lay still.

Nadius saw his head fall back, the body go limp, the eyes develop only a glassy stare. He heard the last, dying gasp as Licentor was gone.

"No! No!" he shouted at the lifeless form. "You can't die yet. You haven't told me the secret!"

— Chapter Three —

As soon as Lydia saw Nadius's face she knew something was terribly wrong. She had been in the atrium when he came into the room, his face ashen, contorted with the expression that reflected the state of his mind. For a moment she said nothing, staring at his anguished face. Then slowly she spoke. "It's Father, isn't it?"

He took a faltering step toward her. "Lydia, he . . . he is—" Then he broke down completely, covering his face with both hands as he sobbed, "He is dead!"

Lydia got up slowly and walked toward him. Any bitter feelings she bore him about the affair with Sybil were forgotten as she put her arms around him. He clung to her, burying his head in her breast, as a child with its mother. "Lydia, Lydia! He is dead!"

Her senses were deadened by the shock of the news, and she felt no emotion as she led her husband to a chair and sat him down, still holding him in her arms. She patted his head and stood up. She walked to the doorway and stepped outside where two men held the reins of a donkey. In the cart, covered by a blanket was a still form. Lydia stood looking at the contents of the cart for several moments.

She walked forward and placed her hand on the blanket, feeling the still form beneath it, her mind not yet fully comprehending what had happened. Then her emotions burst, breaking the barrier which the initial shock had created. She threw herself upon the form in the cart.

"Father! Father! You can't be dead! You just can't! I need you so!"

Euodia pulled her away and took her into the house. The older woman sat her in the atrium with Nadius, and having no words sufficient to comfort her, held her hand tightly to her own breast as both sobbed out their grief.

The older woman put her to bed, sitting beside her and holding her hand, having no words to comfort her. Lydia sobbed until there were no more tears left. Then, exhausted, she at last was still and mercifully asleep. Euodia pulled the cover up over her and silently left the room.

As she passed Nadius, still sitting where Lydia had put him, she turned. "You are master of this house now, Nadius. You must pull yourself together and do something."

He lifted his eyes to her, bloodshot, full of fright as a small child. "Do what? I don't know what to do."

She shook her head as she regarded him. "You are a man. Act as one. Now you have to grow up whether you want to or not. Get up and do something! Anything! But just don't sit there whining!"

She went to the courtyard. Clement and Epaphroditus had removed Licentor's body and were washing it. Clement's face was streaked with tears as he removed his master's clothing. Euodia put her hand upon his shoulder. "Be brave, Clement. I know the sorrow in your heart, but we must be strong for Lydia's sake."

He nodded as he tenderly washed the body. Epaphroditus carefully removed Licentor's sandals, his eyes also streaming tears. "There never lived a kinder, gentler man," he said.

There was no question of where Licentor would be buried. He would lie beside his wife beneath the big trees along the river they both had loved to walk in the cool of the evenings long ago.

Clement went to the storeroom and returned with a bolt of the finest double-dyed purple silk. He handed this to Euodia. "Here, wife. Make his burial clothes. It is only fitting that they be of this cloth. He was of royalty. Not by birth, perhaps, but by the way he lived. No one, not even the emperor, deserves the finest purple more than him."

The next day a crowd assembled in the courtyard, people who had known Licentor all their lives. They had come to pay their last respects to him in death. Soon the cart would take the body to the grave along the river for burial. Nadius had regained his composure, and with the help of some wine was now able to accompany the body to its final resting place.

Euodia saw Lydia, dressed in mourning clothes, come out of the house. She rushed to her side and put out her hand. Lydia took it and looked into her eyes. "It's all right. I can manage," she told her. "I must be there to say my last goodbye to him."

A new strength seemed to have taken hold of Lydia. Her eyes, though red from crying, were dry, and she carried herself straight, with determination in her step. She stood beside the cart, her thin body erect, and received the consolation of the guests. "Where is my husband?" she asked. "He must be by my side."

Nadius came to her. "Lydia, I—"

"Please do not speak," Lydia told him. "We must first bury my father. There will be time for talk later." She took his arm and they walked beside the donkey down the road and northward to the bank of the river Hyllus, where a grove of large trees formed a canopy. There her mother lay in rest, and the ground next to her had been opened, waiting to receive the remains of her husband.

The cart stopped beside the open grave and men gently took the body from the cart and placed it in the dark, moist ground among the roots of the great trees. The ceremony was brief. Flasks of wine and oil and loaves of bread, freshly baked by

Euodia that morning, were placed with the body in the earth. A priest recited a sacred ritual, committing the soul of Licentor to the keeping of the gods of the underworld. The men replaced the earth and sealed the tomb. Later a stone would be carved to mark the spot.

When they returned to the house, the visitors said a few words to Lydia and went their way. Nadius followed her into the atrium and she turned to face him. "Now, my husband, it is time for us to talk."

He stepped to the table and poured wine from a flagon into a goblet. Nadius gulped the red liquid before he turned to face her. "I have something to tell you, Lydia. Something very serious. We no longer have a business."

"What do you mean?" she demanded, taken quite off guard by this.

"I mean, my dear wife, that your father died before he told me the secret. The family secret of dyeing silk." He sat down, his face white and drank the rest of the wine.

Lydia began to laugh. He looked at her, bewildered.

"Is that all that bothers you, Nadius? The family secret?"

"All? Isn't that enough?"

Lydia looked at him for a long moment before she spoke. "Tell me, Nadius, would you have married me if there had been no business?"

He looked away. "Why do you ask such a question? We are married! What more do you want of me?"

"I want an honest answer."

Within his chest raged the pent-up frustrations and anger. He jumped to his feet and flung the goblet against the wall with a crash. "An honest answer? Yes, I'll give you an honest answer! I would not have looked twice at you were it not for your father's damned business! Is that honest enough for you?"

She sat very still. The answer had not hurt, for it was only the confirmation of what she had already known in her heart. She nodded. "Yes, that is honest enough."

"Well, the business is mine now. The papers were drawn up before our marriage. Now I own the whole bloody business, for whatever it may be worth now! And you are my wife! And there's nothing I can do about that either! We will both have to make the best of a sorry deal!"

Lydia smiled at him, and he stopped and looked at her, puzzled. It was not a smile of mirth or happiness or joy. It was an icy smile and it upset him. "What is wrong with you? Why are you looking at me like that?"

Lydia arose and walked to the doorway. Then she turned and faced him again, the strange smile still on her lips. "It is only, my dear husband, that the secret, that precious family secret that you prize so much, did not die with my father."

He took a step toward her, his expression changed. "What? And who else knows it?"

"I do."

He strode toward her. "You do? Thank the gods! Tell me, Lydia. What is it?"

She pulled away from him. "No. I do not think so, Nadius."

"What? You will tell me!" He seized her by the arm and pulled her roughly to him.

"You're hurting my arm—"

His other hand was around her neck. "Tell me, Lydia. Tell me or I'll choke it out of you!"

"Stop it! Stop, Nadius! You're hurting me! I'll never tell you!"

He threw her into the wall and her head struck with a loud crack. Lydia slipped sideways and fell to the floor. Nadius stood over her, his fist raised. "Tell me!" he screamed at her.

Suddenly Lydia's expression changed. She clutched her stomach in pain. "Help! Help me! Get Euodia quickly."

Nadius sensed something more than her physical pain. His eyes went to her hands clutching her abdomen. "Lydia! What is it?"

"The baby! Oh, by the gods, get Euodia quickly! I think I'm losing the baby!"

It was the next day before he was allowed to see her. She lay very still in the bed, her eyes fixed on the ceiling. Nadius walked slowly to the side of the bed and looked down at her. "Lydia."

She did not acknowledge him. Her eyes did not blink. Only the slight movement of the covers indicated that she was alive. "Lydia," he said again, "please speak to me."

A full minute passed without any sign that she had heard him. Then her eyes moved slowly and looked at him. Her expression did not change, her face calm and detached. Then her lips moved. "What do you want from me now?" she asked. "I have lost the baby. Do you want to hurt me more?"

He dropped to his knees beside the bed, his face buried in the covers next to her hand. "Lydia, I am sorry. I am so sorry. Please, Lydia. Please forgive me." He was crying softly, his head moving slightly as his body shuddered. She watched for several moments, saying nothing. Then her hand moved slowly toward his head. She placed it on his hair and stroked it gently.

"Nadius, the child I lost was the only one I shall ever have. I can never bear another child."

He raised his head and looked at her, tears streaming down his face. "It was my fault, Lydia. I did this to you. And I am sorry. I didn't mean for this to happen."

She sighed as she stroked his head. "No, I suppose you didn't."

He took her hand in his. "I haven't been much of a husband to you. But I can change, Lydia. I can change if you give me another chance."

"Another chance? Oh, Nadius, we have been joined together before the gods. For better or worse, you are my husband. Perhaps we can talk about it later, but right now I am too tired. In a few days I should be feeling better. Go away now. Give me time to get over all that has happened."

He arose and stood looking down at her. Then he bent over and kissed her on the forehead. "Yes," he said softly, "rest now. When you are feeling better we can talk about it."

He left the room and she closed her eyes. Sleep did not come easily, and when it did she dreamed of children, children which now she could never bear.

When Lydia awoke, Euodia was sitting quietly next to her bed. "Drink this broth, Lydia. You haven't had any nourishment in you for two days."

She drank the contents of the cup and was surprised how good it tasted. Then Clement and Epaphroditus eased into her room. "I've brought you some flowers," Papie told her and held out a bouquet of wild asters.

"They are lovely," Lydia smiled at the youth. "Thank you." Euodia placed them in a vase of water on her night table near the bed.

The two men stood awkwardly in Lydia's room, neither knowing what to say to her. These people were her family, Lydia thought with joy. The three of them were all the family she had now that her father was gone. Certainly she could not count on Nadius, and she wondered whether he would ever mean as much to her as these three did. Three slaves, destined by the gods to be born of slave parents, Euodia and Clement and their sixteen-year-old son, Epaphroditus, were all she had now.

She had known Euodia and Clement all her life. She could remember when Epaphroditus, little Papie, had been born, though she was barely four at the time. He was like a baby brother to her and so it had been all her life.

After they left, she slept again, this time without dreaming. The next morning she tried to get out of bed, shaky, and managed to pull on her robe before Euodia knew what she was doing. Then she walked slowly out of her room and into the atrium. Euodia was sweeping the floor and looked up in surprise, her face reflecting disapproval.

"I'm hungry," Lydia told her. "I want a big breakfast. There is much work to be done."

When Nadius came into the dyeing rooms behind the house that morning, he was astonished to see Lydia working at the vats. "What are you doing here?"

Lydia raised her hands, stained with the dye and smelling like fish. "There is work to be done," she replied. "The cloth does not just magically appear and dye itself." She turned back to her work. Nadius stood watching her for a moment, then turned on his heels and walked out. He did not return to the dyeing rooms for the next three weeks.

Clement had really been the master of the art of dyeing cloth, although he would have denied it to give the credit to Licentor. But his skilled eyes could detect the slightest deviation in color as he watched over the vats as a hen over her chicks. When the cloth came from the vats, it was a yellow color. Only when the fabric had been carefully hung in the sunlight did the deep purple develop by the action of the light on the dye. The master dyer had to check the drying cloth constantly, making certain that all parts received the exact same quantity of sunlight. And Clement was an artist at this, pulling here, shading a bit here, as the sunlight brought out the colors evenly under his expert direction.

Clement was a very unusual slave, for Licentor and his father before him had been unusual masters. First off, he was an educated man. He could both read and write and also work with mathematics. And as he and Licentor had worked side by side for more than twenty years, Clement had absorbed almost all of the knowledge his master had possessed. They had talked of philosophy, as indeed most Greeks were wont to do. But also they spoke of history and science and geography and a dozen other subjects. In fact, Clement was probably, now that his master was gone, the most intelligent and educated man in Thyatira.

Epaphroditus, his son, now benefited from his father's knowledge. Although the youth was not nearly as interested in the wide range of subjects his father was, he still received an extensive education at his side. But this morning there was something else on Papie's mind as he worked.

"Father," he said in a low voice, "it isn't fair."

Clement glanced at his son for an instant. Then his attention was back to the vat, checking to see that all of the powdered dye was thoroughly dissolved. "This needs more stirring, Papie," he said. "And what isn't fair?"

Papie put the large paddle into the vat and began to stir with long, even strokes. "It isn't fair that Nadius should own the business. He knows nothing about it. It should belong to Lydia now. After all, it was her father's. Why should Nadius suddenly come into our house and give us orders? It just isn't fair!"

Clement pursed his mouth. "My son, if you are looking for fairness in this life, you will be much disappointed."

The youth continued to stir the vat of dye. "But it still is not right. I don't like him. I don't like the way he treats you, Father. I don't know how you can take the way he talks to you."

Clement put his hand on his son's shoulder. "Let me explain something to you, son. I have been the most fortunate of men. For all my life, almost forty years now, I have been privileged to live in this house, to be a part of this family, to work with the finest human being who ever lived. I have a good wife and I have a son I am proud of. I am also a slave.

"Now look around you, Papie. Look at other houses. Look at how their slaves are treated. We—you and I and your mother—are treated much better than most families treat their rightful members. So what if Nadius has come in and tries to push his weight around. Can he dye this cloth? No, my son, and he will come to realize in time just how much he needs us. And there is Lydia. No matter what Nadius does or says, I shall do anything in my power for Lydia. I would give my life for her."

Epaphroditus was silent as he stirred the vat, absorbing what his father had said. But under his breath he still formed the words, "It still isn't fair. It isn't fair."

A month later there was sufficient cloth dyed to fill the orders Licentor had received on his last selling trip. That evening Lydia spoke to Nadius. "Now it is time for you to go to work," she told him. "The cloth is ready. You must deliver it to our customers and obtain their next orders."

Nadius had been drinking heavily. He had kept himself away from the house while Lydia and Clement prepared the cloth, coming home late each evening. He and Lydia had spoken but little to one another in that time. She had not told him of Sybil, and he knew nothing at all about the fact that he was to become a father in a few weeks' time when the peasant girl from Pergamum had his baby.

He nodded to her and downed the rest of his wine. "Good," he replied. "I shall leave tomorrow. Have Clement get the shipment ready at the dock."

The next morning Clement and Papie loaded the cloth on the cart and took it to the dock. It was loaded aboard the ship and the captain was ready to cast off. But Nadius had not arrived and Clement wondered if the irresponsible young man had forgotten.

A half hour later Nadius arrived, his eyes red from the month-long drinking bout. He boarded the ship and the crew cast off the lines. The ship drifted into the current which took it down the Hyllus River.

Clement stood on the dock with Papie, watching the small vessel disappear around the bend. He shook his head and turned to his son. "I have a strange feeling," he said, "and it is not a good one. I feel that some disaster is coming. One which will affect us all."

Nadius retraced the trip he had made with Licentor, calling on the customers who had ordered fabric and taking their orders for the next trip. All were saddened by the news of Licentor's death, expressing deep regret and inquiring as to how Lydia was bearing up on the death of her father. Most of them, anxious to help, increased their orders for cloth to be delivered on his next visit.

This increased Nadius's confidence, both in the business and in himself. He refrained from drinking on this trip until he arrived at Philippi, where he chanced to meet Herteles again at the inn. The two soon became fast friends, spending their nights together drinking at the inn. Nadius, anxious to impress his new friend and to boast of his new wealth as sole owner of the business, insisted on paying the tabs for each night's drinking bout.

It was not until Nadius was ready to leave Philippi and was

checking out of the inn that he realized how much money he had spent. Most of the profits from the trip had been squandered in the nights of revelry with Herteles.

Melisus watched Sybil's time approach and now it was almost upon them. There were no signs that the birth would be anything other than normal, for the girl had been healthy and the old midwife had seen that she had taken good care of herself. She was not alarmed when in the middle of the night she heard the young girl call out to her that the time had come.

For the last week Melisus had insisted that Sybil sleep in her own bed, which was higher than the pallet on the floor. She readied everything she needed for the delivery of the baby and sat down next to the bed to time the contraction pains.

They came closer and closer together, and when the time had come, Melisus prepared to help the baby into the world. Then it came and she cut the cord and slapped the tiny bottom to start the child breathing. A loud wail came from the small throat and Melisus smiled as she turned back to the bed and the new mother.

"You have a fine son," she announced, "a fine healthy boy." She wrapped the child in the soft cloths and put it into the box beside the bed. Then Melisus turned her attention to Sybil and what she saw she did not like. Hurriedly she used clean cloths as a compress to try to control the bleeding, now profuse. But still the blood came, soaking the cloths and the bed in a scarlet pool.

Melisus had seen this happen before. She knew that she must stem the flow of blood or the young girl would be dead very quickly. All her knowledge from over a thousand deliveries was put into play, but to no avail. Still the blood continued to pour from the now pale young girl who lay still and close to death upon the bed.

She had no one to send for help. Indeed, there was no one who could do any more than Melisus herself could do. But twenty minutes later Sybil stopped breathing. And as the child wailed loudly in the box, Melisus stood up, her face in anguish. Nothing more could be done. Sybil was dead.

She carried the small bundle to Lydia's house, tears streaming down her face. "I tried," she cried. "I tried as hard as I knew how. But the gods had deemed it her time to die. I could not prevent it."

As Euodia tried to calm the nearly hysterical woman, Lydia took the soft bundle in her arms. Finally Melisus calmed down enough to tell them what had happened, and Clement and Euodia went back to her cottage to wash Sybil's body and arrange for burial.

"But what of the child?" Melisus asked. "What is to be done about him?"

Lydia held the tiny infant close to her breast. "Do? It is done. He is mine. I lost my baby. But now the gods have given me a son. I will keep him as my own."

Arrangements were made for a wet nurse for the infant. This was a common practice for women who could not nurse their own babies or perhaps did not wish to ruin their figures, as many of the rich women chose not to. Lydia opened the blankets and looked at him. She hummed a tune as she cuddled the tiny form. His hands reached out for her and she knew this child was really her own, a gift from the gods to replace the child she had lost. She now had a son and she knew she could never give him up.

The wet nurse was a jolly woman in her early forties with huge breasts. "I have enough milk to feed a dozen babies," she laughed as she held him close to her to feed him. When he had finished, he fell asleep in her arms. Selsai, the wet nurse, would live in the house until the baby was weaned. Euodia frowned and whispered to Lydia, "She needs a bath. She smells like a pig."

Lydia smiled at her. "I'll leave that up to you. See that she gets one. And she will be sleeping in my old room for the time being." Lydia took Euodia by the arm. "Be kind to her. The baby needs her."

Later that evening, when the baby and the nurse were both asleep, Euodia came to Lydia. "What are you going to tell Nadius now? You'll have to tell him about that girl. You'll have to tell him that the baby is his."

Lydia looked away. "I'll worry about that when the time comes," she said. "But Euodia, isn't he beautiful? So tiny and wrinkled."

Euodia shook her head. "To me all babies look like little monkeys. Even Papie did. I haven't seen one yet that was beautiful, except for you, Lydia. Now you were a beautiful baby."

Lydia laughed. "Go on, now. See to that bath for Selsai. And get her some clean clothes. We can't have her going about in rags."

Euodia left shaking her head. "This place is becoming a regular inn for transients," she muttered to herself. "Used to be quiet around here, but no more."

Lydia smiled as she heard her. She peeked into his basket and looked at him, sleeping peacefully, content. "A baby in the house," she sang softly. "My baby. And no one will ever take him from me."

Nadius arrived back in Thyatira and stood on the dock at the river. He knew he would have to explain where the profits from the cloth had gone, and he did not want to face Lydia to tell her he had wasted them on drink. Then the solution came to him. He would go to Angelicus, the moneylender. He would borrow the money. On the next trip he would make it up and no one would be the wiser.

Angelicus was more than willing to lend him the money.

Nadius was now a man of means, the owner of a profitable business. All Nadius had to do was sign his name to the pledge the loan maker drew up. With the business as security, there was no trouble at all in making the loan. Angelicus counted out the money to him and Nadius went home.

There was no one at the door to greet him, no one knew when to expect his return. He entered the house and his ears were greeted with a strange sound. It sounded like a baby crying. He entered the atrium and saw Lydia with an infant in her arms.

"What is this?" he asked. "Are you minding babies now?"

Lydia smiled at the tiny child in her arms. "Yes, Nadius. I am minding babies. Sit down Nadius and let me tell you about this child."

He sat down, wondering about the strange glow in his wife's face.

"A few weeks ago this fine boy was born to a poor country girl from another town. She had become pregnant during a brief tryst with a young man. When her father found out, he threw her out of the house. She had no place to go and came to Thyatira where the baby was born. But during the birth, the young girl died, leaving this baby an orphan. The gods took away our child, Nadius, and I can bear no other. But now they have given me this beautiful baby boy to raise as my own."

She looked directly into his eyes. "I want this child, Nadius. I want to adopt him and raise him as my own."

He arose from the chair and his expression changed. "Now wait," he said sternly. "I should have something to say about that! And I do not intend to raise the illegitimate child of some country tart. I won't have it, Lydia. Do you hear me?"

Lydia's eyes flashed. "You will have it, Nadius. I want this child and I will have him!"

"You will not!" He slammed his fist against the chair. "Not the spawn of a whore! Is that what you expect me to adopt? Do you really expect me to call that—that bastard—my own son?"

Lydia smiled at him. She held out the baby to him. "Yes, Nadius. I do. Especially since you really are his father."

— Chapter Four —

Lydia named the boy Doronius, which in her language meant "a gift," and to her the child had been a gift, a gift of the gods to replace the baby she had lost. Nadius ignored the boy. Since the day Lydia had told him the child was his, he avoided him as much as possible and had turned sullen and morose.

But Lydia was supremely happy, caring for the baby in every way she could, doing everything for him except that which she could not do, nurse him. Nadius spent most of his time away from the house with his friends at the taverns and gaming halls. When he came home late at night, he slept in a spare bedroom so the child's crying would not disturb his sleep.

And when the orders for the dyed fabric were ready, he had the cloth taken to the dock and left on a ship without saying goodbye to Lydia. At Mytilene he boarded a larger vessel and landed at Troas to call on Pietrius. Nadius was greeted warmly and Pietrius inquired about Lydia's health and how he was finding business. He gave an order for his next requirement of dyed cloth and had poured them both wine when Nadius told him, "There have been increases in the cost of wool and silk. I will have to raise my prices accordingly."

Pietrius raised his eyebrows. "Oh? I had not heard of this. By how much will your increase be?"

Nadius had calculated how high he could go without causing suspicion. "By ten percent," he lied.

Pietrius nodded. "That is not too much. I shall have to increase my prices a bit to the rich Roman ladies."

Nadius left and wound his way in the streets down to the wharves. He wished now that he had raised the price to Pietrius by even more, as there had been no argument over the ten percent. "I told Licentor his prices were too low," he said to himself. "That fool did not know how much the cloth should be selling for. He could have been making much more profit all along."

He boarded a ship for Neapolis and when he arrived he stayed overnight at the inn. The next morning he hired donkeys and carried his goods to Philippi. The next morning he called upon Stetius, his largest customer.

"The cost of wool and silk has risen. I must increase my prices," he told Stetius. "The prices will now be . . . twenty-five percent higher on your next order."

Stetius eyed him for a moment, his expression unchanging. Then he said, "You have the right to charge whatever you will for your goods." But Nadius saw that the order was much smaller than previously. Perhaps the man did not really need as much this time, Nadius reasoned.

At each customer for the remainder of his trip, Nadius increased the prices by twenty-five percent. The only complaint he received was from the man in Thessalonica, but Licentor had told him that this man would always complain about prices.

He counted up his total orders and was dismayed when they amounted to only about half of the preceeding ones. What he needed, he told himself, was more customers. Licentor had informed him of an agreement with a competitor not to sell dyed cloth in the city of Ephesus. In exchange, the competitor would not sell in cities where Licentor did business. "That," reasoned Nadius, "was Licentor's agreement. I shall sell my cloth wherever

I please. Ephesus has a quarter of a million people and many rich Romans." He took a ship bound for Ephesus.

According to the custom of the time, Lydia took Doronius to the temple of Diana to dedicate the child and to invoke the goddess's protection on his life. With her went Euodia and Clement, and the sacrifices were made at the altar as Lydia held the baby before the statue of Diana. The idol looked on impassively, her many breasts protruding from her gilded chest, as the ceremony proceeded.

The priest took the baby from Lydia's arms and held him up. "O, great mother of humanity, look with favor upon this child who has been given to your charge. Protect him from harm and from evil. Give him health and vigor. And he is pledged to worship and honor you all the days of his life."

The customary gifts were given to the temple and to the priests, and the party returned home. "Now I know everything will be all right," Lydia said.

Clement and Euodia exchanged glances. "I hope you are right," Clement replied.

Lydia stopped and looked up at him with a bewildered expression. "Why do you say that? Why shouldn't everything be all right?"

Clement shook his head. "I should not have said that. I meant nothing by it. Forget about it."

But Lydia would not let it pass. "Clement, what did you mean? You have been like a second father to me all these years. Tell me what you meant. Is there anything wrong?"

"No. Not really. It's just that . . . well, since Licentor died I have had an uneasy feeling. There is an entirely different mood in the house. But pay no attention to me, Lydia. It is probably my imagination. I didn't mean to upset you."

Euodia look Lydia by the arm. "It's just that he misses your father so much. Pay no attention to what he said, Lydia."

They walked on in silence as Lydia thought. Clement was right, she agreed silently. The house had certainly been different since her father's death. It had been such a happy place. But now the mood was changed. Of course they all missed Licentor, but there was more to it than that. A blackness, some impending evil, a dark cloud, seemed to hang over them all now. She shuddered as they entered the courtyard. But she would have to make the best of things. The mood would pass. Now that she had little Doronius, laughter and good feelings were certain to return. She would make sure they did for his sake.

She put Doronius to bed and sat thinking. Had she made a mistake in marrying Nadius? Everything had seemed to change after that. And the marriage had certainly not turned out the way she had dreamed. They had not lived together as man and wife since she had lost her baby.

Nadius had not even looked at the baby—even after learning it was really his own. It had been a great shock to him, she knew. In time, Lydia prayed, he would get over it and take the boy into his arms and into his heart. Time, Lydia thought, cures all things.

Nadius arrived at Ephesus and took a room at an inn on the Arkadiane directly across the wide street from the temple of Serapis. He inquired as to who sold the expensive dyed fabrics to the rich of the city and was told the largest and best-known merchant was a man named Lycops who had a shop farther along the Arkadiane near the agora.

The next morning Nadius walked along the street to the agora, the marketplace, and found the shop of Lycops, an elaborate place befitting the wealthy clientele he served. Nadius nodded with approval at the variety of cloth which was on display.

A servant stood near the door to greet customers and Nadius asked to see the owner of the establishment. A few moments later an obese man came from a back room. "I am Lycops," he said. "What can I do for you?"

Nadius pulled a small sample swatch of his best purple silk from his robe and handed it to the man. "Do you have any silk to match this?" he asked.

Lycops moved to the doorway for better light and held up the cloth. His brow furrowed as he turned back to Nadius. "Let me show you what I have," he said as he unrolled some fabric on the table. "This is the finest silk in the city. You will not find better than this."

Nadius ran his fingers over the cloth. "Yes," he agreed, "the silk is excellent. But the color is not good." He held the swatch of his own purple next to the material on the table. The contrast in color was obvious.

Lycops eyed him cautiously. "Where did you get this?" he demanded. "I have not seen color like this for many years."

"I see it everyday," Nadius said. "I own the business where it is produced."

Lycops' eyebrows arched. "There is only one man who can dye silk such as this," he replied. "And you are not Licentor of Thyatira."

"Licentor was my father-in-law. He is dead and I now own the business."

"I tried to purchase his cloth years ago," Lycops said in a low tone, "but he refused to sell to me. I suspect he had an agreement with those in Ephesus who dye cloth."

"Perhaps he did. But now the business is mine. I intend to sell where and to whom I choose. Are you interested in buying silk such as this?"

The proprietor motioned for him to come to the rear of the

shop and led him through a doorway into a private office. He indicated a chair and Nadius sat down facing him. A servant poured wine and Nadius sipped his slowly as Lycops looked at him eagerly. "I have done business with my present supplier for many years," Lycops said. "I would be taking quite a chance doing business with you." He bent his head and felt the swatch of purple silk again, feeling the texture and marveling at the brilliant color. "How do I know that you will supply my requirements? And perhaps your goods are not the same quality as this sample."

Nadius regarded him for a moment, then took a chance to call the man's bluff. He arose from the chair and tucked the swatch back into his robe. "I am a man of my word," he said haughtily. "If you question it, then I shall sell my silk elsewhere in the city. Good day to you."

Lycops hurried after him and seized his arm. "No, please! I did not mean to question your word. Please accept my apology."

Nadius slowly returned and sat down.

"I shall give you an order for your fine silk," Lycops told him. "How soon can you deliver?" He counted on his finger. "Let me see, I shall need five rolls of purple silk and ten of wool."

Nadius sneered, "I thought you were the largest dealer in fine cloth in Ephesus! Apparently I was wrong. If that is your requirement, then I must certainly look elsewhere. My smallest customers use more cloth than that!"

Lycops was perspiring. His eyes were on Nadius. He had intended to give him a small order, hoping that would keep Nadius from selling to his competitors. But it had not worked. And if his competitors could offer this quality of silk, his own business would be ruined.

"Tell me, Lycops," Nadius asked, "how much cloth will you sell in three months? That should be the size of your initial order with me."

The fat merchant blinked at this. Nadius was demanding all or nothing at all. But he could not risk letting his competitors obtain this silk. Certainly the man must be realistic. For his entire quantity of goods, there should be a discount on the price. This time Lycops gambled. "What you are asking me to do is very risky. What am I going to say to my present supplier? He has been as a brother to me! Do you expect me to cut him off without warning?"

Nadius shrugged. "That is your problem, not mine. You must run your business, I must run mine. It is a hard world, Lycops. Every one of us must look out for himself."

"Then there must be discounts on a quantity of that size. My present supplier gives me a large discount. Will you match this?"

"How much discount are you getting?"

"Twenty-five percent."

Nadius gulped at this. "And how much are your requirements a year? What quantity are we talking about for this discount?"

When the man told him, Nadius could hardly contain himself. This one man bought more cloth in a year than the rest of his business combined. Here was an opportunity to double the business volume instantly. But with the discount, he would be selling at a price even lower than what Licentor had been getting from his customers.

He made up his mind hurriedly. "If you place an order with me for your entire requirement of all cloth, I will give you the same discount."

It was done. He walked out of the shop with the order in his hand which had doubled his business. Then Nadius had a sickening thought. Could Clement produce this increased volume of cloth. At the moment he didn't know.

Over a thousand miles from the shellfish beds of the Mediterranean and Aegean seas a storm was brewing. This was not a usual storm. In fact a storm of this intensity occurred only once in about a hundred years.

As it passed over the Black Sea it intensified further, and when it cut across the neck of land that separates Europe from Asia, the counter-clockwise fury of the winds whipped the water of the Aegean into a boiling cauldron, lashing the western coast with mountainous waves.

The creatures of the sea were smashed against rocks and reefs, and the sea animals that clung to the rocks were dashed to pieces, mangled with the fury of the crashing surf and boiling foam. The storm lasted for two days and nights, and when it finally subsided many of the species had been decimated.

Among these were the Murex trunculus and Purpura haemastoma, the smallest of the shellfish whose glands contained the dye used to produce the magnificent purple color. It would be years before these shellfish beds returned to normal.

Nadius had waited out the storm at Ephesus. He had been fortunate not to have been caught at sea when the storm had struck, for many lives were lost as ships were smashed against the rocky reefs of the Aegean. When he reached Mytilene he was greeted with the disastrous news by Busteles. The shellfish beds nearby were no more. His ships would have to travel great distances to obtain the mussels for dye, if they could be found at all.

Nadius boarded the small boat that would take him the rest of the way home with a sickening fear. The cost of the purple dye would naturally be high—much higher than ever before. It might not be available at all. But he must obtain the precious dye. He had gambled his business on his ability to supply the cloth. If he could not, he would lose everything.

When he entered the house, Lydia knew at once that something was wrong. Although they had not spoken to each other much during the past months, the anguish on his face softened her feelings. "What is wrong?"

He flung his belongings on a chair and stalked to the table where the decanter of wine was kept. He downed a goblet full before facing Lydia.

"The storm has destroyed the beds. There may be no dye this year. If there is, the price will be exorbitant."

"Oh, no! Clement was afraid the storm might have affected them!"

He looked at her now with a different attitude, not as a wife he had grown tired of, but as a mature, sensible woman who might have a solution. "Lydia, we may lose everything." He took her hand in his, as a confused child seeking guidance from his mother. "What are we to do?"

Despite her feelings about him, her heart was filled with compassion. "We will survive. No matter what happens, we will survive. It will be all right, Nadius. It will be all right."

"Survive!" Suddenly the old look was back in his face. "I want to do more than just survive! You don't understand. I took orders for twice the usual quantity of cloth. If we can't deliver it, I shall get no more orders from my new customer."

"What new customer? Where have you gone to sell our cloth?"

He filled the goblet again. Then looking out the window toward the green fields stretching to the river, he said slowly, "I went to Ephesus. Lycops has given me the order for his entire requirement of silk and woolens."

"Ephesus! Father never sold our cloth in Ephesus. He had an agreement not to sell there."

"Agreement be damned! I won't be bound by his agreements!" As he shouted this, she drew back from him. He hung his head and reached out for her hand again, pulling her to him. "Lydia, you don't understand the world of business. For the business to grow, we must sell more cloth. I intend to be the largest producer of cloth in the Aegean, in the world. I can't be bound by the way your father did things. I have to run things my own way."

She looked into his eyes. Inside of her she knew him to be weak, lazy, irresponsible. She could not now crush his sudden ambition. If he was to be the master of this house, then he would have to be the one to make the decisions. When she answered him, her voice was level and controlled, "Whatever you say, Nadius. The business is yours. But be careful. Greed can bring disaster. Father was content to make a good living. He wanted no more from life. If you wish to be the biggest, then that is your right. Whatever you decide is the way it shall be."

He kissed her lightly on the cheek, relieved at the manner in which she had taken his plans and his action. He went directly to the rooms behind the house where Clement worked at the vats.

"Clement," he called. "I must talk with you. We have plans to make. Big plans."

Selsai, the wet nurse, held the baby to her breasts and sang to him as he nursed. In a short time she would no longer be needed, she thought to herself. The boy was beginning to eat some solid food now, and soon he would no longer need her fat nipples and plentiful supply of milk.

She would be sorry when that time came. She had enjoyed taking care of this child. She certainly did not understand the master of the house, but that was none of her business, she thought. Still she could not understand how any man could ignore a baby as cunning and as lovable as Doronius. As he finished nursing, she held him on her shoulder to burp him. Suddenly she felt him stiffen and she moved him in her arms so she could see what was the matter.

The child's face was contorted in pain and she looked on in bewilderment as his body shuddered. It lasted for only a few moments and the child was himself again, appearing perfectly normal. Selsai returned him to her shoulder and patted his back. In a moment came the satisfying sound of a belch. She placed the boy in his cradle and stood looking down at him. His face was a reflection of contentment now. What had caused the sudden pain, she wondered? Probably just gas. She would not even mention the incident to Lydia. No need in worrying her over nothing.

Clement could not believe his ears. He was being asked by Nadius to do the impossible! How could he be expected to produce twice the quantity of purple cloth with only half the amount of shellfish dye?

He should not have told Nadius about the process used by many dyers of inferior quality cloth of using substitute dyes for the expensive Murex and Purpura shellfish dyes. It was true that initially the color was almost as good as the double shellfish-dyed cloth, but the color would quickly fade in the cheap process, turning shades of dirty brown.

But Nadius insisted that he do this in the next production of fabric. Licentor would never have allowed such a thing. Clement considered refusing, but he thought of Lydia and the baby. If he refused, he did not know what the reaction of the volatile young man who now owned the business would be. So for the sake of his mistress, Clement held his tongue and consented to do his best with the cheaper method of dyeing the cloth.

Nadius now counted his cash assets and found that they were not sufficient to purchase the double quantity of silk and woolen goods he now needed. He would have to go to the moneylender again for more money. But, he calculated, when this production of cloth was sold, he would have more than enough to pay part of what he owed to Angelicus and still have some money left over.

He sought out the moneylender in the market and found the man more than willing to give him what he needed. Nadius signed another paper, and now half of the business was mortgaged for what he owed the man.

When the fabric arrived, the entire household was busy with dyeing the cloth. When the time came to add the secret ingredient to the batch of silk, Lydia refused to tell Nadius what it was, insisting on entering the vat house alone to add it to the batch. Nadius was furious, stomping off to the tavern and returning late that night very drunk and in a foul mood.

Clement followed Nadius's orders, as distasteful as they were to him. He first used indigo to dye the cloth, replacing the shellfish dye. Only on the second dyeing was the Murex and Purpura used.

When the cloth was ready, Clement showed it to Nadius. He examined the color carefully, comparing it to a swatch of previous material dyed in the proper manner. But he could not tell the difference between the two. Clement had done his work well. And if the color faded with time, then he would face that problem when it arose. But now, feeling confident as the stock of fabric grew each day, he made plans to travel down the river and across the Aegean again to deliver his goods to the customers.

Nadius was very proud of himself. He had pulled off a coup. For Busteles had been right when he told him that his men might have to travel a long distance to find the shellfish. They had, and since the dye must be extracted within three days, they also had to rent the facilities to extract the dye in the far-off lands where they had been found. The price of dye was now twice what it had been the year before.

Nadius had bought little of the dye, telling Busteles that business had fallen off. And two weeks later, he loaded his cloth on the ship and set off, stopping first at Troas and then going on to Philippi to deliver his fabric. At neither place was the quality of the cloth questioned. Clement had done a good job, indeed.

At Ephesus, even the critical eye of Lycops failed to notice anything out of the ordinary in the dyed cloth. The fat man paid for the order and placed another one just as large. Nadius was in high spirits when he boarded the ship for Mytilene and from there to Thyatira and home. But when he entered the workshop and saw the look on Clement's face, he knew immediately that something was very wrong.

Clement held up a swatch of cloth, a sample from the goods which he had just delivered. "It has already begun to turn color," Clement told him. "You will face a hornet's nest when you call on our customers next. What you have delivered to them should all be a dirty brown by now."

Angelicus, the moneylender, pulled the papers from his tunic and gestured with them to the man who sat opposite him at the table. "These are notes covering half the value of his business. I thought you might be interested in them, as you are a competitor in the dyeing of cloth."

The other man's eyes widened as they talked. He had long envied the purple silk Licentor had been able to produce. Gorticus had never been able to discover the secret that Licentor's family possessed, nor had anyone else in the trade. He knew that if he could dye cloth with the brilliant colors on the silken fabric from the Aegean islands, he could become a very rich man.

"But suppose he can pay off these notes. They would be of no value to me then." He sipped his wine and watched the face of the moneylender.

Angelicus smiled a mirthless smile. "He will not be able to do that," he said. "I happen to know that he owes the sellers of woolens and silk much money as well. If he were forced to pay off these debts, he would not be able to meet the notes on the business."

"And how do you intend to make that happen?" Gorticus asked.

The dark man laughed. "That is very simple. They also owe me much money. If I were to call in their outstanding debts, they would have to demand payment from Nadius. He must pay them or he would not be able to obtain the cloth he needs to continue."

Now it was Gorticus who smiled. "You seem to have all the answers, my friend. And how soon will this happen?"

Angelicus lifted his glass. "As soon as you purchase these notes from me. With the twenty-five percent bonus added on, of course. Is it a deal?"

Gorticus lifted his glass in return. "We have a deal. Call in your debts at once. And soon the secret of dyeing silk will be mine."

Nadius could not understand what was happening when the suppliers of cloth all demanded payment for what he owed them. He could not refuse, for he needed more cloth to fill his new orders. Reluctantly he took from his purse the proceeds from the last orders and when the last man had left, the purse was almost empty.

He would have to get an extension of the loan from Angelicus, he reasoned, for now he could not meet his payment to the moneylender. He found the man at his customary place at the agora and approached him.

"I must have some additional time," he told Angelicus. "I will need three more months in order to pay you."

Surprisingly, the dark man did not protest. Instead he smiled at Nadius in a strange way. "I no longer hold your notes," he told him. "You will have to speak with a man named Gorticus. I sold your securities to him. You must know him, Nadius. He happens to be in the same business you are in."

Nadius went home numb. The world was crashing down about him. Now Gorticus would foreclose the mortgages and take over his business. Licentor had told him of that man, how he had envied the secret process. And now the business would belong to him. He was not surprised when on the next day Euodia announced that a man named Gorticus was in the atrium and wished to speak with him.

The next day found Nadius traveling down the river Hyllus to catch a ship bound for Macedonia. He did not believe his good fortune. The man, Gorticus, had been very honorable about the whole affair.

They had gone into the garden to talk, for Nadius had been certain that Euodia would be listening in the house. Gorticus had produced the notes he had signed with Angelicus worth half Nadius's business. They were indeed due, but instead of foreclosing, Gorticus had made him a generous offer. He would purchase the other half of the business for a substantial sum of money. But there was also a condition to this. He must be given the family secret, the long-guarded process of dyeing silk the beautiful and lasting purple colors.

Nadius had agreed, not telling the man he did not know this secret. Nadius would get it from Lydia. Now that the business was gone, she would have no reason not to tell him the secret. They had a month to vacate the property, the house and the workshops where the vats for dyeing the cloth were kept. And in one month, Nadius would have to deliver the family secret process for dyeing silk.

But now his purse was full of the money Gorticus had paid him for the other half of the business. This he did not intend to waste. Perhaps, he rationalized, the whole thing had happened for the best. He was not really suited for the business of cloth dyeing anyway. And now he had bigger and better things in mind.

Two weeks later Nadius arrived back home. He called everyone into the atrium to make an announcement. When they had all assembled, puzzled over the sudden conference, he faced them with a broad smile.

"I have sold the business," he announced. "We are all moving to Philippi in Macedonia. I have bought a gold mine there."

— Chapter Five —

They stared at him, wide-eyed, mouths agape, not believing what he had just said. Lydia was the first to gain her composure.
"You have done what?"
A grin was on his face. "Our fortune is made," he told her. "In six months' time we shall have enough gold to last us a lifetime."
"But you... we... know nothing about gold mining!" exclaimed Clement.
"There is little to know," Nadius said. "The gold is among the gravel and sand in the river bed. All we have to do is wash the soil away and the heavier gold flakes remain. And there is also a mine shaft leading to a vein of almost pure gold beneath the earth."
"But I have lived in Thyatira all my life," Lydia protested. "To me this is home! I don't want to leave here. Especially far across the sea. I was born here, in this house, and you had no right to sell it without even consulting me about it! This was my father's business!"
His expression changed. "Can't you get it through your head that I own it now? It is no longer your father's! It's mine. And I can do with it as I please." He glared at them, his eyes moving to one person, then the next. "I will hear no more about it! It has been done! And I have bought another business, one which shall make me rich. I don't want to go through life with my hands smelling of filthy fish. I don't want to have to bow and scrape to customers. In six months I shall never have to work again!"

He stalked from the room and they looked at one another without speaking. Then Euodia began to cry. "What shall we do?"

Lydia put her arm around her and fought to control her own emotions.

"My husband says we are going to Philippi," she said slowly. "We shall all go to Philippi."

Later that evening Nadius returned home and faced Lydia in the atrium.

"Now you must tell me the secret of dyeing silk," he said. "I must reveal this to Gorticus. It is part of the bargain."

She turned her head away. "Since you have already sold my father's business, I suppose it does not matter now," she said. "But I shall tell him myself. On the day we leave I will tell him the secret. But not before."

He argued with her, but to no avail. Still she insisted that she would be the one to tell Gorticus. "Don't you trust me?" he demanded.

She looked away from him in disgust, not bothering to answer. He walked away. Lydia heard him go out the door, to meet his friends in the tavern, she supposed.

When the packing for the move began, Lydia saw the things she remembered since childhood stacked in piles. They could take only the necessities, the clothing and utensils that would be needed when they arrived in Macedonia. Along with the mine went a small cottage at the site. Nadius had not actually seen the property, so he could not describe what they would find as far as accomodations. But Herteles had told him that the cottage was livable and there was a spring of water nearby. Still, Lydia's heart was torn as she watched the things she had treasured placed on the pile to either be sold or given away.

With a woman's judgment, Lydia sorted out the pots, bowls and kitchen utensils they would need, trying to be as practical as possible. She held in her hand the enameled dishes that had belonged to her mother. "I suppose these are too fragile for use there," she said sadly, putting them with the other things to be left behind. "I feel as though my life itself is in that pile," she told Euodia.

The days sped by until it was time to take the boxes to the dock. Clement and Papie loaded them onto the wagon and set out. Euodia took the baby and rode on top of the boxes in the cart while Nadius and Lydia waited for Gorticus to arrive. Half an hour later he came, and Nadius greeted him warmly. Lydia only nodded slightly to the man who now owned all that she treasured from her youth.

"Are you ready for your journey?" Gorticus asked.

"Our belongings are already at the dock," Nadius told him.

"Then all that remains is for you to tell me the secret process for dyeing silk." He turned to Lydia. "Your husband says that you wish to be the one to reveal it to me."

"What I wish has nothing to do with it," Lydia said coldly. "Since my husband has made a bargain with you, I must fulfill my part in it. But I hope you appreciate the value of this family secret. It has been handed down for many generations from father to son."

"I do," he told her. "And I shall now hand it down to my son for the future generations of my family. It belongs to me now."

Lydia turned to Nadius. "I wish to speak with him alone," she said.

Reluctantly he walked away and Gorticus moved closer to Lydia. "Now," he said, "what is the secret of dyeing silk?"

Lydia pulled him close to her and whispered in his ear. His face registered surprise. "And that is all there is to it?" he asked.

She nodded and he grinned at her. "Extraordinary! No wonder no one could guess what it was!"

Lydia joined her husband and they walked through the gate and down the road to the dock at the Hyllus River. She stopped for a moment before the road bent around a turn and looked back at the house where she had been born and had lived all of her life. Then, with a deep sigh, she turned.

"Let's go, Nadius. There is nothing left for me here."

The ship at the dock had already been loaded with their belongings when they arrived. A few moments later it cast off and they were on their way. At Mytilene they would board the larger seagoing vessel that would take them to Neapolis. From there they would hire donkeys to take their possessions to Philippi.

Lydia stood in the stern of the ship as it proceeded downstream past the grove of trees where her father and mother lay in eternal rest. She felt a deep twinge of guilt and remorse as she noted that the flowers she had placed just this morning on their graves had already begun to wilt.

"It has gone," she said to herself. "Nothing lasts forever."

Euodia put her arm around Lydia. "It all belongs to that horrible man, Gorticus, now," she said.

"Not everything," Lydia replied. "He did not get everything."

"What do you mean?"

There was a faint smile on Lydia's lips as she answered in a low voice. "He did not get the family secret," she said.

"What? But you gave it to him!" She stared at Lydia. "Or did you?"

Lydia put her hand to her mouth to stifle a laugh. "Just wait until he tries it! Oh, how I should like to see his face!"

"Then what did you tell him?"

Lydia pulled the stout woman close and spoke into her ear. "I told him he must eat asparagus for three days, then urinate into the vat!"

Euodia laughed until she choked. "Lydia! You didn't!"

Lydia nodded her head vigorously, "Yes, I did!"

"Oh, I would give anything to see his face. I hope he at least likes asparagus!"

The ship rounded a bend in the river and the scene was gone. That evening they were at Mytilene, and their belongings were transferred to the larger ship bound for Neapolis.

The days spent aboard the ship were trying, especially for the women. Although the ship was large enough to cross the sea, it was too small to allow for either much comfort or privacy. A tarpaulin was dropped between the corners of the large cabin, and only here did Lydia and Euodia escape the eyes of the crew and the other male passengers.

Doronius took the voyage well. Clement slung a small hammock for him and the motion of the ship seemed to soothe the baby; he slept most of the journey. The days were pleasantly warm with the sun's rays tanning them on the deck, but the nights were cool and extra blankets had to be unpacked. The stars hung low and large in the sky and brighter than Lydia had ever seen them against the utter blackness of the Aegean sky. When the moon rose, it sent a silver shimmer over the calm waters as the ship rode at anchor at an island for the night, creating such a dazzling path that Lydia almost tried to step out and walk upon it.

When they reached Neapolis, Lydia was surprised. It was a far prettier town than she remembered, having been here in the company of her father when she was about ten years old. The inn where they found lodging was clean and comfortable. It was reassuring to her that the proprietor recognized Nadius and greeted him warmly. When Lydia's head touched the soft pillow in the clean bed, she fell asleep at once.

Morning came too quickly and the sun streamed through the window of the room. She dressed and looked out the window. In the courtyard the donkeys were already being loaded with their possessions and would carry them to the cottage north of Philippi where the mine was located. Their braying filled Lydia with the desire to be off, to see this property her husband had bought and which he claimed would be the making of their fortune.

Philippi was but a four-hour journey and they reached the city before noon. Here they bought the provisions they would require in the remote wilderness of mountains where the mine was located, and these were added to the donkeys' loads. Nadius inquired about the route to the mine and was advised to wait until morning to start out. Although the distance was not great, the trail in that part of the area was rough and could be treacherous in the dark. They wisely decided to spend the night in Philippi and begin the final leg of the journey early the next morning.

That night as Nadius settled into the bed at the inn beside Lydia, he turned to her for the first time since she had lost her child. "Lydia," he said in an earnest voice, "we are making a new start in a new place. Do you believe we can do the same with our marriage?"

His penitent tone of voice moved her and the feelings she bore him softened, as though these feelings had also been left far across the sea.

"I am willing to try if you are," she told him.

He took her tenderly in his arms, one hand stroking her hair. "I want to make it new," he said. "I want to so badly." Her arms were about him and her lips sought his, eagerly, hungrily. And after they had made love she lay there, praying to the gods that it could always be the way it had been on this night.

The next morning found a chill in the air, and the sun was hidden behind thick walls of grey, winter clouds which had come over the mountains to turn the green of autumn to shades of red and yellow and brown. Soon the snow would come to this part of Macedonia, and the air would drop below the freezing temperature. They had arrived none too soon.

With his map in hand, Nadius led the party, the travelers and the donkey master who led his beasts of burden, up the steep trail and into the mountains north of the city. Soon the trail became less distinct, the way cluttered with rocks. In some places the narrow trail was hardly distinguishable from the dense underbrush of thorns and thicket.

The last few miles were the hardest. "Are you sure this is the way?" Lydia asked.

Nadius looked at his map. "I am certain. But I had no idea the going would be this hard. But we are almost there. Look at the map. We have only a short distance to go." But the short distance took the remainder of the day and the sun was disappearing behind the mountains as they finally descended into a dry creek bed and saw the cottage.

As she stood before it, Lydia did not know whether to laugh or cry. She had formed a mental picture of the cottage, a neat, rambling structure set in a vale with scenic mountains ringing it. In her mind's eye she had seen a growth of wild roses clinging to a rustic fence while in the front a tall shade tree cast welcome relief to a small bench next to the bubbling spring. But for the sight that greeted her eyes, she was totally unprepared.

The cottage consisted of one small room leaning unsteadily against the rocks of the mountain. The front door hung by one lone strap with claw marks scraped deep in the rotting wood indicating it had been torn free by a bear.

The roof had partially caved in, leaving gaping holes open to the sky. Cobwebs and filth covered everything inside, along with the droppings of the dozens of small animals that had visited to inspect it. The floor was clay, and on one wall stood a hearth with a section of the stones broken and lying scattered on the floor.

Clement was the first to break the silence as they all stood looking at their new home in shock. "The roof can be repaired," he said, "and the chimney restored. When the floor is swept clean and the door is set right, it will not look as bad."

But the man who owned the donkeys broke Clement's attempt to cheer them up. He stuck his head in the doorway and made a face. "Are you people really going to live *here?*" he asked incredulously.

Nadius nodded his head. "Yes, my friend. We are going to live here. But not for long! Not for long!"

It was too late that evening to start work on the cottage. As soon as the sun had disappeared behind the mountains to the west, the darkness descended on the valley as a black blanket. They had only sufficient time to gather firewood for the night and prepare to sleep out next to the fire until morning. They cooked their meal on the open fire and not long after curled up in blankets next to it to sleep.

Lydia heard the calls of animals and shivered as she cuddled Doronius close to her. But if she had seen the dozens of small eyes peering out of the darkness that ringed the slight glow of fire, she would not have slept at all.

Morning came with a dim light breaking through the trees on the mountain crests in the east. It spread long arms of red through the sky, gradually lightening the overcast. Then, as the sun itself climbed the peaks, day burst forth as a golden shaft of light that illuminated the valley.

After a quick breakfast of fruit, Clement and Epaphroditus began unpacking the tools they would need to repair the cottage. Nadius paid the donkey master for the use of his animals and bought one of them, which seemed the best of the lot, as they would certainly need the animal to haul and pull and perform the many tasks donkeys can do and men cannot.

After the man had left with his animals to return to Philippi, Nadius decided to inspect his mine. Since he was not in the least handy with tools, his assistance in the repair of the house was not missed. He scrambled up the dry creek bed carrying a clay pan and small shovel.

Lydia and Euodia swept out the interior of the small cottage and in short order had cleaned it of cobwebs and filth. Clement rehung the door, noting with respect the depth of the claw marks and hoping the animal would not return now that the cottage was occupied.

Epaphroditus felled some small pine trees with straight trunks and stripped the branches. Then he and Clement propped up the sagging roof and repaired the rafters. They applied a thick covering of new thatch on the old roof, sealing it against all but the heaviest of downpours and keeping the chill air out of the cabin.

The only feature that Nadius had probably not overestimated was the spring. It was indeed close by the house, and its water was cold and pure. With soft clay from the creek bed mixed with the spring water, Clement repaired the hearth, replacing the fallen stones and cementing them in place with the clay. A fire was then lit in the hearth to dry out and bake the clay to a bricklike hardness.

While the others were working on the cottage, Nadius climbed the creek bed into the mountain. He could see the entrance to the mine shaft far above, and he climbed the hill by grasping the small trees and shrubs that grew from between the rocks of the steep hill. When he reached the mine entrance he saw mounds of rubble that had been taken from the mine. Since he had no lamp, he could do nothing more than peer into the dark mine, its walls and roof supported by timbers. He examined the rocks outside but knew nothing of geology, and they told him nothing. Seeing all he could of the shaft entrance, he descended again to the creek and followed the bed around the other side of the mountain.

He heard the sound of water running and, rounding a bend in the creek, he came upon a waterfall that emptied into a great pool of water. As there was no outlet to the pool, he surmised that the pool fed an underground stream. Then, as he peered into the crystal depths of the pool, he saw something that made him catch his breath.

There in the gravel at the bottom of the pool something caught the slanting rays of the sun, glinting a bright yellow. Nadius removed his sandals and waded out into the water. Then, by holding on to a bush that grew from the side of the pool, he reached down deep into the water and grasped the object that had reflected the brilliant color.

It was in his hand and he shouted as he groped his way back to the bank of the pool and clambered up. He sat in the grass and turned the object over with his fingers, letting the sun's rays play upon it. Then, with another shout, he got up and started running down the dry creek bed in the direction he had come, almost forgetting his sandals until the rocky bottom bruised and cut his feet.

"Lydia! Clement! Look what I have found!" he screamed as he ran.

Now that the room had been swept clean, the two women looked at the meager furnishings of the cottage. Crude pallets were on the floor for sleeping. A rickety table was in one corner with two benches. The room was so small that there was really no more space for furniture. They unpacked and stored the kitchen utensils, pots and pans, and the tiny cabin was now at least clean enough to inhabit. It was certainly not like the house in Thyatira, but they would survive, Lydia thought.

For lighting at night, niches in the walls held lamps filled with oil. Epaphroditus had cut firewood and stacked it neatly along the wall next to the hearth. The spring had been cleaned out, and two large amphoras of cool water had been brought into the house. Little Doronius, just learning to crawl, got himself healthily dirty on the ground just outside the doorway and was the first member of the family to enjoy the luxury of a bath.

Lydia had just finished bathing him when she heard Nadius shouting. He came running down the creek bed, his arms waving wildly. "Look! Look at what I have found!"

They crowded around him as he looked at them with smug satisfaction. "All of you thought I was crazy when I bought this mine," he said excitedly, "but this should change your minds."

He opened his hand. In the palm was a rock, streaked with particles of yellow. "It's gold," Nadius laughed, "and the mine is full of it."

Clement took the rock and held it up to the sunlight. "Yes," he said, "it certainly looks like gold. Thank the gods! Nadius, I owe you an apology. I never thought it would be found so easily."

They danced around the cottage. Nadius took Lydia in his arms and whirled her around and around. "You see! I knew best after all. Our fortune is made! In six months we shall be rich. We shall never again have to worry about anything!"

Euodia carefully unpacked the silver statue of Diana and set it upon an altar in a nitch in the cottage wall. All then paid homage to the idol, Diana's image, thanking her for favoring them with finding the precious metal that would make them all wealthy.

At the base of the mountain another altar was built. This one was dedicated to the god of the mountain who had opened his bosom to them and had allowed them to share his treasure. This was a natural thing for Greeks to do, since to them all things, whether they be storms, mountains, trees or rocks, contained gods and goddesses. And each had to be pacified to render good luck and favor upon men.

Early the next morning Nadius assembled them all. They must organize their activities, for in addition to working the mine, they would need food, and firewood would have to be cut and stored for winter. Epaphroditus was designated the hunter, for he had trapped small animals in the woods in Thyatira and hunted them with bow and arrow. Nadius would work in the mine full time, as would Clement. Papie would spend half his time hunting food and chopping wood and work in the mine the rest of his time.

Lydia and Euodia would take care of the house and little Doronius. They would also be responsible for washing the ore the men would bring out of the mine and down to the creek bed. They would swirl the ore around in a clay pan with water, separating the dirt and soil while the flakes of heavier gold settled to the bottom of the pan.

"We shall work as much as possible during the winter," Nadius said. "And in the spring when the weather clears, we shall work it every day. We must put up with these hardships now. But I promise you, we shall all live in luxury the rest of our lives. This I swear by all the gods!"

But none of them could have foreseen just how hard the work would prove to be. The mountain god did not give up his treasure that easily. They could see the rocks inside the mine glint back yellow in the light of their torches, but when they swung the heavy picks against the walls, it gave but grudgingly. There was a small cart in the mine, used to carry out the ore from the mine tunnel. But in half a day, the two men had barely filled one cartload with ore.

Epaphroditus had better luck with his hunting. He had been in the forests but half an hour when he saw a herd of deer. He crept as close as he dared and aimed his arrow for a doe. His aim had been true and the arrow struck the deer in the neck. The doe jumped in surprise as the arrow struck her, bounded a few yards, and fell dead as the wound took its toll. He hauled back the carcass and hung it in the trees to drain the blood. At least they would have fresh meat for the next week and it was a welcome change from the dried food they had brought from Philippi.

The problem of how to get the ore from the top of the mountain to the creek bed in the valley was solved when Clement found a chute that had been carved in the rock. It was overgrown with brush, but when that was removed, they were able to dump the ore in the chute, which carried it to the creek bed down below. Nadius had been instructed on how to wash away the soil and dirt, and he demonstrated this to Lydia and Euodia. When the first pan of washings revealed yellow stuff in the bottom, they all resumed work with renewed vigor in the afternoon.

The weeks that followed found the group of new miners exhausted at the end of each day of work, their muscles sore and their bodies drained of energy. Only the increasing contents of the jar of yellow metal kept them going as the fall of the year turned into winter and the air grew colder and colder. Soon the snow would come and they would not be able to climb the mountain to the shaft. Nadius pushed them to the limit of their endurance, alternately using encouragement and shouting abuse to keep them moving.

Then one morning they awoke to find the ground covered with the silent snow that had fallen during the night. Nadius looked up at the grey clouds that covered the sky completely. "We can't work today," he told them, and his words were received with quiet thanksgiving by the rest of the party.

It continued to snow all day. Epaphroditus went out early to check his traps while he could still push his way through the drifting snow. He brought in two rabbits from his trapline. These, with the dried venison hanging at the back of the cottage, would have to last them until the snow stopped.

When the sky finally cleared several days later, three feet of snow blanketed the valley. The forest was draped with a curtain of silence, clean and white in the sunlight. Lydia thought she had never seen anything so beautiful, for snow was rare in Thyatira. She went outside in a path that Epaphroditus cleared and looked at the pines, their branches drooping with their burden of soft snow. The air was fresh and still and cold. Only the call of an eagle broke the stillness of the scene as it circled high above the forest, its eyes searching to catch the slightest movement of a mouse or squirrel.

They all relaxed by the warmth of the hearth, glad to rest from the weeks of labor. The baby played before the fire on a blanket, and even Nadius held him as he took his first hesitant but proud steps on wobbly legs, all the while chattering unintelligibly to them. Papie could once more set his traps and stalk the deer in the forest, following the tracks in the fresh snow. In the evening they sat around the embers of the fire and Clement told stories, tales of the heroics of the ancient Greeks, of the battles, of the gods and the poets. But most of all he spoke about Alexander and what was to be the finest hours of their common heritage.

The winter finally passed and the first signs of spring appeared. The snows melted and the air itself was different, a warmness and fragrance in it which came from the shifting to a southernly flow. The rains of the spring came, gently at first, then in torrents. They found the rains had made the path up the mountain more treacherous than did the snows, for it became slippery mud. They were forced to claw their way to the top, holding onto any shrub or tree their hands could reach to keep from sliding down the mountain path.

Nadius was anxious to begin. He and Clement fought their way to the mine entrance and prepared once more to chop at the rock with picks. But at the entrance, Clement saw signs he did not like. He held his torch high and pointed to the roof. "Look. Up ahead. The timbers are sagging."

It was obvious that the snow and rain had seeped through and weakened the roof supports of the tunnel. Water dripped through the ceiling in many places and had eroded the shaft dangerously.

"We can't go in any farther," Clement said. "It is too dangerous. The roof may give way at any minute."

But just then, the flickering light of the torch caught a large rock and it glinted back into Nadius's eyes. "Look there! A huge nugget of pure gold!"

"I see it," Clement replied, "but we dare not go after it. The roof may come down!"

Nadius hesitated, his eyes still on the nugget. Then he handed his torch to Clement. "Here, hold this. It won't take but a moment to get it and bring it back."

He was gone, up the tunnel before Clement could stop him. His hand grasped the nugget, held by the adjacent rocks in the wall of the tunnel. He pulled at the nugget and a small shower of rocks issued from where he pulled. Then the shoring above groaned. A cascade of debris fell about him as he still clutched the nugget in the wall. As he pulled it free and turned to run, a thunder clap shook the tunnel as tons of rocks and earth came crashing down.

"Nadius!" Clement screamed. "Get out of there!" Then he was knocked backward as the entire roof caved in and a falling beam struck him a glancing blow. He shook his head and staggered to his feet, the air about him filled with dust.

"Nadius!" Clement shouted. But his voice could not penetrate the wall of solid rock before him, filling the tunnel completely, and burying Nadius beneath it.

Clement clawed desperately at the rock. His fingers bled as he tried to pull it out of the way. "Nadius! Nadius!" he shouted. "Can you hear me?" He sobbed as he clawed and dug impotently at the wall of rock. But Nadius could not hear him. He lay crushed beneath the tons of fallen rock, still clutching the yellow nugget. The mountain had taken him into its bosom, and he would lay there beneath it until the end of time.

— Chapter Six —

Epaphroditus was at the foot of the mountain when he heard the muffled roar come from the tunnel. He looked up quickly and saw the dust bellow from the entrance to the shaft. "Father!" he said, almost as a prayer. "Father is in there!"

He dropped his bow and ran to the path up the mountain, slipping and sliding as he crawled, sometimes on all fours, up the side of the steep slope, fighting his way to the entrance.

He paused for a moment at the mouth of the tunnel, the thick dust choking him, not being able to see inside. "Father!" he shouted, "are you in there?"

When no answer came he groped his way inside, feeling with his hands along the side of the shaft. Once inside the dust was not as thick and he could see the faint flicker of a torch up ahead. He made out the form of a man, digging and clawing with his bare hands at a wall of rubble.

"Father! What has happened!"

Clement turned, his eyes filled with tears. He pointed to the wall of rock. "Nadius is in there," he cried, "Come! Help me!"

Papie dropped to his knees beside Clement and together they tried to move the debris that had clogged the tunnel. "It's no use!" Epaphroditus sobbed. "We can't do it!" He pulled his exhausted father from the wall and led him out of the shaft.

"What am I to tell Lydia?" Clement asked desperately. "She has already had so much sorrow. First Licentor, then the baby. Now this!"

The two men, one young, the other approaching middle age, came down the mountain. "There was nothing we could do, Father. It was the will of the gods."

The women at the cottage had also heard the dull roar from the mountain. Lydia had picked up Doronius and had run to the creek bed, followed by Euodia. When they reached the steep path, Clement and Papie were already coming down. Lydia saw their hands, bleeding and raw from digging at the rock. When she saw that Nadius was not with them, she immediately knew what had happened.

She sat down on a fallen tree, holding her baby close, her head whirling. Mountain and forest spun around, and she thought she was about to faint. She closed her eyes tightly. "No," she told herself, "I have to face this. I have to stand up and be brave. My baby needs me. I must be strong for his sake."

Clement was standing before her. He tried to speak but no words came. Lydia looked up into his tear-streaked face. "Nadius," she said calmly, "he is dead, isn't he?"

Clement nodded. She put her arm on his shoulder, holding her child with the other. "It will be all right, Clement. It will be all right." She turned and walked slowly back toward the cottage. The others followed a short distance back, too shocked to speak. Lydia put Doronius in his bed and came out of the cabin. She stood in the doorway facing them, her eyes intense as she spoke.

"It had to happen, you know. It had to happen sooner or later. I knew it would." Her voice was calm, her tone even and controlled. "We will have to leave this place. The mountain god has guarded his treasure well. He claimed my husband as payment for his gold. We shall leave. I never want to see this place again."

Clement and Euodia looked at each other, neither knowing what to say. Finally Clement spoke, "At least she will be a rich widow when we take the gold to the buyer in Philippi. It should be worth a fortune."

They quickly packed their belongings, taking only what the one donkey could carry. There were many things left that Lydia would have liked to carry back. "But I suppose they can all be replaced when we are home in Thyatira again," she said.

Early the next morning they left with Epaphroditus leading the donkey out of the valley into the forests. As they reached the top of the first hill, Lydia looked back for the last time. She could plainly see the opening of the tunnel on the mountain, the last resting place of her husband. She swallowed hard, forcing back the tears that had almost broken through her outward composure.

She turned away, holding her child tightly to her breast. The last year seemed as a dream, a horrible nightmare of tragedy upon tragedy. First her father's death, then the loss of her unborn child, the business and her home sold away. Now the death of Nadius. Slowly she followed the donkey on the narrow path, stepping carefully on the unstable rocks. Life must go on, she told herself. At least she still had Doronius. And Euodia and Clement and Papie. She would sell the gold flakes and nuggets in Philippi and they would all return to Thyatira and home. Maybe she could even buy back the house by the river. Clement took the baby from her and she moved down the trail toward Philippi.

It was late afternoon when they arrived and took rooms at the inn. Lydia counted out the money from the purse Nadius had left at the cottage containing the money remaining from the sale of the business. She was surprised that it was so much, although certainly not enough for their passage home to Thyatira.

The next morning she and Clement took the gold to the office of one of the dealers. They were shown into a comfortable room and the dealer carefully dumped the contents of the leather purse on the top of his polished table. His eyebrows flickered as he saw the pile of yellow metal. He extracted a nugget from the pile with tweezers and held it up to the light.

"You say this was your first experience in mining?" he asked, a rather quizzical expression on his face.

"Yes," Lydia answered. "My husband bought the mine only recently. He was killed when the roof of the tunnel caved in only a few days ago."

The man looked first at her and then at Clement. For a moment he said nothing, his brow furrowed as if in deep thought. Then he shook his head. "I'm afraid you have made the same mistake many do who are new to this."

"Mistake? What do you mean?"

"This is worthless."

"Worthless? It is gold, isn't it?"

The dealer swept the pile into a large bin next to the table. "Gold? Well, I suppose you could call it that," he said. "It is called fool's gold."

Back at the inn, Lydia sat dazed with shock. What would they do now? The money in her purse would last for a while. It would buy food and shelter but was certainly not enough for even one passage back to Thyatira. They were stranded in a strange city. What would they do, she cried to herself in frustration.

Nadius had apparently been the victim of a fraud, a swindle! In his greed, he had been taken in by promises of fast and easy wealth. Perhaps she could go to the authorities. Perhaps they could find the man who had sold her husband the worthless mine and get back the money. It was at least worth a try. But she did not know how or to whom to appeal for help. Then she thought of Stetius, her father's long-time customer and friend in Philippi. Yes, she would go to him. He would know what she must do.

As a small girl, she had come with her father on a trip, and they had visited Stetius. The kindly man had given her candy, she remembered, and had held her on his lap. Yes, she would go and see Stetius. He would help her, she knew he would.

The next morning, dressed in her best clothing, which was not all that good for the winter at the mine had ruined most of her things, she inquired as to where Stetius could be found. With Clement, she followed the directions to his home. A servant answered the door and she told him who she was, hoping the man might remember her father. She was shown into the atrium and told to wait.

In a few minutes, a short, thin man with a long and pointed nose entered the room. His eyes twinkled and his face was wreathed with an impish smile. She recognized him at once. "Uncle Stetius!" Lydia exclaimed.

"No," he said, "this cannot be Lydia. Lydia is still a child, not a beautiful and charming woman!" He held out his arms and she went to his embrace. He hugged her warmly, then held her out at arm's length to look at her. "Yes, it is indeed the little girl who sat upon my lap just a few years ago and captured my heart." Then his face grew serious as he remembered Nadius telling him of Licentor's death.

"I cannot tell you of my sorrow when I learned of your father's passing," he told her. "Your husband—what is his name?—told me of it."

"My husband now is also dead," Lydia said. "He was killed in an accident just a few days ago."

Stetius and Lydia sat in the atrium, and she told him of all that had happened. When she had finished he held her hand and said,

"My dear, you have done the right thing in coming to me. Now do you have the deed of ownership to this mine your husband bought?"

She handed him the papers and the location map. He studied these while she waited breathlessly. "Is there anything I can do?" she asked. "Can I get back the money paid for this worthless thing?"

He looked up. "I don't know. These papers say very little. But I am not a judge of matters such as this. We shall go and see the Roman tribune who handles such things. He is a good and just man. He will be able to tell us."

Lucius Marcellus was the administrative tribune of the province of Macedonia. Only the Roman proconsul was of higher status. His duty, in addition to certain routine administrative functions, was the supervision of the magistrates who dispensed Roman law to the citizens.

Marcellus was an exception to the usual Roman administrator. In these corrupt times, bribery and extortion were commonplace. But Marcellus had no need for this, for he was from an old and very wealthy Roman family.

At thirty-five, he was a widower with a daughter of eight. Since the death of his wife, his sister had become the mistress of his house and she was devoted to the young child. Tall, ruggedly handsome, educated and wealthy, Marcellus was much sought after by the Roman households with marriageable daughters. And indeed he would have been a fine catch for any young Roman maiden. But he was not interested in marriage, and his position and his adored daughter kept him occupied and busy.

Any citizen of Macedonia, not satisfied with the decision of the magistrates, could appeal to the tribune for a hearing. Not all did this, however, for Marcellus could increase the fine or sentence as well as decrease or nullify it. And as all sorts of people sought a hearing with him, he was not surprised when his servant announced that the merchant, Stetius, and a woman desired to speak with him.

Marcellus knew Stetius, for his sister, Lucretia, often purchased fabric at his shop. He nodded to the servant, and in a moment the short, thin man and a young woman were shown in. "Stetius, my friend, what may I do for you?"

They shook hands and Stetius introduced Lydia. "This young lady is the daughter of a dear friend who has recently passed away. She has been defrauded by a citizen of Philippi and I knew you could advise her."

The tribune motioned for them to be seated and Lydia told him what had happened. Marcellus watched her intently as she related now Nadius had bought the property as a gold mine and how they had worked the mine to obtain the metal. Her dark, piercing eyes misted as she told of the accident that had taken her husband's life, then of finding in Philippi that they had toiled in vain, that the ore was worthless fool's gold.

His sympathy went out to her. She was a remarkable woman, he observed. A young and pampered daughter of a well-to-do dyer of cloth suddenly being thrust into the rugged life in the mountains of Macedonia, washing ore that was dug from the mine. Her clothing was not rich and somewhat the worse for wear, but she wore it with a bearing that spoke of good breeding and dignity.

He examined the deed, attesting to the sale of the indicated property to Nadius by a man named Herteles. "I know him slightly," Marcellus said. "He is a friend of the proconsul's. I have heard nothing ill of him before."

He indicated the paper he held in his hand, the deed to the property. "There is no mention made here of any mine, only the land. On the basis of this deed, I can find no fraudulent statement, as it promises nothing at all about any gold being found on the property."

Stetius grimaced. "I was afraid of that. When I examined the paper, I could see as much. Then there is nothing we can do?"

Marcellus shook his head. "No. I am sorry. There is nothing that can be done."

They thanked the tall Roman tribune and left, walking slowly back to Stetius' home. "What will you do now?" he asked.

She walked on a moment longer in silence before answering. "I don't know," she said softly.

"Then you must come and live in my house with me," he told her. "My children are all grown and I am lonely by myself. My own dear wife passed away many years ago."

"No," Lydia said. "I can't do that. I appreciate your offer, but I didn't come to you for anything like that. You have done all for me that I can ask."

He started to protest, but the independent tone in her voice told him it would be no use. "Lydia, I miss your father very much. Not only his friendship but his cloth. I have not seen any the equal to it." He considered telling her that the goods Nadius had last delivered to him had been worthless, turning brown after only a few weeks. But he held his tongue, not knowing whether she knew her husband had resorted to inferior quality after taking over Licentor's business.

Suddenly she looked at him, her eyes wide with interest. "Would you buy my father's cloth again, if you could get it? I mean purples of the same quality as he produced?"

"Certainly. I would buy all I could get of it."

For the first time she smiled. "Suppose I could supply such cloth? Would you buy it from me?"

"Of course I would, my child. Of course I would."

She walked taller then, a new briskness in her step. "Then I shall go into the business," she told him. "Back into my father's business. I shall become a dyer of cloth here in Philippi." She kissed him on the cheek and ran down the road to the inn, anxious to tell the others of her decision.

Back at the inn, she called Clement, Euodia and Epaphroditus together. "Clement, could you construct vats to dye cloth here in Philippi?"

"Of course. Why?"

"How long would it take? How long before we could begin to dye cloth?"

"Oh, I guess within a month. What do you have in mind, Lydia?"

Her eyes gleamed. "I have in mind going back to what we all know best. Back into my father's business. Right here in Philippi. Stetius will buy cloth from us, and I am sure some of father's other old customers would."

They were all silent for a moment as the impact of what she said struck home. Then all began talking at once.

"Oh, yes. The beautiful purples again."

"How wonderful!"

"And I can almost smell the familiar odor of the vats," laughed Clement. "But it will cost money to get started, Lydia. We don't have that kind of money!"

"Leave that to me," Lydia told them. "I shall get it!" But the truth of the matter was that she had not the slightest idea at that moment where she would get it. All she knew was that somehow, some way, she would obtain it. She had to.

Over the course of the next week, she visited every moneylender in Philippi. All of them told her the same thing. Without collateral, they could not lend her a single denarius. After she had exhausted all of her possibilities, she tearfully told them of her failure.

"It's no use," she cried. "I don't know now what we are going to do!"

Clement and Euodia exchanged glances. They had anticipated this and had discussed what they would do if it came to this situation. They left the room and were gone for several hours. When they returned, Clement placed a purse before her. "Here is the money, Lydia. Now we can begin."

"Where did you get this?" she demanded.

Clement put his big hand upon her shoulder. "We are the collateral for the loan," he told her.

"You? But what . . . .? Oh, no. You didn't!"

"There was no other way," Euodia said. "And there is a year to repay the loan and the interest."

"Before your father died," Clement said, "he gave me these papers. We, Euodia and Papie and I, have been freedmen since then. We did not feel it right to include Epaphroditus in this, Lydia. But Euodia and I, well, it was the least we could do for you."

Lydia's eyes were filled with tears as she embraced them both. "But suppose we fail? Then you would be—"

"Yes, we would be slaves again. But there are worse things, Lydia. And Euodia and I were born slaves, although we were never treated as such by your father. We have always felt more as your family than slaves."

"And you have been," Lydia protested. "That is why I can't let you do this!"

Clement put the purse in her hands. "You have nothing to say about it. It is already done. Now here, take this and let's get started. You will have to go to Mytilene and make arrangements about the dye. My vats will be of no use without that."

Lydia booked passage on a ship bound for Mytilene. They had seen a house house outside of Philippi, next to the river, that would be ideal for their needs. The next day they rented it and moved their meager possessions into it. As soon as Lydia had sailed from Neapolis, Clement and Papie began to construct the wooden vats in which the cloth would be dyed. Euodia would care for Doronius while Lydia was away.

As the ship sailed across the blue green waters of the Aegean, Lydia's heart beat faster. She felt some strange force drawing her to the emerald islands so familiar to her. And as they came within sight of Mytilene she recognized the docks and buildings and the piles of shells that marked the factory where the dye was extracted. The offshore breeze brought the familiar smells to her and memories of her father when he had first taken her here as a child to buy the dye and the silks and woolens. There were the same whitewashed stone buildings, the magnificent trees, the bright flowers. As her feet were once more on the uneven stones of the quay, she felt a peace within her, and a nostalgia, as though she were once again at home.

Quickly she located the dye factory owned by Busteles, her father's old friend. And even before she entered the workshop, the sights and sounds and odors told her she was back among friends. It is good, she thought, to be home again.

She went in and saw him, working among the vats and cookers that extracted the precious dyes from the shellfish. She waited until he had finished what he was doing and turned and saw her. With a wide grin he hurried toward her, his reddish beard shining in the sunlight. "Ah, my little girl returns! Come here, my child, and let me hug you!"

His big arms wrapped around her slender frame, and she kissed him on the cheek. "Oh, it is so good to see you again," she told him.

"I heard that you had gone to Philippi to live," he said. "Here, let me look at you. And what brings you back to Mytilene?"

"Many things have happened," she said. "Terrible things."

He took her hand. "Come! Let us have some wine and you can tell me all that has happened." They went into his house next to the dye factory and he poured wine for both of them. For the next hour Lydia related all that had happened. At the end of her story she faced him with a serious expression. "And so, I must go back into the business of dyeing cloth. I have no other way to earn a living for myself and my family."

"And you will need dye," he said, his brow knotted. "And this has brought you to Mytilene."

"Yes. I shall need dyes. Will you help me? I have little money. I will need credit for the dyes."

"Credit? What is that? You can have whatever you need! But I must tell you, Lydia, your husband treated many people in a disgraceful way. Him, may the gods have mercy on him, I would not as much as speak to." He regarded her for a moment. "It is a hard thing to say, Lydia, but perhaps you are better off without him."

Lydia's eyes were sad as she answered. "I know he did not love me," she said, "but I cannot find it in my heart to hate him. He was my husband. What he was cannot alter that."

The red-bearded man smiled at her. "From you I would expect no other answer." He got to his feet. "Now let us see to what you will need. And I wish to give you something else." He went to a table and took a quill and inkpot. He wrote something on a scrap of parchment and handed it to her.

"Take this," he said. "Show it to the brokers of cloth when you bargain for the silk and woolens."

Lydia took it from him and read what he had written on the parchment.

"To whoever reads this, greetings from Busteles, manufacturer of purple dyes at Mytilene. Be it known to you that the bearer of this letter is Lydia, daughter of Licentor. Give her whatever cloth she needs. Her credit is good. If she cannot repay you, then I will."

Three days later, with all the cloth and dyes she needed, Lydia boarded a ship back to Philippi.

— Chapter Seven —

"Ah," exclaimed Clement as he examined the cloth he held in his hand. "Yes! Yes, indeed! This is perfect."

The group around him had held their breath as he had carefully inspected the first batch of cloth from the dyeing vats in the house beside the river. They had all waited as the fabric had dried in the bright Macedonian sun and the rays had not only dried the cloth but had changed the color from the original yellow as it came from the vat to the brilliant Thyatiran purple.

"Thank the gods!" Euodia exclaimed.

Clement eyed his wife, a broad smile on his face. "The gods had nothing to do with it," he told her. "Thank the secret that Lydia carries in her head." He looked carefully at the cloth and nodded. "Yes, this is as good as any that Licentor himself could have made."

"Fool," his wife admonished. "Didn't the gods have something to do with your finding the special white rocks that contain the secret ingredient of the process? Be careful, husband, that you do not offend them."

Clement turned to Epaphroditus. "Don't listen to your mother, son. You and I have done this. The marble and wooden statues in the temples do not have smelly hands as we do. Ours have done the work, not theirs."

In the weeks that followed they washed and dyed the cloth, anguishing over each batch. They anxiously tended the cloth as it dried in the sun, watching over it, carefully turning it to bring out the full brilliance of the purple.

When they had finished and were satisfied with their work, Lydia took samples to Stetius. She sat in a chair nervously as he inspected them. His eyes missed nothing, no flaw nor blemish could escape his practiced observation. Then he turned to her, smiling. "It is every bit as good as your father's work, Lydia. You have done well."

She breathed a sigh of relief. "Then you are pleased?"

"Pleased? I am delighted. When can you deliver the material?"

"As soon as you like. This afternoon if it is convenient for you. Clement and Papie will bring it to your shop."

They toasted the new enterprise with wine. Then Stetius' face grew serious. "There is something I must warn you about, Lydia. There is another dyer of cloth in Philippi, a man named Vestus. He has a bad temper and will be furious that you have entered into competition with him. With fabric of this quality, you will cost him much business. Be careful of him, Lydia."

Lydia laughed. "Oh, Uncle Stetius! What man would harm a woman? I don't think I have any cause for worry."

Stetius paid Lydia for the fabric and she returned home. She wanted to pay off the moneylender immediately and get back the papers that pledged Euodia and Clement as collateral for the loan. But Clement was adamant.

"No, Lydia. We need this money to purchase more cloth and dye. There are still many months before the loan must be paid. We can have more batches of cloth produced and sold well before then."

Lydia checked her books again. It was true there were many bills to be paid. She owed Busteles for the dye, the cloth merchants for the woolens and silk. There was the rent for the house by the river and food was needed until the next cloth could be produced and sold. He was right, she finally agreed. They would have to wait to pay off the loan.

She wrote out the orders for the dyes and cloth and obtained the letters of payment for what she owed. These were sent on the next ship across the Aegean, and now all she could do was to await the shipment of her orders. This could take over a month.

Vestus' brow knotted as he examined the cloth. "Where did you get this?" he demanded of the man before him.

"From the shop of Stetius. I hear it was made by some woman who lives in a house by the River Gangites."

Vestus held the purple cloth to the light. He had seen nothing so fine in quality in years, not since Licentor of Thyatira had produced cloth of purple. But that man had died and now he had the business in Philippi all to himself.

Vestus glared at his servant. "A woman? What would a woman know about dyeing cloth? Has she no husband?"

"She has only servants, sir. But I understand she comes from Thyatira."

Vestus scowled. "Thyatira! That explains why Stetius did not order cloth from me last month. But we shall see about the quality of this cloth. It will probably turn brown in a few weeks. Then Stetius will be glad to buy my fabric again."

He fastened the swatch of purple cloth on a wooden post in his garden and every day he examined it carefully. When there was no change in its brilliant color after two weeks, he began to be concerned.

"Only one man knew the secret of color like this on silk. I shall have to see about this."

That afternoon Vestus dragged his huge bulk into Stetius' shop. He saw on display the colored fabrics that had been produced in Lydia's vats by the river. He grunted as he saw the fashionable Roman ladies who were admiring and buying these fabrics. He waited until Stetius had waited on the last one before he approached him.

"It seems you have found another supplier of cloth," he said. "Does our longstanding friendship count for nothing?"

Stetius frowned at the surly man. "Vestus, I believe you presume too much. In the first place, just because I have bought cloth from you does not mean we are friends. In the second place, you have charged me exorbitant prices. And in the third place, it is my right to buy from whomever I choose. Now if you have anything else to say to me, say it quickly. I am a busy man."

Uninvited, Vestus plopped his heavy frame in a chair. "I hear my new competitor is a woman." He spat out the word as if it were an oath.

Stetius stood over him, his face livid. "No, Vestus. She is not a woman. She is a *lady!* A very fine lady! Something you would not understand! Now, please get out of my shop. I have work to do."

The big man lifted himself from the chair and glared at Stetius as he left the shop. "You will come begging to me, Stetius! You will come crawling to me, sniveling, to buy my cloth. You will see!"

Stetius poured himself some wine, his hands still shaking with anger. He downed the wine and shook his head. "That man is capable of anything. I must make Lydia take my warning seriously." He sat down and tried to calm his nerves. It took a half hour before he was able to get back to work.

The door of his shop opened again, but this time Stetius smiled broadly when he saw who it was. "Marcellus," he exclaimed, "it is so good to see you. Please come in and sit down."

The tall Roman tribune extended his hand after the Roman fashion and Stetius shook it warmly. "I have come to buy some fabric for my sister," he said. And added self-consciously, "I wish to surprise her with it."

Stetius poured wine and the tribune sat in the chair just recently vacated by Vestus. "You are indeed in luck," Stetius told him. "Let me show you this fine fabric. It is the finest purple I have seen in years."

Stetius pulled a length of silk from his display table. "Hold it up to the light. Have you ever seen anything so rich and beautiful?"

The tribune glanced briefly at the cloth. "Yes. It is indeed fine cloth. Cut me enough for a gown for my sister. And have it delivered to her dressmaker, will you?"

"Done, my friend," Stetius beamed. "Now sit here with me and rest yourself. Let me pour more wine for you."

They talked for a few moments about common things, the fine weather, the death of a prominent Philippian, small talk, polite and meaningless conversation. Then Marcellus's face grew serious. "Tell me," he asked, "that girl you brought to me, the one with the deed to the worthless mine. How is she getting along?"

Stetius grinned at him. "You will not believe this, but the cloth you just purchased was dyed in this splendid color by that very girl. She has opened a business here of dyeing cloth."

"Business?" Marcellus exclaimed. "A woman running a business?"

"There is nothing so strange about that. Her father was the best dyer of fabric in Thyatira, in the whole Aegean. And the servant who assisted her father is with her."

Marcellus sat back and smiled. "Well, I suppose it is not that extraordinary, then. It is just that, well, she did not seem to be the type who would be capable of running a business."

"You have the exact word which describes her," Stetius told him. "Extraordinary. She is a very extraordinary woman."

The tribune sipped his wine. "And where is her business located? I think I would like to observe this process of dyeing cloth sometime."

"She has rented the old stone house just off the Egnation Way by the Gangites River. Near the old temple of Apollo."

"Yes. I know the place. A huge, rambling structure."

"That's it. And I am sure," grinned Stetius, "that she would be most happy to show you how the cloth is dyed." He put down his goblet and smiled with inner satisfaction. "Very happy, indeed."

Lydia felt the need to offer a sacrifice to the gods for her good fortune in establishing her business in Philippi. She asked Clement to come with her, but he refused. "I will not offer anything to a statue for what we have done ourselves," he told her. So accompanied by Epaphroditus, Lydia went to the nearby temple of Apollo.

As they approached the building they noticed it had fallen into disrepair. Weeds grew in the path and there were cracks in the foundation of the stone structure. The odor of garbage struck their nostrils as they entered the building. The interior was dark, musty and empty. No priests were in attendance at the altar standing before the statue of the god.

One side of the building contained living quarters for the priests, and after waiting for several minutes, Epaphroditus went through the door that led into those quarters in search of a priest. He knocked at a door and, when there was no response, he opened it. He peered in cautiously.

From a bed in the corner of the room came the sound of a snore. Epaphroditus cleared his throat loudly until the man in the bed stirred and sat up. "What do you want?" he demanded.

"To offer a sacrifice."

The priest grunted and shook his head to clear it. He reached for the container of wine beside his bed and drank deeply. Then, after a loud belch, he rolled out of bed and stretched. "You have money, don't you?"

"Yes," Epaphroditus replied.

"Then give it to me."

"My mistress has the money. She is waiting in the sanctuary."

The priest wiped his mouth on the sleeve of his robe and followed Epaphroditus into the sanutary. He held out his hand to Lydia. "Pay me," he said.

Lydia produced a coin and handed it to the priest. He examined it carefully and grumbled. Then he put it between his teeth and bit it. Satisfied that it was genuine, he walked to the altar. He dipped his hand into a clay bowl and brought out a handful of moldy grain. He threw the grain upon the altar and chanted for a moment. Then he walked away and started back to his room.

"Is that all?" asked Lydia.

The priest glared at her. "That's all you get for one drachma. What did you expect, to have a bull killed?"

Epaphroditus took her arm and led her from the temple. "Come on, Lydia, let's go." They went out into the sunlight and down the path. Neither spoke until they had traveled far enough from the temple where the stench of garbage could no longer be noticed. "Perhaps my father was right," Papie said.

Lydia nodded. "I feel worse now than when we came. I wonder if that priest really thinks Apollo noticed what was done."

"Or cares," said Papie.

They walked along the road back to the house by the river in silence, each tasting the bitter emptiness of the experience.

He guided his horse along the road toward the river. "This is stupid," Marcellus told himself. "Why am I here?" But he had not been able to get that girl out of his mind. The story he had told Stetius about being interested in the process of dyeing cloth had fooled no one. It was obvious it had not fooled the seller of fabric and he certainly had not fooled himself. No, it was that he wanted to see her again, pure and simple, and he would be miserable until he had.

The old stone house came into view from the road. Behind it the Gangites River meandered peacefully to the sea, its banks lined with tall, shady trees. It was a pleasant sight, he thought, quiet and serene. As he turned his horse from the road onto the dirt path that led down the hill to the house, he saw a man standing in the bushes watching the house. But when the man saw him coming, he turned and quickly ducked into the trees. Curious, Marcellus thought. Who would be so interested in this place?

From the house, the approach of the horse and rider had gone unnoticed by the women working in the back. Lydia and Euodia had just pulled a length of cloth from the vats and were wringing it dry when he dismounted and tied his horse to a small tree.

He walked around the house and saw a child, secured in the same manner as his horse, to another tree near where the women worked. Since they could not watch him constantly, Lydia had tied a piece of rope about his waist to keep Doronius from the ever-present danger of falling into the river.

The dye had stained both women's arms a deep yellow to their elbows. Lydia's hair blew in the breeze, and now and again one of the strands blew across her eyes. With her hands busy wringing the fabric, she tried to blow it up out of the way. As she did this for the hundredth time that afternoon, she looked up and saw him watching her, an amused smile on his face.

"Well," he laughed, "you may not have found the yellow metal, but you found something else the same color."

Her heart sank. She could not have looked worse, she thought. She and Euodia strung the piece of fabric on a line between two trees to dry, and she turned to face him, wiping her hands at the same time on the long apron she wore. "This is an unexpected pleasure, Your Excellency."

He walked to the vat and peered in. "Stetius told me you had entered the dyeing business. In fact, I have purchased some for my sister. I was very interested in the process."

"Oh," she smiled. "Then let me show you how it is done." She began to explain the complicated procedure used to transform ordinary fabric into the shimmering shades of purple, saffron and hyacinth so popular with the Romans. He nodded as she spoke, his eyes on her face, which had become animated by her enthusiasm.

"I see," he said. "It is very complicated. I had no idea there were so many steps involved."

"Oh, but I have explained only the initial procedure. Then you have to—"

He held up his hand. "I think I have heard enough for today. I am confused enough for one day. But let us talk about you. Have you been well?"

"Me? Oh, I am never sick. But Your Excellency must forgive my lack of manners. May I get you some wine? Some fruit, perhaps?"

"That would be very nice," Marcellus said, "and perhaps we could sit in the shade of the trees beside the river to drink it."

Euodia immediately went toward the house to fetch the wine as Lydia and Marcellus walked toward the river. "Mama! Mama!" cried Doronius.

Lydia untied him and picked him up. "This is my little man," she told the tribune. "His name is Doronius. He was a gift to me from the gods."

"He is a fine, healthy boy. You are very fortunate. I have a daughter. She will be nine next month."

"Then you and your wife are also fortunate," Lydia smiled.

"My wife is dead," he said.

"Oh, I am sorry."

"It has been five years now. The pain is still there. But time is easing it somewhat."

"I hope it does. My husband has been dead for only a few months."

Marcellus looked at the boy in his mother's arms. "Does he favor your husband? It helps to have a child who resembles the loved one who is gone. My daughter looks very much like her mother."

Lydia stroked Doronius's hair, gleaming golden in the bright sunlight. "Yes," she said, "he favors his father very much."

Euodia brought the wine and took Doronius from Lydia's arms. "It's time for his nap," she explained. "I'll take him back to the house."

Lydia unrolled a cloth on the grass and poured the wine. As she handed the goblet to Marcellus, her hand briefly touched his, and she felt a strange sensation in her fingers. He had felt it also and his eyes looked deeply into hers.

"Lydia," he said, "do you ever wake in the night, lonely and restless? Have you ever out of habit reached across the bed and been startled to find it empty?"

She watched the swans on the river a moment, pondering her answer to his question. "No," she finally told him. "My husband was . . . well, our marriage was not very good."

Marcellus finished his wine and arose. "I must go," he told Lydia. "I have to hear a case this afternoon."

"So soon? You have not been here very long."

"I must attend to my duties. Thank you for the wine. And the tour of your factory. May the gods favor your business."

He mounted his horse and was gone. Lydia watched him ride up the hill. At the top he turned and waved to her. She waved back, vigorously, her heart fluttering in a strange way. Will I ever see him again? she wondered. As she entered the house, she was conscious of Euodia's inquisitive look.

"What brings a Roman gentleman to see you, Lydia? And a tribune, at that!"

Lydia felt her face suddenly flush. She turned away so Euodia would not see it. "He is a friend of Stetius'," she said. "He was merely interested in how cloth is dyed."

Euodia smiled at her. "Of course. That was all he was interested in. All Roman gentlemen are interested in the dyeing of cloth."

Euodia smiled as she saw the reddish glow on Lydia's face deepen. She put her arm on Lydia's shoulder and winked. "I think he is very handsome," she said. "And very nice."

"Fool!" Marcellus exclaimed aloud as he spurred his horse along the road back to Philippi. "Why did I go there in the first place?"

He shook his head, angry with himself and feeling foolish at the emotions that surged inside his chest. "She is a recent widow. A poor Greek woman who cares only for her son and her business. And I am a Roman officer, a man with a daughter and responsibilities. Stop being such a fool," he told himself. "Forget about her."

And as he reined his horse at the entrance to his home and handed the leather thongs to a servant, he resolved he would not see her again. He would not be a fool again. She was only an insignificant Greek woman, and not an overly attractive one at that! No, he resolved, he would not be a fool again, no matter what the emotions within his heart urged him to do.

For three days he kept his resolve. Yet a dozen times a day he found his thoughts wandering back to the grassy river bank and to the intriguing smile of the young woman who dyed cloth. Each time he caught himself and felt foolish once more. Each time he shook his head, swearing by the gods he would think of her no more. But again and again he did until at last he gave up. Calling for his mount to be brought to him, he rode toward the rambling stone house by the bank of the river Gangites.

He neared the house and again saw the man in the trees watching, and again the man vanished into the thick brush as he approached. The first time he had dismissed this, but it had happened again and he was certain that someone was very interested in what was going on in Lydia's house. Who could possibly be curious about her? He would have to look into this matter. Perhaps Stetius would have an idea who it could be.

When Marcellus tied his horse, he saw no sign of her. At the back of the house two men worked at the vats. He walked toward them. "Is Lydia at home?" he inquired.

The older man nodded politely, seeing the trappings of his office as a tribune of Rome. "She is inside the house, sir. Would you like me to fetch her?"

"No," Marcellus told him. "I can see you are busy. I shall go to the door myself." He walked to the door and found it standing open. He heard the sound of her voice, singing softly, and stopped to listen. Then he heard a child's voice and she laughed as she answered. She was putting the child to bed. He heard her walk inside the house and he cleared his throat. A moment later she came to the door, her face registering surprise when she saw him.

"Oh, it is you!" she exclaimed.

"I didn't mean to startle you."

Lydia brushed back her dark hair. "You didn't startle me. It's just that, well, I seem to look a mess every time you see me. You must think I always look this way."

"You look fine," he smiled. "I came only to ask you something. Will you come to dinner at my home tomorrow evening?"

"Dinner? Me? I don't know—"

"My sister will be there," he interrupted, "and I would like you to meet my daughter. Will you come? I'll send my carriage for you."

Lydia blinked at him. "I don't know . . . . I have nothing to—"

"Please say you will come. I want you to."

Lydia suddenly felt like a schoolgirl again. "All right. I will come."

"Good. My carriage will be here in the late afternoon." He turned to leave. Then remembering the man he had seen in the trees, he turned back to her. "Lydia, why should anyone be watching this house? I have seen a man up there." He pointed to a line of trees near the road. "He was watching this house. When I approached, he hid."

"A man watching this house? I don't—oh, it couldn't be!"

"Tell me! Who is it?"

"I'm not sure. But Stetius warned me about someone. But it's not possible! The man is also a dyer of cloth. Stetius said he would resent my competition."

He took her hand in his and looked down at her. "Lydia, there are men in this world who are capable of anything. Make certain your doors are bolted at night."

He mounted his horse. "Until tomorrow."

She whirled and ran inside the house. "Euodia! You'll never guess where I'm going tomorrow!"

— Chapter Eight —

Lydia was ready an hour before the carriage arrived. Euodia had made her a new gown, fashioned from the leftover pieces of saffron-dyed silk. They had labored far into the night, cutting and stitching in the dim light of the small oil lamps until their eyes could take no more. Early in the morning Euodia had arisen to finish the dress.

Lydia's hair had been washed and set, piled high on her head after the fashion of the Roman ladies, with a single gold ornament, which had belonged to her mother, placed in the back. As Euodia fussed about her, adjusting the gown, smoothing the last strand of hair into place, Lydia was suddenly afraid.

"What if his sister doesn't like me?" she asked. "What if my manners are not proper for a fine Roman table?"

Euodia squeezed her hand. "You have nothing at all to fear. Just be yourself. Of course she will like you! She can't help but like you."

Lydia looked into the polished bronze mirror that also had been her mother's. "I am so plain, Euodia. I look like a farm girl next to those lily-white Roman girls."

"If lyou are not good enough for them," Euodia smiled, "then they have no taste at all!" She picked at a loose thread in the gown and removed it. "You are beautiful and charming and sweet. And if they don't like you, so that? We do."

Lydia hugged the older woman. "You are right. I'm being as silly as a schoolgirl. It doesn't matter what anyone else thinks of me except the ones I love. I have you and Clement and Papie and Doronius. I'm no silly young girl. I'm a widow with a business to run."

Clement called from the doorway. "The carriage is coming!" Lydia drew a deep breath and looked outside. Down the dirt road she could see the splendid carriage with shiny brass trimmings, drawn by two gray horses. The driver reined to a stop in front of the house and a footman stepped out from the carriage and opened the door for her.

Then they were away at a trot, up the dirt road and toward the city. Lydia saw the houses whip past the carriage window and she became lost. She had never been in the Roman section of Philippi, where magnificent stone mansions sat among terraced gardens, each more elaborate than the next. Finally the carriage turned off the road into a drive that led up to the most beautiful house of all.

The carriage stopped in the circular drive next to a fountain bubbling with clear, cool water. Bright flowers bordered the green lawn. When the footman opened the door, she stepped out into a world she never knew existed.

As she entered the atrium, Marcellus came forward to greet her. His eyes registered approval of her appearance as he smiled. "Lydia, you look lovely. Your gown is beautiful. Come, I want you to meet my sister."

He took her arm and she was swept into a large room. On a divan reclined a tall, blonde woman, her face painted with cosmetics after the Roman fashion. "Lydia, this is my sister, Lucretia."

Their eyes met and, although a smile was on the face of the Roman woman, Lydia saw ice behind the painted eyes, a cold and forbidding look that said many things.

Lucretia extended her hand. "How good of you to come," she said, but behind the greeting was a warning. What you see here is mine, it told Lydia.

"It was good of you to invite me," Lydia answered.

"For that you must thank Marcellus," Lucretia said dryly, though her lips still curled in the artificial smile. Lydia read the meaning. How dare you invade the sanctity of my private domain, it said.

"Marcellus tells me you are in business. Of dyeing fabric, I believe."

"Yes. In fact, the gown you are wearing I believe was dyed in my vats. May I look more closely at it?" Lydia touched the gown and smiled. "Yes. This is our purple. The cloth must have come from the shop of Stetius."

Lucretia shrugged. "You would have to ask Marcellus that. He bought the fabric for me as a present."

A servant entered and placed a tray on the table. "Here, Lydia," Marcellus said. "Try one of these."

Lydia turned to the tray on the table, glad to be away from the confrontation with Lucretia for a moment. She took one of the small pieces of delicacy from the tray. "This is delicious," she smiled at the tribune.

Another servant brought wine. It was unlike anything Lydia had ever tasted before. "This wine is from Italy," Marcellus told her. "It is blended with honey. There is none like it in the world."

A small girl entered the room, brought by a woman Lydia assumed was the child's governess. She was about eight or nine with long blonde hair and an alabaster complexion. "And this," Marcellus beamed, "is my daughter, Tia."

Lydia saw the deep blue eyes. There was no ice behind these. Lydia held out her hand and took the small, white one in hers.

"I am so glad to meet you, Tia. Your father has told me so much about you."

The child smiled a reply, then turned to her father. "May I stay up and eat with you and Aunt Lucretia this evening?"

"You'll have to ask your Aunt Lucretia about that," he said.

Tia looked at the woman on the divan. "May I, please?"

"It's way past your bedtime."

"Just this once. I'm not sleepy. I'm really not. I had a long nap this afternoon. Please!"

Lucretia's face softened and she smiled at the girl. Lydia saw that it was genuine. "Well, for a little while. But when I tell you to, you must promise to run right off to bed. With no more arguments."

"I promise. Thank you," Tia beamed.

In the Roman style, they all reclined on divans placed around a long table. The servants brought the courses of the meal. Lydia had never seen so much food on one table. She was not used to eating in this position and Lydia wondered if she could. She observed how the others balanced their plates, and she did the same as she tried to cut her meat. Her hands shook and a section of her roast pork slid off the plate and onto the floor. Her eyes caught Lucretia looking at her, a smile of scorn on her ruby-painted lips.

"Oh, I'm so sorry," Lydia apologized.

Tia smiled at her. "I do that all the time," she told Lydia.

Lydia smiled back in gratitude. "Do you, dear? Then I don't feel as bad about it."

A servant briskly removed the piece of meat from the floor and placed another on Lydia's plate. This time she was more careful. The dinner progressed slowly. Marcellus tried to keep the conversation flowing, but Lydia was concentrating so much on her manners that she scarcely could answer him. Lucretia talked with Tia about things Lydia could not possibly know, and she was excluded from their conversation. Finally, after what seemed to Lydia to be an eternity, dinner was over and Tia was ordered to bed by her aunt.

She ran to her father and kissed him, then stood before Lydia and curtsied. "It was very nice to meet you," she told Lydia. Then she was out of the room and down the hall to her bedroom.

"What a lovely child," Lydia said.

"She is the image of her mother," Lucretia said dryly. "I shall never understand why the gods allowed my dear sister-in-law to die so young. She was so full of life. So beautiful. There can never be another like her," and she looked directly at Lydia. "Never!"

Lydia looked at Marcellus. "It's getting late. I had better go home."

"Late? Why the evening has just begun," he protested.

"We have just received a new shipment of cloth," Lydia lied. "We must begin work early tomorrow morning. I really must go."

"But, Lydia—"

"If she must go, Marcellus, then she must go," Lucretia interrupted.

He nodded. "I'll have the carriage brought around," he said. "And I shall accompany you home."

Lydia saw the expression on Lucretia's face. A sudden chill struck her spine. It was not just an expression of displeasure, but of hate, disgust. She said her thanks to the blonde Roman woman and was glad to get out of the door and into the carriage. Marcellus helped her in and climbed beside her.

"All right, driver. But take it slowly. We are in no hurry and it is a pleasant evening for a ride."

They rode through the darkness and Lydia felt him take her hand. "I hope you liked my sister," he said. "And my daughter."

"Tia is a sweet child, Marcellus."

They rode along in silence for a few moments. "What did you think of my sister?"

"She . . . she is very beautiful."

"You didn't like her, did you?"

Lydia drew a deep breath. "No, Marcellus. I did not dislike her. But I think she dislikes me."

"What? Why do you say that? What did she say to make you think that?"

"It isn't that she said anything, Marcellus. But a woman . . . instinctively knows when another woman doesn't like her. And I can understand how she feels. It isn't just me. She has you and she has Tia. Any woman who comes into her house she feels is a threat to her."

The tribune shook his head. "Women! I'll never understand them! Of course she likes you, Lydia. Anyone would. You are mistaken about her."

"Have you invited other women to your home since your wife died?"

He frowned. "Yes. There have been a few. Why do you ask?"

"And what was Lucretia's reaction to them? Be honest now."

He rubbed his chin. "Well, she did say one of them didn't like Tia. And another one—well, she had heard some scandal about her that she would not tell me about."

"Do you see what I mean? She will have something to say about me, as well. But it isn't important. Forget I brought this up. I didn't mean to."

"Not important! Why would it not be important?"

"Because, Marcellus, she would be right. I could see tonight that you live in an entirely different world from mine."

"What do you mean, different? How is it different?"

"I have never had such a fine dinner, Marcellus, and I thank you for it. But I was, well, uncomfortable. I'm not used to food like that. I'm just a plain person. I didn't even know which utensil to use. I live in a plain and simple world, not the Roman one."

"But—"

"There can't be any buts, Marcellus. It just wouldn't work. Lucretia is right in protecting you. And protecting Tia. Until the right woman comes along, she will go on protecting you."

"Protecting me from what?"

"From yourself, Marcellus. From yourself."

The carriage rounded the bend in the road and cut off down the dirt entrance to the house by the river. As the horses stopped, Lydia looked out. "That's strange," she said. "I don't see any lamp lit inside. And I don't see anyone."

Marcellus stepped from the carriage. "I'd better have a look around."

With Lydia a step behind him, he bounded up onto the porch and flung open the door. "Hello," he called. "Is anyone here?"

From the darkened room came a sobbing reply. "Thank the gods you've come! Men came. They smashed the vats. When Clement and Papie tried to stop them, they beat them, too. Come quickly! I think Clement is dead!"

The footman brought in a lamp from the carriage, and Lydia saw Clement on the floor, his head and face a mass of blood. "Oh, dear gods!" she exclaimed. Euodia was huddled in a corner clutching Doronius to her. With his back to the other wall, Epaphroditus sat dazed and bleeding.

"Restor, quick! Take the carriage and fetch a doctor here!" Marcellus ordered the driver. The man cracked his whip and the horses were off, galloping up the hill and toward town. Marcellus put his ear to Clement's chest. "He is still alive," he said, "but just barely. Get water and a cloth. We have to stop the bleeding!"

Lydia tore her gown and gave him the cloth. She ran to the well and brought back water. She dropped to her knees beside

Marcellus and Clement. "You mustn't die, Clement!" she cried. "Oh, Marcellus, don't let him die!"

Marcellus did what he could for Clement, holding the cloth as a compress against the wound on his head which had been bleeding profusely. "See to Epaphroditus," he told Lydia.

"I'm not hurt badly," the young man said. "Don't worry about me. Just help my father!"

It seemed an eternity before they heard the sound of the horses' hoofs on the road and the carriage arrive with the doctor. A tall man ran into the house, followed by the driver. "I was in luck, sir," the driver told Marcellus. "The doctor was at home."

"Quickly, man! See to him!"

The doctor checked Clement's wounds. "Raise his legs," he told them. "And put something under his head. Hand me my bag. He needs a potion immediately. He has lost a lot of blood."

The doctor gave the semiconscious Clement a dose of medicine from a foul-smelling bottle. Almost at once Clement fell asleep, but his breathing was more regular. "We can move him to a bed now," the doctor said. Marcellus and the footman lifted him carefully and carried him to his bed. "If he lives until morning, he will survive," the doctor told them.

Euodia knelt by her husband. "You can't die, Clement! You just can't!"

The doctor then checked Epaphroditus's injuries and, although the young man was covered with blood, his wounds were not serious. They washed the caked blood from him and he joined his mother at his father's bedside. "We must ask the gods to spare his life," he said.

Euodia shook her head. "The gods do not care. If it were up to them, he would surely die. He must fight this battle for himself."

Marcellus took Lydia's arm. "The man I saw watching

this house," he said. "He must have had something to do with this. What was the name of the man Stetius warned you about?"

"His name was Vestus. But you can't believe he would—"

"Can you think of anyone else who might want to harm you?"

"No."

"Then it must have been this man Vestus." His face glowed with rage. "We live under Roman law, Lydia. If Vestus is responsible for this, he will not go unpunished."

"Lydia! Come quick! Look here." Epaphroditus's voice came from the storeroom. She ran to the rear of the house. Papie had a remnant of cloth in his hand, slashed to bits with a knife. "Look at our cloth. It has all been cut to ribbons!"

"The new shipment!" Lydia cried. "It is ruined. All of it."

Marcellus's face was grim. "Then it had to be Vestus," he said. "No one else would have cared about your cloth!" He took a step toward the door and motioned to his driver. "I shall be back later," he told Lydia. "Right now I have to attend to this man Vestus."

She heard the carriage rattle up the road and sighed as she surveyed the ruins of her fabric. Behind the house she found the vats smashed, useless, their wooden sides smashed to splinters.

Lydia sat on the ground and put her head in her arms. "We are finished," she said. "And what's worse, the moneylender's loan is due in a month. There is no way we can repay it now."

Marcellus had rousted the man out of bed and he sat rubbing his eyes as the tribune told him what he wanted him to do.

"You, Lorestus, are the chief tax collector of the province. I have saved your neck countless times when you exceeded your authority. Now I am calling in your debt to me."

Lorestus blinked his eyes and tried to shake away the effects of the preceeding night's wine. "But of course, my friend. I shall be most happy to do whatever you want. Just tell me what it is."

"Do you know a man named Vestus? He is a dyer of cloth."

The tax collector yawned and scratched his stomach. "The name seems familiar. Oh, yes, I know who you mean."

"Do you have his tax records for the last five years?"

"Certainly. All taxes are paid directly to me. I have a complete list of all taxes paid for the last ten or twelve years."

"Good. Then this is what I want you to do. Remove the records of this man, Vestus. Hide them somewhere. Then summon him to you and tell him that he is delinquent in his taxes for the past five years. I want to be there when he hears this."

Lorestus smiled a wry smile. "He must have offended you greatly, Excellency. The penalty for not paying taxes for that length of time is confiscation of all property."

Marcellus nodded. "I know the penalty, Lorestus. Just make certain that he also becomes aware of it."

Lydia and Euodia had kept the vigil all night beside Clement's bed, and when the first streaks of morning began to paint the eastern sky, they watched his breathing with increasing hope. "He's going to make it," Lydia whispered. "I know he's going to live."

Euodia had been holding his hand and he stirred slightly. His eyes opened for an instant, then closed again. "Did you see that, Lydia?" Euodia exclaimed. "He opened his eyes."

Clement groaned and opened his eyes again. This time they were on his wife's face. "Eu-odia," he said in a low voice. "My head—it hurts."

Euodia kissed his hand. "It's all right, my darling. Everything's going to be all right now. Just lie still."

Clement's eyes searched his wife's face. "Is Papie all right?"

Euodia smiled, with tears of joy streaming down her face, "Yes, he is fine. But lie still, Clement. You lost a lot of blood."

"Who were those men? Why did they do this?"

"I don't know who they were. But the main thing is that you are all right. Nothing else matters."

Lydia and Euodia looked at each other, and their expressions silently said that they would not tell him about the smashed vats and the slashed fabric. There was no need of his worrying about them, or that now there would be no way to repay the moneylender. The collateral, their freedom, would be taken from them and they would be sold as slaves.

That afternoon found Marcellus in the office of the chief tax collector, waiting for Vestus to appear as summoned. He had returned to the house by the river and was relieved to find Clement recovering.

"I have known you for many years," Lorestus said, "but never before have I seen you do anything not strictly in accordance with the law. But asking me to remove a man's tax records is, well, highly irregular to say the least."

"There are some things, Lorestus, in which the law is best served in unusual ways. I believe you will see that happen in this case."

At the appointed time Vestus arrived, somewhat anxious as to what purpose he had been called before the chief tax collector. He smiled nervously at Lorestus, then trembled visibly when he saw the tribune present. "Excellency," he said to Marcellus with a formal bow, "I trust you are well."

Marcellus grunted a reply, his face frozen in seriousness, which upset the already shaking man even more. "Sit down, Vestus," Marcellus told him. "You are in serious trouble."

"Tr-trouble? I don't understand."

Marcellus nodded to the chief tax collector. "Tell him the charges. Then let us hear his defense against them."

"Charges? What charges? I have done nothing!"

Lorestus unfolded a document and began to read. "It has come to the attention of the legally appointed collector of imperial taxes that Ignatius Vestus, a citizen of Philippi and a dyer of cloth goods, has for the past five years been deliquent in paying taxes due to the empire. It is ordered that he be brought to account before these charges and, if he can furnish no proof of the payment of said taxes, his property, holdings and all possessions be confiscated and sold to recover the unpaid taxes and whatever fines and assessments be levied against him by the administrative tribune of the province, Lucius Marcellus."

Lorestus looked up at Vestus. "And what do you have to say, Ignatius Vestus, to these charges?"

"I—I—I do not know what to say! I have always paid my taxes."

"The records say otherwise. Do you have receipts for the taxes you claim to have paid?"

"Receipts? Of course not. No receipts were ever given to me."

Lorestus shook his head sadly. "If you have no proof of payment, then the tribune Marcellus has no choice but to levy fines and assessments against you in addition to the back taxes you owe. Your property, all that you own, must be confiscated to pay them. If this does not cover your debt, then you will be sold as a slave."

The dyer of cloth was stricken with terror, his face ashen with fear. "But—but I am innocent! There has been a mistake! You cannot do this to an innocent man!"

Marcellus turned to Lorestus. "Perhaps there has been a

mistake here. Perhaps—and I just say perhaps—the tax records are in error."

"Yes," cried Vestus, "they are indeed in error!"

"Could not a search be made through the records, Lorestus? Maybe the missing records could be found."

"Yes! Yes, please look in the records again. I swear to you, as an honest man, I have always paid my taxes to Rome."

Lorestus rubbed his chin. "Well, I don't know. It would take a great deal of time to search through all the records for the past five years. But if you order me to do this, Excellency, then I shall."

Vestus was almost on his knees before Marcellus. "Please, sir, I am an honest man. A good citizen. A family man who obeys the law. Please ask that a search be made."

Marcellus's eyes narrowed. "You claim to be a good citizen, Vestus. What do you have to put forth to substantiate that claim?"

"To substantiate it? Let me see—"

"Can you point to one good deed you have done to a member of this community? Some charity, perhaps?"

"Charity? Let me see—"

"I have always heard that each trade takes care of its own members. Is this true, Vestus?"

"Yes, sir. It is a custom. If a member of one's trade falls upon hard times, other members rush to his aid."

"Well, then. Have you rushed to the aid of the widow, Lydia? She is a member of your trade. A dyer of cloth."

Vestus's eyes bulged. "Ly-Lydia? I do not seem to recall that name."

"Then let me refresh your memory. The merchant Stetius and you had a conversation about her. When he no longer bought your cloth, but hers. Now do you remember?"

Vestus swallowed hard and his mind raced. The tribune

seemed to know a great deal about his activities. Could he also know about his hiring men to wreck the widow's vats and destroy her stock of cloth? There had been a fight at the house and some of the widow's servants had been injured. How badly hurt were the men who had resisted his hired thugs? Finally he nodded his head and admitted, "Yes, I do recall Stetius telling me about some woman who was dyeing cloth. Perhaps her name had been Lydia."

Marcellus bent forward so that his face was very close to the trembling, perspiring man. "Don't you think, seeing as how this widow is a member of your trade, you should offer her some assistance? And that you should really insist that she accept it? Why don't you rebuild her vats which were destroyed by hoodlums, and replace her cloth which has been ripped to shreds?"

Marcellus's face was but an inch away from Vestus's now. "Don't you think you should do this, Vestus? After all, she is a member of your trade!"

The veins in Vestus's neck bulged, his head throbbed. "Yes," he said. "I—I think perhaps I should . . . ."

Marcellus handed him a small scrap of parchment. "Here is the inventory of the cloth that was destroyed. I think it would be most generous of you to replace it. But after all, you are a good citizen. You claim to be, that is."

He took the scrap of parchment without looking at it, his eyes still riveted to Marcellus's piercing stare. "Yes," he stammered, "I—I—think—"

"And Vestus," Marcellus said very slowly and deliberately, "if that widow lady, Lydia, as much as stubs her toe, I shall hold you personally responsible. Do you understand me?"

Vestus nodded his head in agreement. "And the tax records? Will there be a search made? Will they be found?"

"We shall see about that," Marcellus stated. "After the vats have been rebuilt and the cloth replaced."

Vestus bowed and hurried away, not stopping until he had returned to his shop. He gave orders to those who worked for him which puzzled them greatly, for none of them ever remembered Vestus as being a charitable man.

Lydia awakened the next morning to an astounding sight. A small army of workmen had arrived in carts, led by a centurion. She came out of the door and the centurion saluted her smartly. "The tribune Marcellus sends his regards, madam. These men will repair the damage to your vats. In the carts you will find cloth. Please check it to see that all you lost has been replaced."

By the end of the day, the vats had been rebuilt and the storehouse once again contained the woolens and silks, ready to be dyed. When all had been done, the centurion accompanied Lydia on an inspection. "Is everything satisfactory, madam?"

"Yes," beamed the astonished Lydia. "Please thank the tribune for me."

"I believe you may do that yourself, madam. If I am not mistaken, he is riding down the road right now."

A grinning Marcellus reined his horse. "Is everything finished?" he asked the centurion, returning the officer's salute.

"Yes, sir. We are about to leave."

"How did you accomplish this?" Lydia asked.

Marcellus laughed. "I really didn't do anything at all. It was all out of the goodness of Vestus's heart. You know that people in the same trade are supposed to be honor-bound to take care of their own. All I had to do was to remind him of this fact."

"You must be a very convincing reminder," Lydia told him.

The tribune dismounted and took her hand. "I hope I am," he said, his face now serious. "I hope to convince you of something."

"No, Marcellus. Please don't talk about that now. I'm too confused and my gratitude would perhaps influence my answer."

"Very well, Lydia. But I shall be back. And I will be very convincing, I promise you."

She watched him ride up the road, the trail of dust kicked up by his horse following in his wake. Her heart and her head were torn apart by this tall, handsome Roman. Her head told her it would never work. Her heart told her differently.

Marcellus rode directly home. Things had happened so quickly that he had not seen his sister since the night when Lydia had come for dinner. Now he saw her in the atrium and she smiled when he entered, then returned her attention to her needlework.

"I have been wanting to ask you, Lucretia, what you thought of Lydia."

She raised her eyes slightly, then lowered them to her work. After a moment of silence, she answered. "What does it matter? She is your mistress. I have nothing to do with it."

He did not believe what he had heard. "Mistress? Is that what you think she is? My mistress?"

"Dear brother, I am a grown woman. I know what men need. And you have been five years without a wife. What you do about it is no concern of mine."

He shook his head in amazement. "Lucretia! Lydia is a lady, a fine lady. She is no—no—"

"Whore? Go ahead and say it, brother. I have heard the word before. You shan't shock my sensitive ears."

He stood dumbfounded by her reaction. He knelt beside her at the divan. "Lucretia! Look at me! What makes you think that Lydia is such a woman? Look at me, Lucretia, and tell me."

She kept to her work. But inside was the fear, the clutching fear, the terrible feeling that he would find another woman, perhaps marry her and take Tia away from her. She couldn't lose

Tia! Since her sister-in-law had died, she had been mother to this child, to hold, to care for, to love and to be loved in return. She could not—would not—lose her now. And she would do anything to prevent it!

She sighed heavily and finally answered him. "Marcellus, I am just trying to protect you. To protect Tia. You are very vulnerable. Believe me, I understand. If you desire this woman, then take her. But let it be in her bed, not one in this house."

He stood up and looked down at her, confused, hurt by what she had said. Lydia had been right! Lydia had told him she would feel exactly this way! But Lucretia was so wrong about Lydia. How could he make her understand his feelings, his intentions, about Lydia?

He walked from the room, still shaking his head in confusion. But one thing was certain—he could not bring Lydia here again. There was no telling how Lucretia might treat her, what she might say to her. Perhaps in time his sister would understand. He hoped she would with all his heart.

For the next two weeks Lydia was too busy to think about anything but work. With Clement injured and bedridden, Lydia, Euodia and Papie had to dye the cloth all by themselves. From early in the morning until late into the night, Lydia toiled at the vats.

First the fabric had to be sized with the secret ingredient if it were silk. Then came the first dyeing, then the cloth must be dried properly. Then came the second dyeing, then the exposure to the sunlight to bring out the brilliant and lasting purple color. She had lost all sense of time and days when they finally finished the last batch and hung the cloth out in the sun to dry and develop its color.

With a sigh, Lydia and Euodia sat down on the ground next to one of the vats. Clement, with the assistance of a walking stick, had been able to get out of bed and supervise the final, critical steps of the process. Now he nodded his head in satisfaction, "It is good," he told them. "It is very good."

Lydia looked up at him. "Clement, I am glad to hear you say that, but honestly, if it were not good right now I could care less. I'm exhausted."

He hobbled away on his walking stick, shaking his head. "What's this world coming to?" he growled in mock anger. "A little work and everybody's tired. You certainly can't get decent help nowadays."

Vestus signed the papers and the man handed over the money. He had sold his property in Philippi and would be leaving the next day for Thessalonica where his brother lived. He would open up his business of dyeing cloth there.

He had decided it was not safe for him in Philippi, not since the tribune Marcellus had taken such an interest in that widow. She had ruined his business here, had taken away his best customer, and if the slightest misfortune happened to her he would be held responsible. It was best to get out of Philippi while he was able.

But no one, he bragged, ever got the best of Ignatius Vestus. He would get even with that widow, Lydia. And with that cocky tribune, too. If it took the rest of his life, he would get revenge. This he promised himself.

As soon as the dyed fabric was taken to Stetius and Lydia had the money for it, she went directly to the moneylender and paid off the loan. At sixty percent interest it took most of what she had, but at least the threat of slavery no longer hung over the heads of Clement and Euodia.

That evening she relaxed for the first time in weeks. The day had been oppressively hot and the evening had brought no respite. She put Doronius to bed on the porch where a slight breeze made it bearable for sleeping. With a sigh, she sat down on the steps.

Suddenly she heard voices coming from near the bank of the river. People were singing, but a strange kind of singing she had never heard before. Her curiosity aroused, she got up and walked toward the river to hear better. She could see a small fire burning on the bank, not for warmth on this hot and humid night, but to give one of the men light to read by. This man was chanting in a language Lydia did not understand. She crept closer, to where she could see and hear, and sat down on the grass and listened.

In the dim light she could see there were only a few people on the bank listening to the man. Most of these appeared to be women. Then she was startled to hear the man speak in Greek.

"I know most of you do not speak or understand Hebrew," he said, "so I shall use the language you understand. I want to tell you about how God used our father, Moses, to free us when we were slaves in Egypt, how Moses led them out of this bondage and into the land which God had promised to give them from the time of Abraham."

As Lydia listened, she was drawn closer and closer into what this man was saying. He spoke of God. Not as a god, but as though all who listened to him knew there was only one God. And this was an entirely different kind of God than Lydia had ever heard about. This God actually cared about people, even to the extent of helping to free them when they had been slaves in a foreign land.

She sat spellbound as the story went on. The man told how God had led the people across the desert wastes, feeding them with a food called manna, which dropped from the sky at night. And this God actually appeared before them, as a cloud by day and as a pillar of fire by night. Then, when he had called Moses to the top of a mountain, this God gave to him a set of rules by which the people must live. He called these the Ten Commandments.

As the speaker enumerated these rules, Lydia felt a strange sensation inside herself. Yes, she thought, these are really rules from God. Not to kill. Not to steal, lie or cheat. The kind of God the man described would certainly have given this set of rules for people to follow.

The man went on. Now he was speaking about a promise God had made, a promise to send His Anointed One, who would lead the people, all people, out of the bondage they were now in. He would lead them toward a rich and full life. To freedom and hope. The prophets had described this Anointed One. He would be a man of compassion, of love, caring for all men and capable of breaking the bonds of those who believed in him and to restore them to their true heritage which God had ordained for them.

Lydia listened with her eyes closed, feeling a warm sensation inside. She could believe in a God such as this man described, a loving, caring God. Then she heard herself saying, "God, if this is true, then I want to be a part of your kingdom. I believe what this man says about you. If you are real, then please let me know it."

She opened her eyes and was conscious of someone standing before her. She recoiled, startled. "Oh!"

"I am sorry. I did not mean to frighten you."

Lydia recognized the man who had addressed the group. "I—I was just listening to you speak. And to the singing. I did not mean to intrude."

"All are welcome here," the man told her. "God's message is for all people, Greek as well as Jew."

"Thank you. I believe what you say. I believe you speak of the true God. I have long doubted the stories of the gods who are supposed to live on Olympas. They are mere superstitions, invented by foolish men. But your God is different, caring about people, watching over them. I can believe in such a God."

"We meet every week here at this time," the man said. "There are only a few of us here in Philippi. A few Jews and the rest Greeks such as yourself, who have heard and have believed in our Lord. I must go now, but if you wish to be with us next week you will be welcome."

The man disappeared into the darkness. The people on the bank had also left, and Lydia sat alone, thinking about what she had heard. She felt something new stir within herself, a warmness, a sensation she had never felt before. She went back to the house and found Euodia.

"Euodia," she said, "I have just heard a man tell of the true God. Next week you must come with me and hear more about this God."

— Chapter Nine —

The man leaned his powerful arms on the stone parapet above the water and looked far across the Aegean Sea. He could easily make out the forms of several of the islands that lay as stepping-stones, spanning the blue waters that separated Troas on the Asian side from the Macedonian Greece to the west. He ran his hand through his reddish-brown hair in deep thought, then turned to his companion.

"Last night," he said, "I had a dream. A strange dream."

Silas moved closer. "And what was the dream, Paul?"

Paul turned his eyes once more to the sea and pointed across the water toward Europe. "In my dream I saw a man of Macedonia. He was far off and yet I could see him clearly in the distance. His arms were outstretched, as though pleading with me."

Paul turned to his companions, Silas, Luke and the young man, Timothy. "And do you know what he said to me?" The apostle's eyes filled with moisture as he spoke. "He said, 'Come over and help us.'"

Silas peered across the water. "To Macedonia?"

Paul nodded. "That is what he asked."

"But we cannot go to Europe," Luke interjected. "Not without the permission of the Jerusalem church. Not after they decided to restrict our work to Asia, at least for now."

Paul sat on the low stone wall. "That is what they told us," he agreed. "But I can't get that man's face out of my mind. Nor the sound of his voice. He was like a starving man begging for food."

"But there is so much left to do here in Asia. There are so many who need our help," argued Silas.

Paul squinted as the sunlight struck his eyes, still red and swollen from a recent infection. "The seeds have been planted here. But over there is ground that has not yet known the seed of truth. Over here there are those who will continue to sow, but no man has yet tilled the soil to the west. Over there," and he gestured toward Macedonia, "they have not yet heard. Not one soul! Someone must go!"

Silas put his hand on Paul's shoulder. "And someone shall go, Paul. When it is time."

"Time! Who is to decide when the time has come? Is it to be those cowards in Jerusalem? Men who have never taken the name of Christ beyond the borders of Judea? Are they to decide whether that man in Macedonia will die without the knowledge of Jesus? To die and be cast into hell because no man would take the word across this thin stretch of water to him?"

"But someone has to make decisions, Paul. You, yourself, agreed to that. We are to abide by these decisions."

"Bah!" Paul snorted. "Someone in Jerusalem? While we sit here and look across the water at an entire continent of pagans who have never heard the name of Christ? We are to listen to someone in Jerusalem who hides, cowering in fear from both Roman and Jew?"

He stood up and looked again at the green islands, reaching like a chain of oases from Asia to Greece across the Aegean. "The time has come to act, not cower in fear."

"And what does that mean?" asked Silas.

"That," said Paul slowly, "means that tomorrow I intend to take ship to Macedonia. The man in my dreams has waited long enough. I believe the Holy Ghost is leading me and I shall not hesitate for any man." He turned and looked at each of them for a moment, his eyes bright with enthusiasm. "If any of you wish to accompany me, you will be welcome. If not, stay here and rot until those pompous asses in Jerusalem deem it the right time. But tomorrow I shall go to keep my appointment with that man in Macedonia. He has waited long enough."

For several months Lydia had been going to the bank of the river whenever the group had met. At first only Euodia had gone with her, and she had also believed in the God of the Jews. Finally they persuaded Clement to come with them. He admitted that what he heard of this invisible God who cared for people sounded true, but when the leader told him about the covenant God had made with his people—with the sign of this covenant being the circumcision of all males—he had protested. "If I must submit to that, then I can never be one of them."

But he still came to the river bank and listened, and he encouraged Epaphroditus to come as well. Now they all sat on the bank of the river Gangites, Lydia holding the sleeping Doronius on her lap, as they heard the leader tell the stories of how the invisible God had waged war for them, cared for them, and punished them when they strayed from His word.

Still, Clement refused to do more than listen. "There is more to the God than we have heard about," he told them. "I feel it, especially about this Anointed One that the God will send into the world to free men from their bondage."

Syntyche opened her eyes and stretched. The bed of straw, all she had been given to sleep on, reeked with the stench of filth and crawled with lice. She sat up and scratched the sores where the vermin had bitten her during the night. The young girl sat still, feeling an awareness that for her was strange, knowing for a brief few moments who she was and what was happening to her.

Syntyche was a slave, owned by two brothers of Philippi who made money from the power of the demon who had taken possession of her. This demon could tell the future, and anyone for a drachma could have his fortune told. Syntyche never saw this money, for the men took it all.

This morning was a rare occasion, for the demon who had taken over her mind and body totally controlled her most of the time. And as she now realized what was happening to her, she sobbed, appalled at her wretched surroundings and what her life had degenerated into. A deep revulsion for her own self engulfed her.

She was kept by the brothers in a pigsty of a room behind their house and given only sufficient garbagelike food to keep her alive. The men, whenever they desired, took her into the house and used her body to satisfy their lusts. The demon reveled in this way of life, and it was only on the brief occasions when Syntyche was rational that she could feel remorse and disgust at what she had become.

The door to the hovel was suddenly thrust open and one of her owners threw a few scraps of food inside. "Come on now! Hurry and eat this! Then get out to the marketplace and go to work. If you don't bring back at least ten drachmas today, I'll beat your worthless hide!"

She started to cry. But then the demon awakened within her and she felt herself falling, falling into blackness as the demon assumed complete control over her again.

Clement awoke and sat up in bed. Euodia stirred beside him. "What's the matter," she asked. "Are you ill?"

He rubbed his eyes. "No, I am not ill. But I had the strangest dream," he told her. "I dreamed I was standing on a high hill overlooking the sea. On the other side I could see a man. Somehow I knew this man could help us. How, I do not know. But I was begging him to come over to Macedonia." He shook his head, trying to clear his mind. "It was the strangest dream I've ever had. Even now it seems so real to me."

As the ship put into port at the island of Samothrace, Paul felt a sense of anticipation and exhilaration. Finally, he knew, his real mission had begun. The years of missionary traveling and work in Asia, the establishment of churches on Cyprus, and at Antioch, Lystra, Iconium and the other cities had been in preparation for this.

The ship dropped anchor for the night in the harbor at Samothrace, and Paul, Luke, Silas and Timothy went ashore to stretch their legs. Paul was in high humor. He sang and laughed as they walked the streets near the harbor. Silas, who had known him for years, had never before seen him in such good spirits. "What did you give him, Luke? Did you slip one of your potions into his wine?"

"No," the physician laughed, "but I wish I had one that would do it. Unfortunately, most of mine are purgatives."

Timothy, who adored Paul, only smiled at Luke's joke, but the Apostle roared. "And all his potions are so foul-tasting that his patients are forced to recover in self-defense so they will not have to suffer a second dose."

They stopped at an inn for dinner, and Paul asked the blessing both before and after the meal, thanking God for providing their needs and for allowing them to venture forth onto this great and untouched continent of Europe with the news of Jesus Christ. They returned to the ship to sleep, spreading their pallets on the deck. In the morning the ship weighed anchor again, bound for Neapolis on the coast of Macedonia.

That evening they made port and stopped at an inn for the night. The next morning they started off early, climbing the road toward their first destination, the city of Philippi. As they walked, Luke kept them informed of the history of the area, pointing out where Octavian and Antony had met Brutus and Cassius in battle.

"How is it that a physician knows so much about history?" Silas asked.

Luke smiled at him. "An educated man should know about many things. And besides, history is the most fascinating of subjects. Have you never read Thucydides's s history?"

Silas frowned. "I never heard of him!"

Luke shook his head. "What a bunch of dolts I am forced to travel with! One of the most famous Greeks of all time and you have never heard of him!"

Timothy spoke up. "I know who he is. I read his history in school."

"Ah," smiled Luke, "all is not lost! Here we have an educated young man. Now tell me, Timothy, have you also read anything by Xenophon?"

"Only his *Anabasis.*"

"Then you are in luck. I have a copy of *Memorabilia.* You will have to read it. It is marvelous."

And so as the four men approached the city of Philippi, Luke and Timothy were lost in a conversation about history and philosophy. Paul silently contemplated the great challenge that lay before him, and Silas complained about the blisters that were developing on his feet.

The agora, or marketplace, in the center of the city was crowded with people, shoppers, vendors, merchants, and with those who were there just to exchange the gossip of the day. It was through this crowd that Marcellus made his way, bound for the section of the square where the magistrates held court, meting out Roman justice and hearing the cases brought before them.

Syntyche was in the agora as usual, calling to the passing men, inviting them to have their fortunes told. "You there," she, or rather the demon which possessed her, called out to a man carrying a basket of grapes on his shoulder. "I have something to tell you concerning your future. For a drachma I will tell you."

The man passed by, barely glancing at her, for she was in the same place every day and had called to him before. "It is about your wife," Syntyche called. "She has been unfaithful to you. Her name is Drucilla."

This caused the man with the grapes to stop. "How do you know my wife's name?" he asked. "And what do you know of her?"

A cackling laugh came from the young girl's throat as the demon spoke through her. "It will cost you a drachma to find out."

The man hesitated and the demon spoke again. "What I know will save you much trouble in the future. Give me the coin and I will tell you all I know about her."

"Tell me first," the man replied. "If it is worth a drachma, then I shall pay you."

"Give me the coin first. But I will tell you your own name so you will believe I really know. It is Horace. Your name is Horace. Now do you believe me?"

He put down the basket and pulled out his purse. Handing a coin to Syntyche, he demanded, "Now tell me about my wife! Who is her lover?"

She put the coin safely away in a pocket of her rags and her face was grim as she faced the man. "His name is Agatius. He is a seller of meat. Your wife and he have been lovers for over a year. When you are away from home, he visits her. Go home now and you will find them together."

The man's face contorted with anger. "I shall do that," he told her. "But if what you say is not true, I shall be back for my money." He picked up the basket of grapes and hurried away.

Marcellus had witnessed this exchange and shook his head as the man ran home. No doubt the slave girl was right, but the incident could mean trouble if the man actually caught his wife with the other man. Adultery was a common occurrence in Philippi, as were crimes of passion when the act was discovered.

He strode through the agora toward the corner where the magistrates held court. Standing behind the magistrates were the *lictors*, each with the bundle of rods and an axe which were the tools of their profession and the symbolic emblem of Roman justice. The rods were to administer the scourging, the usual punishment for minor offenses. The axe was for punishment of capital crimes. But depending upon the particular mood of the magistrate, even minor crimes were too often severely punished. It was Marcellus's duty to see that the magistrates meted out equal punishment for equal crimes. Roman justice, although harsh, must also be fair and equitable.

It was into this crowded marketplace that the party of travelers arrived in Philippi. They pushed their way through vendors shouting the merits of their wares and the din of a hundred loud discussions. Paul knew exactly what he was looking for and searched the stalls and shops that lined the agora for the sign, indicating that the owner was a Jew. Here he would inquire about the location of the *beth tephila*, the house of prayer, which in Greek was called the synagogue.

Paul had gone around most of the agora before he spotted the sign he was looking for, a universal sign used by Jews throughout the *Diaspora* to denote to other Jews that a brother was in residence there. He entered the small shop and greeted the man inside. "May the blessing of the Lord be upon your house."

The man's face brightened in acknowledgment. "And upon you, brother."

"I am Paul, a Jew from the city of Tarsus in Cilicia. My companions and I have just arrived in Philippi. Could you direct me to the house of assembly and prayer?"

The man shook his head. "We have none here. There is not even a *minyan* here. Just a few old men and women and some Greek proselytes."

"Oh," Paul said, "not even the ten adult males required to hold a service? I am sorry, brother. But the Lord looks with favor upon you, I am sure."

"We meet on Sabbath at the bank of a river to the west of the city. We would be honored if you could be with us tomorrow at sundown."

"We would be pleased to attend. Is there an inn west of the city where we could find lodgings for tonight?"

"Lodgings? For brothers? My home is small but I would be honored if you and your companions would stay with us."

Paul knew this was impossible, for Luke was a Gentile. Under Hebrew law, Luke could not enter a Hebrew home without defiling it.

"No, brother. We could not impose upon you. But direct us to an inn and we shall join you on the morrow at sundown at the river."

They left the shop, traveling to the west and following the directions to an inn. As they passed where Syntyche stood, the demon within her grew agitated. "These men are the servants of the Most High God, who shows you the way of salvation!" she shouted after them.

A few people in the crowd turned and looked at them as the demon cried out, but the citizens of Philippi were used to the slave girl screaming all sorts of things at passers-by, and they paid little attention to her.

The sun was just disappearing behind the western horizon when Lydia and her family walked down the path toward the river. Euodia had Doronius by the hand as she walked beside Clement. Epaphroditus, who showed the least interest in the services, lagged behind.

As they approached, Lydia saw there were more people than usual at the river bank. There were more men, and she saw some of them, strangers, talking with the Jewish shopkeeper who was in charge. They found seats on the grassy bank and waited for the meeting to begin.

"We have guests tonight," the shopkeeper announced. "They have come from across the sea, from Asia, and have asked to speak to you. But first we shall sing a few songs and have a prayer."

They sang the now-familiar psalms and the shopkeeper led the prayer. Then a stocky man with reddish-brown hair arose to address the group.

"My name is Paul," he said in a deep and resonant voice. "My companions and I have come to bring you good news. God, who is always faithful in His promises, has also been faithful to send into the world Him who has been promised by the Scriptures."

There was a gasp from the audience and Paul waited a moment before he continued. He held up his hand. "The Messiah has come," he said.

Again there was a gasp from the assembly. "He was born in Bethlehem of Judea as was prophesied by Micah, and of a virgin as was foretold. In fact, He has fulfilled every one of the prophecies made by the prophets, the spokesmen of the Lord God.

"Yet the priests of the temple recognized Him not. They plotted against the Anointed One of God and had Him crucified."

There was a murmur in the crowd. "Killed? The Messiah was killed?"

Paul raised his hand to quiet them. "But God raised Him up from the dead and He was seen by many."

"Raised from the dead?"

"Yes," Paul replied. "God raised Him from the dead and He defeated death so that you"—and he gestured to include them all—"could also have victory over death and have life eternal."

"How can this be?" a man asked.

"Tell us more," another demanded. "What happened then?"

"This Anointed One was actually the Son of God, the only begotten Son of the Father."

"God's Son? God has no son!" a man cried out.

"Wait! Hear him out!" the shopkeeper shouted. "Let Paul speak!"

He continued, telling them briefly about the life of Jesus, about His ministry, and His death. He described the miracles Jesus had performed, raising Lazarus from the dead and restoring the sight of the blind. Paul's powerful voice kept the small crowd of men and women spellbound.

"And so," Paul concluded, "we have come to you with the good news of the resurrected Christ, taken up to heaven by the Father, but with His promise that whosoever believes on His name, and that God raised Him from the dead, would have eternal life and salvation."

Lydia had sat motionless while Paul spoke, her heart beating rapidly. She had felt an intense emotional experience, as though this man, Paul, had been sent straight from God himself. Yes, she thought, the God in whom I now believe would have done just that. He would have sent His own Son as a sacrifice to save the world from sin and destruction. She hoped Paul would go on speaking all night, telling everything connected with this marvelous thing.

But the crowd was growing restless. It was late and most of them were anxious to go home. The shopkeeper stood up. "We shall hear of this another time," he said and closed the meeting with a short prayer.

The crowd dispersed. Only Lydia and her family remained on the bank of the river. The four strangers turned to go back toward the city.

"Wait," Lydia heard herself saying. "Sirs, may I speak with you?"

Paul smiled as she approached, and Lydia thought she could make out a glow, an aura about his face in the moonlight. "Yes?" he said.

Lydia cleared her throat, the words coming hard. "I . . . I believe what you have said. About the Christ. I . . . I believe He was . . . the Son of God."

Paul's hand reached out and touched her arm. "Blessed are you, young lady, for you are the first to believe on this vast continent of Europe."

Clement had risen and was standing close to Paul, his eyes searching the apostle's face. "It cannot be!" Clement exclaimed. "You are the man in the dream!"

Paul turned and looked into Clement's face. "Yes," he said, "and you are the man of Macedonia who was in mine."

"This is the man I told you about, Euodia," Clement said

excitedly. "The man I saw far off. The one I asked to come and help us. Truly," he said, his voice full of emotion, "these men have been sent by God!"

Lydia faced Paul again. "What must I do to obtain this salvation you speak about?"

Paul indicated the river. "You must believe and be baptized in water, for the forgiveness of your sins and a symbolic death to the things of this world."

"And must I be circumcised?" Clement asked.

Paul shook his head. "You are a Greek. The rite of circumcision does not apply to you. Christ will circumcise your heart, not your flesh."

"Then baptize me," pleaded Clement. He turned to his family, "And these as well, if they agree, for you truly have been sent by God and I believe with all my heart that you have told us about the Christ."

So Paul baptized them all in the shallow waters at the edge of the river, even the child Doronius, who accepted this unexpected bath as though he knew what it was all about.

"And where do you stay in Philippi?" asked Lydia.

"We have rooms at the inn."

"Please, sirs, if you have judged me to be faithful to the Lord, come into my house and abide there."

At first Paul refused, not wanting to inconvenience the young woman, but she persisted, not wanting them to stay at the inn. Finally, after conferring with the others, Paul accepted the invitation, and they all moved into Lydia's house and remained there while they were in Philippi.

With the light of the lamps, sleeping space was found in the spacious house for the four men. Beds were a luxury in those times, and the travelers, as most people of their time, were accustomed to sleeping on a pallet on the floor. Lydia and Euodia brought them blankets and robes to sleep on, and soon the house was still, with only the sounds of sleep heard in the rooms.

Early the next morning Lydia arose. She found her guests already up. "Good morning," she greeted them as she entered the atrium.

"Good morning, and may God bless you for your hospitality."

Euodia brought melons and fruit, and they ate in the spacious atrium after Paul had blessed the food. Lydia was very curious about these four strange men. They seemed to have come from different parts of the world. But it would not be polite to ask personal questions of them. Lydia was glad when Paul, who seemed to sense her curiosity, volunteered the information.

"You have quite an assortment of guests," he told her, "for we come from various places and circumstances. I was born in Tarsus of Cilicia of Hebrew parents of the tribe of Benjamin. I was raised as a devout Jew by my father, a tent maker who taught me his trade.

"It was thought that I possessed some aptitude for learning, and in my youth I was sent to Jerusalem to study at the school of Gamaliel, the grandson of Hillel, who was also a great teacher.

"After the crucifixion of Christ, I believed as did most Jews, that His followers were heretics and strove to suppress them by force. But then, on the road to Damascus, Jesus himself appeared to me in a great and blinding light, and I was led by Him to see that He was indeed the Son of God.

"Since that time I have labored to teach this truth to others. With, unfortunately, only small success to date. But I shall try as long as breath is left in these bones and flesh."

Paul pointed out another of the men who sat in the atrium. "Now Silas comes from an old and distinguished Jewish family. He was one of the first converts of the Jerusalem church, seeing Peter's powerful works at Pentecost." Lydia looked over at Silas, a man of medium height with dark black hair and a beard to match.

"Silas is a merry fellow, never tiring of jokes and songs, but when it comes to the work of the Lord, none is more serious than he. When I appeared at the Jerusalem church to argue the question of what Gentiles would have to do to be admitted to our fellowship, Silas took my side and spoke well before James and the others."

Then Paul indicated Luke, and Lydia could see this man was Greek like herself. He was tall and somewhat thin, with a gentle manner and eyes that seemed to take in everything. He spoke little, but when he did, his words were well chosen, wise and directly to the point.

"Luke was one of the first Gentiles to accept Jesus as Lord," Paul said. "He had come to Judea to study under the Hebrew physicians. They are, as is well known, the finest physicians in the world, having great knowledge of herbs and plants as well as understanding the workings and nature of the body.

"Luke was visiting his cousin, Cornelius, a centurion stationed in Caesarea. He was there when the Holy Spirit showed to Peter that Gentiles should be admitted to full fellowship with us in the Lord. Cornelius was a devout man and believed in God. In a dream he saw Peter and sent men to bring him to his home. At the same time, Peter had a dream, and in it the Lord made it plain that everything God has made is clean in His eyes.

"After Cornelius had been baptized, and all his household with him, he witnessed to Luke concerning the things of Christ, and Luke also believed. Years later I met him by chance when he was called in to treat a disorder I have now and again with my eyes. We became friends, and he decided to join Silas and me in our travels and work for the Lord Jesus."

Paul then looked at the young man, Timothy, and he smiled with pride as he told Lydia about him. "Timothy was born in Lystra of a Greek father and Hebrew mother. This devoted mother and his saintly grandmother led him to study the Holy Scriptures while his father insisted he read the great Greek historians and philosophers. As a result, he has had a very wide and extensive education.

"He came to know the Lord Jesus when I spoke to the Jews at Lystra, and he and his mother and grandmother were baptized into the faith there. Later he asked to travel with me and learn more of the things of Jesus in preparation for becoming an evangelist and pastor.

"And since I have never married and so have no son, Timothy has become my son in the Lord, and I am very proud of him."

As Lydia listened to the voice of Paul and heard what he told her, she began to see him as a very unique person, one whose charismatic personality either drew people close to him or, if they had closed their minds to God, caused them to hate him with fierce passion.

As for herself, she felt drawn to this strange man who had suddenly appeared in her life. When she had first heard him speak, just the night before, she knew from the first that he could not possibly tell a lie. And she believed everything he had said. Then, when Clement told them Paul was the man in his dream, everything seemed to have been confirmed. Clement was not one to take anything for granted. No one could easily fool him. When Paul related to them that he had seen Clement in his dream at the same time, there was no way anyone could deny that Paul had been sent by God.

Lydia felt the peace within herself that Paul had told her Jesus would bring. It was not that she was no longer concerned about things—far from it. But the knowledge in her heart that God cared about her, that He would take care of her no matter what happened, that Jesus had given His life *personally* for her as well as for every man, woman and child in the world. This was the peace she knew, a strange, knowing, believing peace.

And she was hungry to learn as much as possible about Jesus and the one true God who had sent His Son into the world. She sat at Paul's feet entranced, hanging on every word, hungering to know more and more.

During the following days, Paul and Silas went into the city speaking to all who would listen about Jesus, God's Son, who had given His life so that they might have salvation. Many listened to them, for Greeks are always eager to hear of new and strange things, but when Paul finished speaking they mocked him and made sport of what he had said.

But the slave girl, Syntyche, followed after them, calling, "These men are the servants of the Most High God," for the demon who controlled her knew who they were and why they had come to Philippi.

In the evenings, Lydia sat at Paul's feet while he told of his experiences to her, Clement, Euodia and Papie. They were astonished when he told them he had at first persecuted Christians, and it had taken a personal encounter with the risen Jesus on the road to Damascus to set his feet on the proper path.

Paul and the others had been living at Lydia's house for about a week when Marcellus arrived. Lydia introduced the tribune to Paul and the others and they spoke briefly. But later when Marcellus had a chance to talk with Lydia alone, he asked her, "Lydia, who are these men?"

"They have been sent to us by God from Asia," she replied.

Marcellus frowned. "They have what? Surely, Lydia, you are joking. You can't possibly be serious about that!"

"But I am. The man with the reddish-brown hair is Paul. He had personally met Jesus, the Son of God. His mission is now to tell the whole world about the Christ who has brought salvation and eternal life to all who will believe in Him."

Marcellus looked incredulously at her. "By the gods, Lydia, you really are serious about this!"

"I hve never in my life been more serious about anything. I have found the one true God, Marcellus, and my life has been changed."

The tribune shook his head. "You are changed, all right! You have completely lost your mind!"

"Don't you believe in God, Marcellus?"

"God? Which god do you mean? The priests would have us believe in a dozen gods. Even the emperors are now gods. Why do you need another one, Lydia? Just pick out one of these if you must suddenly get religious. But don't make a fool of yourself!"

"If I am a fool, then I hope all the world catches my malady. It gives a peace I have never known before."

He took a deep breath. "You know nothing of these people. They may be criminals for all you know. And you invite them, men you had never before laid eyes on, into your house as guests. I thought you, above all people, would have better judgment."

She put her hand on his arm. "I appreciate your concern, but it is unnecessary. Paul, Silas and Timothy are scholars. Why one of them, Luke, is a physician."

Marcellus shook his head in bewilderment. "Lydia, Lydia. Paul says he is a scholar. Luke claims to be a physician. These people appear out of the night and have you under a spell. What you are doing is dangerous! Can't you see that?"

"They are nto dangerous at all. And please keep your voice down, they may hear you."

Marcellus made an angry noise. "I can't watch you taken advantage of like this, Lydia. I care about you. I care very much. Can't you see that inviting strange men into your home is a dangerous, a foolish thing to do? I'm going to ask them—no, insist—that they leave at once!"

She grabbed his tunic with both hands. "No! You can't do that! They are my guests and this is my house! I won't allow you to insult them!"

He looked at her for a long moment. "But Lydia—"

"No, Marcellus! They will stay!"

He saw that further argument would do no good. "Then I shall go, Lydia. When you have come to your senses you will see that I am right."

She watched him mount his horse and trot up the road toward the Egnation Way, which led into the city. At one point she started to call to him, to ask him to come back, at least to talk with Paul, to listen to him tell of the Christ. But then she knew it would do no good. Slowly she turned away from the door and went back into the atrium with her guests.

In a few moments she was again sitting at Paul's feet as he told of the miracles he had witnessed which God had given as a sign of His power. She completely forgot about the scene with Marcellus as she was caught up in the story by Paul's words.

The next morning Paul and Silas went as usual into the city. Again Syntyche followed them, the demon crying out that they were sent by God to show men the way of salvation. Paul knew what he heard was the voice of a demon and became more and more irritated as the day went on.

Finally he could stand it no longer. He whirled about and pointed his finger at Syntyche. "In the name of Jesus Christ I command you to come out of her!"

The crowd of onlookers gasped in amazement as the girl was suddenly thrown to the ground. Her eyes bulged and she thrashed wildly in the dust. From deep within her there came a terrifying sound which grew louder and louder. Then with a piercing scream, something seemed to issue from her mouth and scamper off into the confusion of the crowd.

Syntyche lay still on the ground, a new expression on her face. She sat up, still in a daze and looked at Paul. "Thank you," she said. "It is gone. At last I am free."

Paul reached down and helped her to her feet. "And you shall no longer be bothered by him, child. Jesus, the Christ, has set you free and now beckons to you to follow Him in the way of salvation and eternal life." And as Syntyche took Paul's hand, she felt a new joy fill her heart.

"I believe," she said, "that Jesus is who you say. He is the Son of the Living God."

Someone in the crowd ran to the brothers who owned the slave girl and told them what had happened. The two men had been drinking as usual and ran clumsily to where Paul and the girl stood, surrounded by the crowd of onlookers.

"Seize them!" one of the brothers shouted. "Take them before the magistrates. These Jews are workers of witchcraft!"

Suddenly several arms were around Paul and Silas, and they were dragged roughly to the part of the agora where the magistrates sat. The brothers bowed before the judges and one of them spoke.

"These men are Jews and are spreading subversion to the people. We, as Romans, ought not to hear such things. These men bring nothing but trouble to our city."

The crowd roared in agreement. The magistrate ordered Paul and Silas stripped of their clothing. "Give them a beating," he told the lictor who stood behind him. The lictor was more than glad to oblige, and he selected a heavy rod from his case. He brought it high in the air and down across Paul's back.

"Wait!" Paul tried to say, but the blow knocked him to the ground. The lictor struck Silas as well, raining blow after blow on the both of them until they had each received the legal limit of thirty-nine strokes with the rod.

The magistrate had been counting and raised his hand for the lictor to cease. "Now throw them in prison," he said, "and charge the jailer well, lest he should let these men escape."

The supple, whiplike rods had laid their backs open, and their wounds oozed blood as they were dragged out of the agora to the prison. This was an old stone structure, dating back almost to the time of Alexander. The thick walls and heavy iron doors were impregnable. The prison itself consisted of three rooms located beneath a steep hill. The jailer lived in the rooms atop the jail. He watched the prisoners, but after they had been locked into the iron wrist and leg shackles, there was not really much for him to do, for the shackles were also welded to the wall and floor. All he had to do was bring food, which his wife prepared, for the prisoners twice each day.

After Paul and Silas had been locked securely in the irons, the lictor delivered the magistrates' admonition to the wide eyed and trembling man. "And if these men escape, your own life will be the forfeit."

"Yes, sir," the jailer told him. "You can depend on me."

The lictor left and the jailer looked at his two new prisoners. "Are you men murderers?" he asked.

"Murderers?" Silas gasped as the irons bit into his flesh. "Do we look like murderers?"

Paul looked at the heavyset man. "We have done nothing but serve God," he said, "and for that crime we are as you see us now."

The jailer checked the lock on the heavy iron door and turned to walk up the steps to his quarters. "In these times, friend, anything can be a crime. I just keep this place. I have nothing to do with putting men in here. I'll bring you food and water in the morning."

The man left and Paul sat back. Suddenly his resonant voice broke the stillness of the dark prison with a song. Silas shook his head. "Have you lost your senses?" he demanded. "How can you sing hymns at a time like this?"

Paul chuckled. "My friend, this is not the first time I have been in prison. Nor is it the first time I have been beaten. Once I was stoned and left for dead. I have found it to do no good to worry about circumstances, for God has put my life on a path of His own choosing, and nothing can possibly interfere with God's plan until I have finished my course."

Silas groaned. "But here we are, bound hand and food. There is no telling how long we will remain here. Luke and Timothy have no idea where we are or what has happened to us. And you sing songs! You are a remarkable man, Paul. Or a crazy man. As yet, I don't know which one."

Paul burst into song again. Then he laughed. "Silas, my friend, just sit back and watch God work! Relax. He knows we are here. I don't know what He will do, but I know we shall not be here for long. There is too much work remaining to be done. Watch, my friend, and see what God does."

Just then they felt the first tremor as the earthquake struck.

— Chapter Ten —

When Paul and Silas did not return, Lydia became concerned. "What could have happened to them?" she asked.

Luke tried to reassure her. "God watches over them, Lydia. Do not worry. They will be all right."

But when they did not return when it grew late, she called Epaphroditus. "Go into the city and see if you can find out anything about them." So the young man left in the darkness and walked the several miles into Philippi. When he inquired about the strangers named Paul and Silas, he was told of the trouble in the agora and that they had been beaten and cast into prison by the magistrates.

There was nothing he could do for them himself. He began to run through the streets and out the Egnation Way back to the house by the river. He had just passed through the marble arch when he felt the ground move under his feet and he stumbled and fell. An earthquake! He had felt them before.

In less than a minute it was over and the ground was once more solid and steady. He got to his feet and ran again, not stopping until he arrived at the house by the river to see lamps burning as Lydia and the others awaited his return.

Quickly he told them what he had learned. Paul and Silas had been beaten by the lictor and thrown into prison. "Beaten?" questioned Luke. "They are both Roman citizens! No magistrate can have them beaten without a trial!"

Nothing could be done until morning, however, and Lydia tried to get some sleep. But she only tossed and turned in her bed, going over in her mind what she would say to the magistrates in the morning.

When Syntyche returned to the house of the brothers who owned her that evening, she was met by their fury. She would not have gone there except that she knew no other place to go, for she had no family, no relatives, no friends. All she could remember was being a slave and even that recollection was hazy, for the demon had taken possession of her when she had been but a child.

One of the brothers struck her with his fist and knocked her sprawling to the ground. "You are of no use to us now!" he shouted at her. "Don't expect us to feed you. Get out, you worthless scum! And don't come back!"

She wandered the streets, alone, hungry, not knowing where to turn. Then she thought of the man who had cast out the demon and remembered the words of the demon when it had used her voice to call after them. "These men are servants of the Most High God who show you the way to salvation."

She thought of what Paul had told her about Jesus, God's Son, and that He cared about her. But Paul had been thrown into prison. Syntyche went to the stone building where the prisoners were kept. She beat on the iron door with her fists but no one came to see what she wanted. She sat on a rock across from the entrance to wait until morning. Perhaps then she could get in and ask the man, Paul, what she should do now.

Darkness fell and the moon came up, casting eerie shadows on the cold stone walls of the prison. But somehow Syntyche felt a warmth within her and she knew she was doing the right thing by sitting here and waiting.

Orcas, the jailer, had just turned down the lamp and was preparing to join his fat wife in the hand-hewn frame of a bed with the straw and pine-needle mattress. He scratched his stomach and stretched. Also in the single bedroom of his quarters lay his five children on mats on the floor. He smiled as he saw them, all sound asleep, and was content that at least for the time being he was able to feed all of them.

His leg ached. This was usual, for it had been badly mangled by a heavy log in an accident. He sat on the edge of the bed and massaged it. Before the accident he had been a woodcutter in the hills north of Philippi. But the tree that had fallen the wrong way and crushed his leg made it impossible for him to continue in that line of work. With a family to support, he had been very fortunate to find employment as a jailer. It paid little, but the house was furnished and he was at least able to feed his family.

His thoughts drifted for a moment to the men in the cells below his family quarters. The two new ones were strange, he thought. They were certainly not criminals. He heard that the crazy girl who told fortunes had followed them around, telling everyone they were servants of God. He felt sorry for these men, for he was at heart a kindly man, but there was nothing he could do for them except feed them and provide them with water. Orcas was kind to all his charges, even those awaiting trial for serious crimes.

These did not remain long in his prison, for Roman justice was swift and final. It was not the policy of Rome to feed and keep prisoners. The guilty were executed quickly, the innocent—and few were ever found innocent—were set free.

He stretched out in his bed, feeling the warmth of his wife's body next to his. She was a good woman, he thought. He would have liked to provide better for her and for his children, but the accident had settled that. Still, this was a secure life. Secure, that is, unless a prisoner were to escape. He shuddered at the thought, for the magistrates would deal harshly with him if that happened. The penalty for a jailer who allowed a prisoner to escape was death. Few Roman prisoners ever escaped.

Orcas had just dozed off when the room began to sway. He heard the groan of the tortured earth as it shook, the crash of stones falling. He sat up immediately. The prison! Suppose the quake had loosened the walls and the prisoners got out!

He scrambled from the bed, his mind racing, and felt in the darkness for his sword. Quickly he was down the stairs and at the door of the prison. The sight that greeted his eyes caused his heart to skip a beat. The cell doors had sprung and were standing open! They were loose! The prisoners had escaped!

When the quake struck, Paul felt the shackles around his legs open and drop off. At the same time the door of the cell sprang open.

"Paul!" Silas cried. "God has freed us!"

But Paul hesitated. He stood up but made no move toward the open door of the prison. From the other cells he could hear the voices of the other prisoners. They had been frightened by the earthquake, but apparently their cells had not been opened by the force.

"Paul, quickly! Let's get out of here!"

"Wait, Silas. God has spoken to me. Stay where you are. We are not to flee as scared rabbits. God has a better way."

Orcas was peering into the darkened cell where Paul and Silas stood, but in the dim light he could not see them. "They have escaped!" he cried. "Now the magistrates will slay me!" He drew his sword and held the point toward his own chest. "It is better to kill myself than to be tortured to death at the order of the magistrates!"

"Stop!" Paul shouted to him. "Do not kill yourself! We are still here!"

Orcas lowered the sword with trembling hands. "Still there?" he asked. "Why did you not escape when you had the chance?"

Paul felt his way in the darkness until he stood at the jailer's side. "God sent the earthquake," he told Orcas, "but for a different reason. He wished to show the rulers of this city His great power. It was not God's plan for us to run away. His hand is upon us, protecting us. Nothing can happen to us without God's permission."

Orcas dropped to his knees before Paul. "Then tell me about this all-powerful God," he begged. "Tell me what I must do to be as you are, to obtain God's favor."

Paul lifted the crippled man to his feet. "I shall do that gladly. It is not the will of God that any man should perish."

They went up the stairs to the jailer's quarters. The quake had awakened the whole family and the children were huddled in their mother's arms in fear. "Come, wife," Orcas told her, "bring the jar of ointment. Let me tend to the wounds of these men of God. And bring food and drink for them as well."

He tenderly rubbed the soothing ointment into the bleeding gashes, which the rod had made on their backs. And after he had tended to their injuries, he bade them sit at his table as his wife brought meat and wine for them. Then Orcas and his family stood and waited, expectantly, for Paul to tell them of this powerful God who controlled even earthquakes.

Suddenly the door flew open and Syntyche stood in the doorway, frightened and shaking. "I am seeking the man who cast the demon from me," she said. "I must hear more of this Christ Jesus from whom even demons flee."

Early the next morning Lydia, Luke, Timothy and Clement went into Philippi and waited in the agora for the magistrates to appear. All about them in the marketplace people were talking about the earthquake of the night before. Finally the magistrates made their way into their customary station and Lydia walked toward them, her face resolute and angry.

"Who is this woman?" one of them asked another.

"She is a friend of the tribune," he replied.

"Sirs, I must speak to you on an urgent matter," she said to them. The chief magistrate motioned for her to come forward.

"And what is that?" he inquired.

"The men you had beaten and imprisoned yesterday, what is their crime?"

The magistrates looked questioningly at one another. "And what interest could you have, madam, in the affairs of some troublesome Jews?"

"They are not troublesome, and they are guests in my home," Lydia said sharply. "What did they do to deserve this punishment?"

"They incited a disturbance," the chief magistrate replied. "They received a just punishment for this. We tolerate no trouble in this city. We are under just Roman law."

"Then tell me," Lydia demanded, "is it just Roman law to scourge a Roman citizen without a trial?"

The magistrates looked puzzled at this question. Finally the chief magistrate answered, "Of course not. A Roman citizen may not be beaten unless he is convicted at a fair trial."

"Then why have you done so to these two men? Both are Roman citizens by birth!"

"What? Why did they not tell us that?"

Lydia's face contorted in anger. "Did you give them a chance?

Did you give them an opportunity to speak in their own behalf? Or did you just order them beaten?"

A look of horror was on the face of the chief magistrate. He had committed a grave mistake. It was strictly against the law to beat a Roman citizen. Only Caesar could order such a punishment without a formal and fair trial. The magistrates were in very serious trouble, and this woman who accused them was a friend of the tribune who handled such matters.

"We did not know," he protested. "We shall set this error right at once. Sergeant," he said to an orderly. "Go immediately to the prison and set the two men free. Go! Hurry!"

Lydia sighed with satisfaction. She had won her case and Paul and Silas would soon be free. She turned to see the wide grin on Luke's face.

"Well done, Lydia. You are a wise and forceful woman. I am proud of you," Luke told her.

The group waited in the agora for Paul and Silas as the crowd buzzed with excitement over this sudden development. Many of the Greeks were glad to see the haughty magistrates get their comeuppance, and they made crude jokes about it within the hearing of the red-faced judges of Philippi.

The lamps in the jailer's quarters had burned all night. Paul told Orcas and his family how God had sent His Son into the world, and how Jesus had been crucified on the cross at Jerusalem and had risen from the dead. When they had heard and had believed, Paul took water and baptized Orcas and his wife and children and the slave girl, Syntyche, and they all received the Holy Ghost.

Silas taught them songs and they spent the night singing and asking questions of Paul. Although none of them had slept, when the sun came up in the morning, none was tired, for they were all filled with the excitement of salvation.

The sergeant who had been sent by the magistrate came to the door and told Paul and Silas they were free to leave the prison, that there had been a misunderstanding. Silas thanked God and was eager to go back to the house on the river. But Paul told the sergeant, "No, we shall not leave this place until the magistrates who condemned us come in person to apologize and personally set us free."

The sergeant was dumbfounded. "But, sir. They will not do that!"

Paul sat down and crossed his arms. "Then we shall stay in prison. I am certain that soon the Roman authorities will learn that two Roman citizens are being held illegally. And that they have also been beaten."

The man reluctantly returned to the agora and explained in a whisper to the chief magistrate. The judge's face grew crimson with rage. But he was trapped and, as much as he despised going personally to the prison, he had no choice. The magistrates walked slowly through the crowds toward the stone building that housed the prisoners, followed by Lydia, Luke, Timothy, Clement and the people of Philippi.

When they arrived before the stone wall, the chief magistrate called out, "You in there. You are both free to go."

Paul's head appeared at a window. "Then you, sir, must come in and free us of these bonds." Paul and Silas had returned to their cell and had replaced their shackles.

Humiliated, the chief magistrate entered the prison. He loosed the shackles from Paul and Silas. "Now go! Leave this city! You are not welcome here!"

Paul did not budge. He looked at Silas and winked. "My friend, did that sound to you like an apology? To me it sounded more like a threat."

The magistrate took a deep breath and fought to control his temper. "All right," he growled, "I apologize. Now please go!"

Paul smiled. "That was better. Come Silas. We have much work to do. And to you, sir, we shall indeed leave this city, but not because of your demand. Our work here will soon be over and we must journey elsewhere."

That afternoon at Lydia's house was the first meeting of what would become the church at Philippi. Orcas and his family, Syntyche and two of the Greek women who attended the services at the river came. Several others who had heard of the powerful God who had opened the doors of the prison for Paul and Silas were also in attendance.

Luke examined the wounds on the backs of Paul and Silas caused by the lictor's rods and cautioned them to rest until they had completely healed. Paul agreed, but only because he knew he must strengthen this new church before moving on to fresh fields. And each day people came to Lydia's house, and Paul preached to them, expounding on what they had to know to be able to resist the temptations of the world about them and the persecution from those who sought to destroy their new faith.

There were no physicians in Philippi. Only two men who were actually butchers posing as doctors, but who knew nothing at all of the art of medicine. It was one of them who had treated Clement. When it was learned that Luke was a trained physician, people began to come to Lydia's house to consult him, and the wise physician administered doses of both the medicinal and spiritual kinds to them.

Timothy, only a few years older than Epaphroditus, found a close relationship growing with him. The two worked side by side at the vats, for Paul insisted that if they were to enjoy Lydia's hospitality they would also help with the chores. Timothy witnessed to the younger boy concerning what he had seen and heard in his brief travels with Paul, and since he was himself half Greek, he understood the cultural bars to a young Greek's total acceptance of the new faith. He was able to lead Papie through reason and logic as well as Scripture to a deeper commitment to Jesus as Lord of his life.

Silas and Clement found much in common to discuss. Silas had lived for most of his life in the Asiatic area of Greek culture, although of Hebrew lineage. He was physically strong, matching the vigorous Clement in lifting and hauling the heavy loads required to prepare the batches of dyes and cloth. Clement found the dry wit of his new friend refreshing and never tired of hearing the tall tales that Silas had heard at the knee of his father. After telling the story, Silas would look sidewise at Clement, a half smile on his lips, trying to determine whether Clement had swallowed the story or knew it was only fabrication.

Lydia found as many excuses as possible to be with Paul. The man had captivated her, and his deep wisdom and knowledge of the Lord intrigued her. Often, when everyone else had gone to bed, she would find some question to ask Paul about the Scriptures that had prophesied the coming of Christ or the meaning behind the parables Jesus had taught.

Paul never lost patience. At each question his mind would begin to whirl, his enthusiasm building, and he would not only answer her question, but, losing track of time, go on to tell her additional things as he thought of them.

As she sat at his feet listening, Lydia studied the lines of his face, carved by toil and hardship. As he spoke, his expression changed, conforming to the mood of what he was saying. At times, Lydia thought, his face was exactly what an angel should look like, and at other times as she pictured the patriarchs he spoke of. But she also saw in his face a picture of a tired and lonely man who very much needed the comfort of home and family and the nurture of those who loved him.

She asked him once why he had never married and his answer did not surprise her. "I have been too busy," he had said. "And besides, it would not to fair to any woman to be married to a man such as I, destined to travel over two continents, moving from place to place, and never being able to provide adequately for wife and children."

Then he had chuckled, "Besides, what woman would have me? A short, chubby, long-nosed, hairy man with a short temper and no sense at all when it comes to pleasing women."

She had almost answered. She had almost protested that what he had said was not true, that he was a very attractive man, a good and very special person, but she had caught herself just in time. But that night Lydia slept little, thinking about him and wondering where his work would lead him. To an early death, she supposed, for it was dangerous to travel through so many wild areas where robbers and murderers lurked. And to speak the way Paul spoke was to invite enemies, bitter enemies even in the cities. Finally she dozed as the first rays of the sun caught the highest leaves of the trees outside her window. And Lydia dreamed, a confusing, troubling dream in which she saw both Paul's face and Marcellus's. When she awoke she was deeply troubled.

To Lydia, the days went by rapidly. Paul and Silas were now recovered from the beating, and she knew any day now Paul would announce it was time for them to leave.

Daily the believers met in her home. Paul introduced at these assemblies something he called "Communion" or "the Lord's Supper." He took bread and broke it into pieces, giving them all a small piece. He told them this represented the broken body of

Christ, who gave His life for them on the cross. After they had eaten, he filled a cup with wine and passed it around the table for each to sip, explaining that this symbolically represented the blood Christ had shed for the redemption of their sins. All found a deep and mystical feeling in this, a feeling of being very close to the Lord they had never seen who had died for them on the cross.

Each day Orcas and his family came. Travel from the jail to Lydia's house was a painful ordeal for him, for his mangled leg hurt badly after this walk of several miles. After he had dragged it slowly down the hill from the Egnation Way, he would collapse in pain until he had rested it. On this day, however, another pain showed on his face. "Paul," he cried to the apostle, "they have relieved me of my job as jailer!"

What would the man do? He could no longer work at his trade as a woodcutter. His crippled leg would not allow it. The position he had held as keeper of the jail was the only opportunity he had for employment. How would he now support his family?

When Paul heard this news he knelt in prayer, his face buried in his hands. After a long while, he lifted his face and looked at Orcas.

"Come here, my friend. The Holy Spirit has led me to a solution of your problem."

Orcas sat down and Paul knelt before him. "Come, all of you," Paul told the others. "Join hands and pray with me. Pray that God will restore Orcas's leg."

He placed his hands on the man's mangled limb, massaging it as he prayed. The others, their hands joined, prayed as well. And as Paul's hands moved over the leg, Orcas felt a warmth flow into it and a tingling sensation; he felt the bones moving, the flesh rearranging itself. Then Paul leaped to his feet.

"Rise, Orcas! Receive your healing from the Lord!"

He looked up at Paul and grasped the apostle's outstretched hand. He arose slowly and for a moment stood still as no one in the room dared to breathe. Paul's face was bathed in a smile. "Walk, my brother. Your faith in the power of the Living God has restored your leg. Walk!"

Orcas took one hesitant step, then another. He looked down at his legs and a wide grin spread across his face. "The pain is gone," he told them. Then he walked, slowly at first, then more rapidly. "Look! Look at me! I can walk again! And it doesn't hurt anymore!"

He strode around the room, laughing, like a child with a new toy. He bolted out of the open door and ran. He ran up the hill and back again. He leaped and jumped. Then, when his elation had subsided sufficiently, he returned to the house. "Thank you!" he cried. "Thank you, Paul!"

Paul held up his hand. "No, Orcas. Do not thank me. I have no power to do anything. It is God who has healed you. Thank Him!"

And they all did. They knelt together in the room and thanked God for the manifestation of His power and love. Orcas sobbed out his thanks as Paul's hand rested on his shoulder. "Now, Orcas, you are no longer dependent on the job as jailer."

"Yes," Orcas exclaimed, "I can cut wood again. Oh, yes, thanks be to God, I can cut wood again!"

Then the day came when Lydia heard the words she had been dreading. They had finished dinner and had passed the cup when Paul's face grew serious. "In the morning," he announced, "we must go."

Lydia did not look up, fearing that if she looked at Paul she would burst into tears. She fought to control herself as Paul continued.

"I have given much thought to your well-being. And I believe you need more time before you are left entirely alone, without the guidance and encouragement of those older in the Lord than yourselves. I have decided that Silas and I will go on to Thessalonica while Luke and Timothy stay here with you for the time being."

"So soon?" exclaimed Clement. "Can't you stay awhile longer?"

"Yes, please stay. For another week, at least," begged Euodia.

"No," Paul told them, but then his face brightened. "We shall return. You have not seen the last of my homely face, not heard the end of Silas's jokes."

There was laughter at this and everyone felt better. Everyone, that is, except Lydia. But she had regained her composure and stood up. "Then it is time I gave you something," she told Paul. She left the room and returned with a leather purse. She handed this to Paul. "Take this. You will need it on your travels."

Paul looked at the purse, heavy in his hand, and then again at Lydia. "I cannot accept this, Lydia. Your generosity has been too much already."

But she refused to take it back. "Please," she begged, "God has provided well for me. My business is growing so fast we can hardly keep up with it. And for what you, all of you, have given to me, how can mere money repay that debt?"

Paul looked into her dark, deep eyes. Slowly a smile came across his face. He placed the purse in his tunic and nodded. "All right, Lydia. I accept this for our Lord. And He will richly bless you for it."

Early the next morning Paul and Silas were gone, up the hill and down the Egnation Way to cross the river on the road leading to Thessalonica. The goodbyes had been brief. Paul had kissed her on the cheek and thanked her again for her hospitality. Lydia stood and watched them until they were out of sight around the bend in the road, her eyes brimming with tears. Clement came and stood by her in silence, his big hand on her shoulder.

"We shall all miss him, Lydia."

She buried her head in Clement's chest and felt his comforting arms around her. He had become a second father to her, this man she had known all her life. "Oh, Clement, you don't know. No one knows."

His rough hand stroked her hair. "I believe I do, Lydia. I have seen the way you looked at him. I know you very well, my little girl. But I also know it cannot be."

Late that afternoon Syntyche came to the house. "Orcas and his family had to leave the quarters at the prison," she told them. "They have gone north of the city to stay with his brother. He will cut wood again in the forests. I had no place else to go, so I came here."

Lydia put her arm around the girl. "You were right to come here. We have plenty of room. You will stay here with us."

But from the very first day, Euodia made it clear she did not want Syntyche in the house. "She is a tramp," Euodia told Lydia. "You are certainly not going to let her stay here permanently!"

"But she has nowhere else to go," Lydia said. "And she is a sister in the Lord, Euodia. I can't turn her away."

"I still don't like it. That story about being possessed by a demon! I still don't believe it. She's trash and I don't want my son around her."

Lydia's mouth was tight as she replied. "Euodia, we have never before had a disagreement, but this is something I must insist on. Syntyche will stay with us as long as she wishes. Do you understand that? And you are to be nice to her!"

Euodia grunted. "This is your house, Lydia, and what you say goes but I don't trust her. And Epaphroditus's eyes go silly everytime he sees her. Be nice to her? All right, Lydia, if you say so. But mark my words—"

"That's enough," Lydia interrupted. "Don't you have work to do? I refuse to discuss it anymore."

Euodia went to the kitchen, mumbling to herself as she worked. "Be nice to her? That hussy! Just wait. Lydia will be sorry she ever laid eyes on that vixen. That pretend-to-be-so-sweet little tramp."

"What did you say?" Clement asked her.

"Nothing! Nothing at all! And don't stand there looking at me like that! Go find something to do!"

Clement left, shaking his head. Something had certainly upset his wife. She was not acting like herself at all. But being a wise husband, Clement steered the right course, which was to stay away from her for as long as the mood lasted.

Two days later Marcellus rode down the hill to the house. Lydia had not seen him for weeks and had begun to think he would never come again to her house. She was genuinely glad to see the handsome tribune and went out to meet him as he dismounted and tied his horse to a tree.

"Welcome," she smiled at him. "You have been a stranger lately."

"I have been away from the city," he told her. "My work takes me to other places in the province. I have heard of the trouble your guests have caused. Have they left yet?"

"My guests did not cause the trouble," Lydia said, her irritation evident in her voice. "Your magistrates caused it. And yes, Paul and Silas have gone."

Marcellus smiled at her. "Well, now. That's the best news I've heard all day. That Jew, Paul, was a troublemaker. You are well to be rid of him."

Lydia's eyes flashed fire. "Paul is not a troublemaker. And he is not a Jew."

"Not a Jew?"

"I mean he is but he isn't. He was but he is not now— Oh, I can't explain it."

Marcellus scratched his head and grinned at her. "It seems simple enough to me," he told her. "Either the man is or is not a Jew. What's this about him being one before but not now? A man either is or isn't one. It's as simple as that."

"Paul is a Christian," she said. "It's a new religion. It came out of Judaism but is different. Many Jews have become Christians, and many Greeks as well."

Marcellus frowned at her. "Lydia, you amaze me. I thought you were an intelligent woman. But the first charlatan who comes down the road with a new religion causes you to lose all your senses. Don't tell me you've become one of those—what did you call them—Christians."

Lydia took a deep breath. For an instant she was tempted to deny it. But something inside her would not let her deny her new faith. She looked him directly in the eye as she answered in a firm voice, "Yes, Marcellus. I am one of those . . . what-do-you-call-them Christians!"

He saw the jut of her chin and the determination in her eyes. For a moment he was tempted to laugh, but he knew that would just provoke her more. Perhaps she would forget about this nonsense after a while, now that the trouble-making Jew had left. Instead he said, "Well, aren't you going to offer me a drink of cool water, at least? It has been a hot and dusty ride."

At this, she relaxed and smiled at him. "Of course. I have been rude. Come inside. And Marcellus, let's not fight. I don't want to fight with you."

She poured water from an amphora, and they sat in the atrium where the shade and breeze would refresh him. Lydia looked into his handsome face, his bright-blue eyes, the dimple under his chin. He was clean-shaven, as most Romans were, and his skin was browned to an almost golden shade by the sun. One lock of unruly hair blew down over his forehead as it always did, and she felt the urge to brush it back, as a mother would do to her child.

"And how is Doronius?" he asked.

"Fine. Euodia has him down near the river. He loves to play there in the shade of the willows. And your family? Is Tia well? And your sister?"

"All are well. Tia is growing so fast I can hardly believe it. She is quickly becoming a young lady."

Lydia, glad that the conversation had left any disagreeable subject, smiled at him. "Yes, children grow all too quickly. And it is a pity. I wish sometimes I could keep Doronius at this age forever."

Something lying on the table caught Marcellus's eyes and he picked it up. "A medical book? Don't tell me you are reading this? Are you also planning to become a doctor, Lydia?"

"No. That belongs to Luke. He is a very skilled physician. He has studied both at Athens and at Jerusalem. He is a very learned man."

Impressed, Marcellus put down the scroll. "And what of your other remaining guest? Who is he?"

"Timothy is but a few years older than Epaphroditus. He has given his life to our Lord and has become a disciple of Paul's. He is a fine young man."

He looked intently at her. "And this Paul? What do you really know of him?"

Her face brightened as she thought of him, and Marcellus read in her expression an emotion that disturbed him. "Paul is the most wonderful, devoted, unselfish man I have ever met." Then realizing this statement included the tribune in its comparison, she added, "Except for you, of course."

Her smile and laugh did not fool him. "And he has completely converted you to his new religion," Marcellus said, "and has made you a Jew like him."

"I told you before, Paul is no longer a Jew. He is a Christian."

"There is no difference. Both are troublemakers. In fact, the emperor Claudius has expelled all Jews from Italy for causing trouble in Rome."

Lydia shook her head. "But he is different. He is—"

"Did he ask you for money, Lydia?"

She stared hard at him. "Money? No, he didn't ask for money. I just gave—"

"You just gave it to him, eh?"

"Yes. I gave him money when he left. He will need it for the Lord's work."

Marcellus took her hand. "Lydia! Lydia! You are the most generous person I know. But you are also the most gullible. Don't fall for the tale of every charlatan who comes by. Don't—"

She pulled her hand away from him and stood up. "You can't talk that way about him! I won't let you! He is a—a—very wonderful person. You will see for yourself when you meet him."

"Meet him? I thought he was gone."

"But he will be back. I don't know when, but he will be back."

Marcellus walked to the door. "Yes, Lydia. I am most anxious to meet your most wonderful Paul. Please let me know when he returns. I have much I would like to say to him!"

He mounted his horse and galloped up the road. "Marcellus!" Lydia shouted after him. "You don't understand!"

Out of hearing range, he turned and waved at her before he rode out of sight. She watched him disappear and a dull feeling rose in her chest. What had happened to her? Why was she so torn apart? So utterly bewildered? And why did she see Paul's face, even when she was talking with Marcellus?

— Chapter Eleven —

Paul and Silas traveled along the Egnation Way, one of the great Roman roads that linked the provinces with Rome. Paved with stone, it also had hostels spaced a day's journey apart for travelers to rest and find food. They passed through the cities of Amphipolis and Apollonia but did not tarry there, for Paul had decided to press on to Thessalonica. He had a relative there, a man named Jason, and he had instructed Luke and Timothy to follow in two weeks and to meet him at Jason's house in Thessalonica.

As they approached this city, coming down out of the hills, they could see the beautiful blue-green waters of the Thermaic Gulf stretching out until it met the Aegean Sea. Thessalonica was a busy port, carrying on trade with all parts of Greece, and it had grown to a size of about 200,000 people.

As the road wound down through the foothills into the flat country of the coast, they passed through a beautiful archway, decorated with five carved bull's heads commemorating the victory of Octavius and Antony at Philippi. An inscription on the arch, called the Varder Gate, stated that Thessalonica was a free city, made so by Octavian for the city's support during the battle against Brutus and Cassius. This meant that Thessalonica was not bound by the rule of the Macedonian governor, and the people were free to elect their own magistrates and five *politarchs* who led the *demos,* the people's assembly.

Paul was surprised when he inquired about his distant cousin Jason's whereabouts. The first man he asked knew where Jason lived. (But later, when the apostle saw the house, he realized his cousin had become a wealthy man, and it was only natural that the people of the city knew him.)

Paul was amazed at the size of the city and its prosperity. The agora was large and bustled with commerce. Stalls of every kind lined the square—sellers of fresh fruit and melons, vegetables and berries, all kinds of meats and fowl. Shops displayed fine clothing and sandals, many of which were made in distant lands and brought to Thessalonica by the ships that moved constantly in and out of the magnificent harbor.

They followed the directions to Jason's house and found it in one of the finest sections of the city. As with most houses there, it was surrounded by a wall, which enclosed an open courtyard. As they entered the gate, they saw a marble fountain surrounded by exotic flowers. The garden was immaculately kept, with trees and shrubs and many types of blooming plants. This was truly the house of a man of great means, thought Paul. He was glad to see that his relative had done well, but he remarked to Silas as they knocked on the door, "I hope his soul has been as well cared for as his garden."

A servant answered the door. "Inform your master that his cousin Paul of Tarsus has come to visit him."

The servant conducted them into an airy and bright atrium, every bit as magnificent as the outer courtyard. Cool water was provided for them to wash in and fruit was brought on a silver tray. Moments later a man of about Paul's age entered the room.

"I am Jason," he told them. "Which of you is my mother's cousin's son?"

Paul stepped forward and the man embraced him warmly. "I

have heard about you," he told Paul. "You are the studious one. Were you not sent to Jerusalem to study with Gamaliel?"

Paul nodded and the man stepped back. "Let me look at you," he said. "Yes, you are certainly my cousin. But the years have treated you kindly. We are about the same age, but I have grown fat and bald. You still look strong and fit. And with a full head of hair."

"This," Paul said, "is my companion and fellow worker in the Lord, Silas."

"Ah," Jason smiled. "Then you are both rabbis. Welcome to my humble home, Reb Silas."

"No," Paul corrected him. "We are not rabbis. And this is not a humble home, Jason. It is magnificent."

Jason smiled, pleased with the compliment. "Yes, I have prospered in business. This is a good city and I have done well, as have many of our people here. There is a large Hebrew population in Thessalonica, and it has grown even larger since many Jews were deported from Italy on order of the emperor."

"I am pleased that things go well for you, Jason."

Jason looked at Paul with a puzzled look. "You said you were not rabbis, but you did say you were workers for our Lord. In what manner do you serve the Lord if you are not rabbis? Are you teachers? Have you been sent to teach in our Hebrew school here?"

Paul and Silas exchanged glances. "In a way we are teachers," Paul said, "but it will take quite a while to explain to you what it is that we teach."

"Then let us hear what it is over dinner," Jason beamed. "But now come, let me show you to your rooms. You must be tired after your journey. Refresh yourselves, then we shall talk about this matter which brings you to Thessalonica."

The new Christians had met as usual that evening at Lydia's house. Now that the overpowering presence of Paul was gone, Timothy had come into his own and had taken charge of the meetings. Each day brought him more confidence, and Lydia saw the change taking place in the young evangelist. His voice became stronger, his manner more assured, and his faith beamed through his boyish smile as he told of Jesus and His ministry on earth.

It had been decided that Clement would become the leader of the group at Philippi when it was time for Timothy to move on and join Paul again. Skillfully, Timothy brought Clement more and more into the leadership of the assembly as they gathered to pray and study.

On this particular evening Orcas had brought both his brother and uncle. The former jailer had become a powerful and effective witness since his leg had been healed. Those who had known him could readily see that something outside the realm of the ordinary had happened. And Orcas had also changed, with a new and dynamic personality and the ability to speak forcefully about his new faith in Jesus Christ.

During the meeting Orcas's brother and uncle heard and believed, and Timothy took them to the bank of the river and baptized them. "Next time I'll bring my wife and children," Orcas's uncle told Timothy. "I want my whole family to receive this."

Finally all departed for home and Lydia's house was quiet. She went to bed and lay awake, thinking of Paul, wondering what he was doing, whether his forceful preaching had got him in trouble in Thessalonica the way it had in Philippi. She prayed, although the custom of nightly prayer was still strange to her, for the Greek gods had been remote and unhearing.

"Father," she asked, "protect him and bring him back safely to me—us."

She had just drifted off to sleep when the banging on the door jolted her back into awareness. For an instant she was not certain whether she had heard it or had been dreaming. Then she heard Clement's voice and she slipped out of bed to see what the matter was.

As she pulled her robe about her, she ran down the stairs. "Clement, what is it?" she called.

"It's Marcellus's driver. He wants Luke to come with him right away. Marcellus's daughter is very ill. The driver says she may be dying."

Now the entire house was aroused. Luke came through the door. "What is it, Lydia?" he asked.

"It's Marcellus's carriage driver. He has come for you. He says Marcellus's daughter, Tia, is very sick."

Luke darted back inside. "I'll get my things," he said over his shoulder. In a moment he was back, carrying the bag in which his medicines were stored. "All right, driver. Let's go," he said.

Lydia hesitated for only a second. "Wait," she shouted after them. "I'm coming with you."

At Jason's house in Thessalonica the lamps were still burning. During an excellent dinner Paul had begun to tell his cousin about Jesus and their conversation continued long after the servants had cleared the table. Jason listened without much comment and Paul wondered whether his words were having any effect.

Paul studied his cousin's face for any sign of either belief or unbelief. When he related what had happened on the Damascus road, where he encountered the brilliant light and spoke with the risen Jesus, he saw Jason's eyebrows raise, but otherwise nothing else was indicated by his expression. Finally Paul was finished. He had nothing more to tell Jason and he raised his goblet and drained the last of his wine.

"And that, my dear cousin, is the entire story. There is nothing more I can tell you."

It was then that Jason's face became animated. "And if what you say is true, Paul, then our long-awaited Messiah has already come."

"That is true."

Jason sat very still and Paul could see he was pondering what he had been told. He rubbed his chin, then nodded his head. "It is no wonder our dear fathers in Jerusalem didn't recognize Him. Those pompous fools have been looking for the wrong messiah, one coming out of the priestly class, one of their own kind."

Paul's eyes lit up. "Exactly! But God's ideas were entirely different, and if they had really known the Scriptures they would have seen this. God's Son was the most humble of men, full of love and compassion. Not the false piety of the priests. But Jason, you say *if* what I say is true. Don't you believe what I have told you to be true?"

Jason sat back and looked into Paul's eyes. He lowered his head and examined the wine in his goblet, swirling it around in the glass. Then he again lifted his head and looked at Paul. "Yes, cousin. I do believe you, for the following reasons: First, there is absolutely no reason for you to lie to me. Before you had this encounter on the road to Damascus, you had a most promising career. You could have remained in Jerusalem, a Pharisee, with wealth, position, reputation, respect—everything a man could desire could have been yours.

"But you gave that up, Paul. And you instead have chosen to live from hand to mouth, traveling about with no home, no wife and family, no worldly security, and you will probably suffer a miserable death at the hands of either robbers or their kinsmen, the priests. You must be totally convinced that this man, Jesus, was the Son of God to give up all you had for what you are now.

Yes, Paul, I do believe you, for no man could possibly invent such an incredible story as you have told me. It has to be the truth."

The carriage bounced along the road for what to Lydia seemed an interminable length of time. Luke said nothing during the trip, but Lydia sensed that the physician was in prayer. Finally the driver swerved into the gate of Marcellus's house and reined the horses. Immediately someone opened the carriage door and Lydia heard Marcellus's voice. "Hurry, doctor! She is very ill!"

Lydia dismounted from the carriage, and for an instant her eyes met Marcellus's. His face showed gratitude that she had come. The tribune took Luke's arm and hurried him into the house. "This way," he said. "She is in here."

Lydia followed, and as she entered the house she saw Lucretia standing by the door of Tia's room. The Roman woman's face flashed for an instant and Lydia read the meaning. What are you doing here? Lucretia's expression had said. You are not welcome here.

Luke entered the girl's room, and Lydia caught a brief glimpse of her lying white and still upon her bed. Lydia's mother's heart went out to her. She was indeed ill, very ill. Lydia knew the color of a child who was extremely sick, dangerously so.

She did not enter the child's room but stayed by the door. Lucretia passed her and shut the door behind her. Inside, Luke swiftly examined the child, his trained eyes taking notice of signs not noticeable to the untrained observer. Although his face indicated no emotion, he did not like what he saw.

Tia had a high fever. On her chest were splotches of red. He asked a few questions, and Lucretia told him that Tia had complained of a headache the day before the onset of the fever. She had developed chills and the headache had become severe.

Each day for three days she had grown progressively worse, her fever increasing steadily.

"Bring basins of cool water," Luke told them. "We must reduce the child's fever." He mixed a potion and coaxed her to drink it. In a few moments she fell asleep, a result of the potion, and he felt her pulse and nodded in satisfaction. When the water was brought into the room, they bathed her carefully in its coolness. Then he faced Marcellus and Lucretia. "Come outside," he said. They left the sleeping child and came into the room with Lydia.

Luke's face betrayed no emotion as he spoke, but his eyes radiated warmth and compassion and love. "I won't try to deceive you," he told them. "It is very serious. I have seen this disease many times. It is especially dangerous for a child."

"But she will recover, won't she?" demanded Lucretia.

"That, madam, I cannot say for certain. Many children do not survive. In fact, most of them do not. This illness takes many lives each year. Our medicines help, but they are not cures. The disease must run its course. If the child is strong enough, she may survive. But I cannot assure it."

"But is there nothing which can be done, doctor? Anything?"

Luke's face softened. "We can only wait and watch," he said.

Lucretia went into Tia's room and sat beside her bed. A servant brought in fruit and wine. Luke accepted a small glass of wine. Lydia wanted nothing. They sat and waited, counting the minutes as hours until the first glow of morning came through the windows. Luke periodically checked her during the long night. There was no change in her condition. Despite frequent bathings in cool water, the child's fever still raged undiminished.

Marcellus sat with his head in his hands, and Lydia wanted to go to him, to comfort him. But with Lucretia there, she dared not. All she could do was to sit and pray for the small child who lay near death in the next room, a child so dear to a man she was very fond if—perhaps, she admitted, that she even loved.

Suddenly Lucretia was in the doorway, her face ashen. "Doctor," she cried, "come quickly! I think she is gone!"

In Thessalonica Jason's house was just stirring. Paul had arisen early, bright and full of energy. Silas rose reluctantly, his eyes red, yawning from too little sleep. Paul led the prayers and they went in to breakfast. Jason's servants had prepared the table, and they savored the fresh fruit, tangy and sweet, and the cakes hot from the oven.

Jason joined them a few moments later. "Good morning," he said, "I hope you slept well."

Silas yawned again. "Yes," he said, "for what there was of it."

"I wish to see the synagogue here," Paul told Jason. "Will you take me there?"

"Certainly. But I can't guarantee what sort of reception you will get. Your message is sure to provoke much controversy."

"I understand that only too well," Paul replied, "but I must deliver it. If they will not hear . . . ." He shrugged his shoulders.

"And what happens if they don't?" asked Jason. "Then what will you do?"

"God will show me what to do. I shall stand in the marketplace and speak. Or along the roads. Some will hear and believe, for God's words do not return void. There are always some who will believe."

Luke rushed to the child's bedside. He placed his hand on her neck, his body tense and his eyes searching for any movement, any sign of breathing. He glanced at Lydia, who had followed him into the room, and his eyes revealed the worst. "She is dead," Luke said in a low voice.

Lydia's mind suddenly went back to Paul and the healing of Orcas's leg. She felt the power of the Holy Spirit guiding her, and she knelt beside the bed, taking one tiny hand in her own. With her other hand resting on the child's forehead, she began to pray.

"Father, in the name of your Son, Jesus, we ask you to restore this child."

Luke's hand was on Lydia's shoulder as he joined her in prayer. Marcellus and Lucretia stood in the doorway, watching, their eyes full of grief at the sight of Tia lying still and breathless on the bed.

"Raise her up, Father. Restore her to life and we will give you all the honor and glory and praise. In the name of Jesus of Nazareth, heal her."

There was silence in the room. For a long moment no one dared to even breathe. Then, suddenly, there was a slight, hardly perceptible movement. Slowly Tia's arm moved and she sighed a low sigh as her eyelids fluttered.

She gazed up at her father, Marcellus, and said, "I had the most beautiful dream just now. I was walking in a lovely meadow with a man clothed in white. For an instant He held me in His arms, and I felt such love from Him. Then He put me down and told me to walk back in the direction I had come. Then I woke up. But I can still feel the warmth of His arms about me and His love."

Marcellus dropped to his knees beside her bed and held his daughter in his arms. "Oh, Tia, my darling," he said, his eyes flowing with tears. "It's all right now. Everything is all right now."

But Lydia saw the look on Lucretia's face, and she knew that everything was not all right. Luke examined the child. The rash had completely gone and her temperature was normal. The child had awakened famished, for she had not eaten in days. Food was brought and she devoured it eagerly.

She looked up at Lydia. "You are the nice lady who came to dinner," she said in recognition. "When are you coming back again?"

Lydia smiled at her. "I don't know, dear. Perhaps when you are feeling better."

Marcellus took Lydia's hand. "I don't know what you did or what happened her," he said. "but I thank you for my daughter's life."

"We did nothing," Lydia told him. "God restored Tia to life."

"God? Which God? I wish to thank Him."

Lydia's face was serious. "There is but one God, Marcellus. He is the God of all people, Roman, Greek, Jew, everyone."

"Then I thank Him," Marcellus said, "whoever He is."

"Someday you will understand what has happened," Lydia told him, "but for now, enjoy your daughter. And would you ask your coachman to take us home? I have my own family to care for. My son will soon be awake and wondering where I am."

In the coach riding back to the house, Lydia laid her head back. "Luke, is it always like this?"

He looked at her quizzically. "Like what?"

"I mean this morning. I felt so close to God. It was wonderful. We called on Him and He answered. He restored a dead child to life. Is being a Christian always like this? To feel so warm and close to God?"

The physician rubbed his chin and gazed at her before he answered. "I wish I could say that it was, Lydia, but it is not. This morning was a rare thing, a mountaintop where you were able to reach out and almost touch God.

"But there are other days, Lydia. Dark days. You will find that being a Christian also means hardship, persecution. Like Paul, those of this world will hate you. No, not hate you exactly, but hate the Jesus who abides within you." Luke slowly shook his head. "No, Lydia. It is not always like this. I wish it were."

Lydia nodded. "But times like this morning make it all worthwhile, don't they? I mean, even a little while on the top of the mountain makes it possible to bear the other days, far down in the valley of hardship and persecution. Even death."

He patted her hand gently. "You have matured rapidly, Lydia, for a new Christian. It is good that you see things in perspective. But the end of what Paul calls 'the race' is the reward. We shall be with Jesus in heaven, and all that we must endure here in this world will be worthwhile then. The reward is worth all that Satan and this world can throw at us."

They arrived home and the driver reined the horses in front of the house. Doronius ran out to meet his mother and Lydia picked him up and hugged him. They went into the house and Lydia looked at them, all staring at her. "All right," she said, "let's get to work. There is little time."

Luke laughed at her. "No, Lydia. We Christians have all the time there is. You see, we have eternity."

On the next Sabbath in Thessalonica, Paul and Silas were taken to the synagogue by Jason. On the previous day Paul had met several of the leaders of the local Jewish congregation. They had been very impressed by his credentials, especially since he had studied under Gamaliel in Jerusalem. Paul had not thought it wise to discuss his real reason for being in the city, for had they known he was a Christian they might not have let him speak before the assembly.

At sundown they entered the building, a magnificent structure of marble, and took their seats in the congregation. As he looked around, Paul was surprised to see so many converted Greeks.

There were also many women, sitting in their separate section, and many of these were Greek proselytes.

The service began with the familiar chants, prayers and songs. No matter where a Jew might travel, the services at the local synagogue were so much alike throughout the world that he would feel at home anywhere.

After the Scriptures were read, the leader of the synagogue invited any visitors present to speak. Most visitors would give a brief and almost routine exhortation. As a visitor who had studied at Jerusalem, the leader expected Paul to exort the congregation to hold fast to their faith, that the Jerusalem Fathers and the Jews of the diaspora were one in the law no matter how far they happened to be from the temple in their homeland. This is what the visitors had said in the past, and the leader anticipated nothing different from these men.

"Men and brethren," Paul began, "I come to bring you joyful news, news of the fulfillment of the ancient and beloved Scriptures." He continued by quoting the Scriptures that had foretold of the Messiah, and his skillful oratory kept them spellbound, trying to determine just what this joyful news might be.

"And so I bring to you news that Messiah has come, Jesus of Nazareth, who was crucified and arose from the dead for the redemption of your souls from sin. God, His Father, raised Him up on the third day—"

At this there was a loud murmur from the congregation. "He was killed?"

"How could Messiah be killed?"

"You say he was raised from the dead?"

The commotion was such that Paul had to wait for it to subside before he could continue. The leader of the synagogue, not expecting any such thing from a student of Gamaliel, was horrified. What would the congregation think of him for allowing such a man to speak? Quickly he stepped in and closed the service. "We shall hear from our brother at another time," he announced over the din.

Jason hurriedly pulled Paul from the front of the building and ushered him out a back door. "That's enough for today," he said. "We had better get out of here fast."

Several people had seen Paul leave and came running after him.

"Stop!" one of them called after him.

"Quickly," Jason shouted, "let's go home!"

But Paul shook off his cousin's arm and faced the people who were pursuing them. "Wait a moment, Jason. Let us see what it is they want."

"Wait, sirs! We would like to hear more of what you say. Tell us more of this Jesus whom you say is the Christ."

Jason relaxed and they waited for the people to catch up with them, two men and three women. Paul greeted them warmly and Jason could see on their faces, not any threat, but genuine interest. "Come along with us," Paul invited. "My cousin's house is close by. There I shall answer all of your questions."

At Jason's house they sat around Paul and Silas as they heard more of Jesus, how He was crucified and buried only to be raised upon the third day as He said He would be.

"I believe you, sir," one of the women said. "What must I do to partake of the eternal life which Jesus has promised?"

"And I, too, believe," a man said. "Tell us what we must do to be saved."

All five were baptized later in the day, along with Jason and the members of Jason's household. The church in Thessalonica had begun. Paul, not knowing how much or how little time he would have there, made the new converts promise to return the next evening for more teaching.

That evening the Christians of Philippi met as usual at Lydia's house. Shortly after they had arrived and in the middle of a hymn, Marcellus reined up his horse in front of the house and came in.

The small congregation was startled at the appearance of a Roman tribune. But when Lydia greeted him warmly, their fears were banished, although they remained ill at ease in the presence of such a high official.

Timothy and Clement were leading the services. Luke did not take an active part, reserving his words for when his encyclopedic mind was called upon to correct a point of history or to interpret a point of Scripture.

"Sit here with me," Lydia invited Marcellus as she pulled the tribune into the group and introduced him to those present. He had not expected to find so many people at Lydia's house, and certainly not a church service. He had come to talk with her, since he had not had the opportunity to do so since Tia's sudden and miraculous recovery from her illness.

As Timothy began to preach, Lydia kept a nervous eye on Marcellus. She wanted him to hear about Jesus, but she worried that too strong an approach might turn him completely away and he would reject everything. But Timothy's gentle manner and soft-spoken approach, unlike Paul's fiery rhetoric, could offend no one. She saw the tribune's eyebrows raise at different points in Timothy's message, indicating that he was at least listening.

At last the meeting was over and the congregation departed, saying a timid goodbye to the Roman officer as they left. Luke, always conscious of the right thing to do, yawned and pulled Timothy by the arm.

"Come," he told him, "it's time for us to go to bed."

"Bed," Timothy started to say, "but it's still early—"

A sudden yank on his arm and Timothy got the message. "Good night," he said and followed the physician to bed.

Lydia and Marcellus were alone in the room. But because the house was occupied by so many people, she knew that their conversation would be overheard. "Come," she said to him, "let's take a walk by the river."

They walked down the path to the bank of the Gangites. The night breeze wafted the sweet scent of myrtle through the air, and the sound of frogs and crickets could be heard. When they reached the bank of the river, Marcellus took both her hands in his and faced her in the moonlight.

"There are things I must say to you, Lydia. Please don't interrupt me until I have said them."

She looked at his handsome face in the moonlight, a serious expression on it. "Yes, tribune? Have I broken the Roman law?" she joked.

"Please don't jest, Lydia. What I have to say is serious. For both of us."

She nodded and wondered what she would say when he had finished, for in her heart she knew what he would ask her. "As you well know," he began. "I have been a widower for several years. But for my sister, I do not know what I would have done in raising my daughter. It is not easy to bring up a child alone." He stared off into the distance for a moment before continuing.

"But I have been very lonely. I did not think it possible to find anyone who could take my wife's place, someone I could feel about as I felt about her. But then I met you, Lydia, and—"

"Please, Marcellus, don't—"

He held her hands tightly. "Please let me finish. I have been thinking about the future, yours and mine. I am a man of substantial means. I could provide well for you and your son.

There would no longer be any necessity for you to work. My house is large. Your servants, Clement and his wife and their son, would have a place there, also."

He looked down at her. "Well, Lydia. Will you?"

"Are you asking me to marry you, Marcellus?"

"Of course I am! What do you think all this has been about?"

She pulled her hands away from him and turned, looking down the dark river. The moon's silvery image shimmered on the water, and in the distance a dove called its lonely sound.

"I don't know what to say, Marcellus. There is so much to consider. We come from backgrounds which are so different...."

"Don't say no, Lydia. If you can't answer right now, then at least think about it. But don't say no tonight."

She turned to him and his arms were around her, pulling her close. "I won't say no tonight, Marcellus. Give me some time to think about it."

His lips were on hers and she felt the closeness of his body. She was at first too startled to respond, but in an instant the warmth rose in her, and she put her arms about his neck and kissed him back, willingly and fervently.

Suddenly she freed herself and stepped back. "No, Marcellus. I don't trust myself. I do care for you. Very much. You have honored me with what you have asked, but I must consider many things before I can answer."

"All right, Lydia. But don't keep me waiting too long."

She put her arm in his and they walked back toward the house. "No, I won't keep you waiting long. In a few days I'll give you my answer."

He was gone in the night and Lydia waited until she could no longer hear the hoofbeats of his horse. Then she went into the house and undressed for bed. She lay down and closed her eyes.

"But why," she asked herself, "when Marcellus kissed me, was it Paul's face I saw?"

— Chapter Twelve —

Each night Paul and Silas held meetings at Jason's house. During the day they preached in the marketplace and on street corners, and there were always several who were interested in hearing more. These were invited to Jason's house in the evenings, and the attendance grew daily. Those who were converted brought their relatives and friends. By the end of the first week Paul counted over twenty newly baptized Christians of what was to become the church of the Thessalonians.

On the Jewish Sabbath Paul again went to the synagogue and was invited to speak once more to the congregation. This time there was no open hostility, but the leaders had prepared a defense against what Paul preached about Jesus being the Son of God and the Messiah. After Paul had finished speaking, one of the leaders arose and refuted Paul's claims by twisting the Scriptures and interpreting them to suit his argument.

Paul could have cut the man to shreds in front of the congregation, but he chose to remain quiet, stating instead that he would answer the statements made by the leader the next week. But there again were those in the congregation who wished to learn more, and these were invited to come to Jason's house, where Paul showed them in the Scriptures all the prophecy concerning the coming of Jesus.

Now the Jewish leaders were becoming concerned about Paul. This man had a greater knowledge of the Scriptures than they had, and in addition could use the skill of a Greek orator in presenting his views to the audience. He was becoming a threat to their leadership, and something, they agreed, must be done about the situation.

They would be ready for this man on the next Sabbath. The leaders recruited a mob of ruffians who would do anything for money. Next week Paul would get a much different reception after his oration. The mob of ruffians would see to that.

Lydia knew the time was growing near when Timothy and Luke would be leaving Philippi. More and more Clement had been taking over the meetings, so that now he was quite at ease speaking to the growing number of men and women who attended.

She had not yet given Marcellus an answer to his proposal of marriage and could not make up her mind. One night she asked Luke to walk to the river with her. She had worked hard all day, and the cool night air was refreshing. At the edge of the river she turned to Luke and asked, "May I ask your counsel on a matter?"

The wise physician smiled. "Why, certainly, Lydia. And what is this matter?"

"Would it be correct for a Christian to marry a non-Christian? I know what Paul has said concerning marriage, that it would be better not to marry at all, but he gave his permission for those who so desire."

Luke was silent for a few moments, collecting his thoughts. "I have heard Paul also speak about a man and a woman being unequally yoked," he replied. "It would be better for a Christian woman to marry a believer."

Lydia was still, watching the moon come up over a grove of trees on the far side of the Gangites. "I know that would be much better," she said, "but could not the Christian woman influence the man after they were married?"

"That is possible, I suppose. But marriage in itself requires a great commitment, especially for a Christian. If one of the partners does not believe in God, there is no basis for a proper commitment."

The stillness of the night was broken by the sound of a nighthawk far down the river. Lydia shook her head in frustration. "Marcellus has asked me to marry him," she told Luke. "I have promised to give my answer soon."

"Lydia, a physician is trained to observe, to recognize the symptoms of many diseases, to take note of how a person walks and talks, the brightness of the eyes. I have observed you, Lydia. Love is very much like a disease and it manifests itself in typical symptoms."

Lydia faced him. "And have you observed these symptoms in me, doctor?"

Luke took a deep breath and considered his words carefully. "Yes, Lydia, I have seen these symptoms in you. But tell me, is it truly Marcellus you have fallen in love with?"

She sighed and sat down on the grassy bank, closing her eyes and feeling the emotions stirring within her and the quickened pace of her heart. "You are a very observant physician, Luke. I suppose you have already diagnosed my malady."

"I believe I have."

"And what is the prognosis, doctor?"

He lowered his tall frame and sat beside her on the grass, and his hand rubbed his chin. "In this case, not very good."

Again she sighed. He knew, she thought. He has known all along. Had it been that obvious, her attraction to Paul? She wondered if Paul suspected.

"Then what am I do do?"

"Marrying a man you do not truly love is not a cure, Lydia. But we doctors do not have cures for all illnesses. I can't prescribe a potion to help you in this case."

They sat in silence for many moments. Then Lydia asked, "Do you think Paul knows? Has he said anything to you?"

"No. I believe Paul is oblivious to things such as this. His mission takes paramount place in his life, and in his thoughts."

Lydia sighed deeply. "I am a fool," she said.

He put his hand on her shoulder and patted her gently. "No, Lydia, to love is not being a fool. Not to love, that is being a fool."

"Paul will never marry, will he?"

"Never is a long time, Lydia. I cannot answer that one way or the other."

"But you think not."

"I do not believe Paul will ever stay in one place long enough to even consider it. He is a very special man, Lydia. Our Lord has placed a great responsibility on his shoulders. And Paul will never forget that responsibility, not for a single moment."

Suddenly the tears came and she could not help herself. She buried her head in his chest and cried out the things she had held back for so long, things she could have told no one before. "Oh, Luke. I am so lonely! I don't want to go through life alone. My marriage was so short. It was far from good, but at least it was something. I don't want to be alone for the rest of my life."

As she cried on his shoulder, he gently stroked her hair, comforting her as he would a crying child. "It is good to cry, Lydia. It is good to get out all the things you have kept in for so long. Go ahead and cry. Cry them all out and you will feel better. That I can promise you as a physician."

For a long time they sat there, Lydia sobbing out her innermost thoughts to the kind and understanding physician. Then, when she had completely emptied herself, they prayed together for the

Lord to comfort her and guide her in living according to His will for her life.

Finally they went back to the house and Lydia went to bed. For the first night in a long time she slept well, for now she knew what she would have to do and what she would answer Marcellus.

A friend had come to Jason and warned him of what the synagogue leaders were planning to do on the next Sabbath. Jason immediately told Paul of the mob that was going to provoke a riot against him if he spoke again.

Paul considered this threat, then replied, "My most important task is to speak once more at the synagogue, or those who have believed me will think me a coward and forsake the truth. But I am concerned for your safety, Jason. Silas and I will leave your house tonight."

That evening, under the cover of darkness and against the protests of his cousin, Paul and Silas left Jason's house and found rooms in another part of the city in a believer's home. But on the Sabbath he went again to the synagogue and addressed the congregation.

Paul refuted the words of the leader who had twisted the Scriptures, and those who heard him were astonished at his knowledge and the strength of his argument. He saw many nod their heads in agreement as he proclaimed Jesus to be the Son of God, the long-awaited Messiah and their Savior. But on the faces of the leaders was scorn and anger. As soon as he had finished speaking, he and Silas quickly left by the rear door and hastened to the home where they were staying.

A short time later the mob the leaders had paid swarmed around Jason's house, demanding that Paul and Silas be turned over to them. When Jason called from a window that they were not there, the angry crowd threw rocks at the house and at the windows. They brought a log and used this as a battering ram to break down the barred gate of the courtyard. The mob swarmed through the gate and into the house, smashing everything in their path.

Although they searched the house from top to bottom, they could not find the men they sought. Furious, they seized Jason and forced him to go with them to the agora, where by prior arrangement waited several of the city's magistrates.

"This man has been harboring the strangers who have the reputation of turning the world upside down," they charged. "Disturbing every city they have entered, they teach against Roman law, saying there is another king beside Caesar, a man called Jesus. They are guilty of inciting revolt."

This was a serious charge and the magistrates could not dismiss it lightly. The charge was recorded, but since no one could point out a single incident of riot in the city of Thessalonica as a result of Paul's teaching, all the magistrates could do was to impose a bond on Jason and several other men who had been brought to court. These men had to pledge their money and property, to be forfeited if any disturbance occurred.

When the men were released, they went back to Jason's house to discuss the situation. Then Jason went to see Paul where he and Silas had found refuge.

"My dear cousin," said Jason. "We have had to put up all that we possess as bond against trouble in this city. I know you do not preach uprising, sedition or revolt, but even so, the leaders of the synagogue will make this happen and our property will be taken from us. For our sakes, we urge you to leave this city."

Paul agreed immediately. He was certainly not willing to risk harm to others by his presence, and this could also destroy all that he had so far accomplished in Thessalonica. "There will be two men coming from Philippi," he told Jason. "I have told them to seek me at your house. When they arrive, tell them to continue on to Berea, where we shall now go. They are to meet us at the synagogue there."

He embraced Jason. "Thank you, dear cousin, for all you have done for us and for our Lord. Continue on in this work. I shall write to you when I can and I shall send another to counsel you in the matters of our Lord Jesus. May the peace of the Lord be with you all."

That night, disguised as women, Paul and Silas left Thessalonica and began the two-day journey to Berea.

The time had come for Timothy and Luke to leave Philippi and join Paul and Silas. Clement had now been firmly established as the leader of the young church that met at Lydia's house, and Timothy was confident the congregation would not only survive but grow.

Marcellus had come to say farewell to Luke. The tribune had been astonished when the physician had refused his offer of payment for the treatment of his daughter's illness, telling him that he had really done nothing. God, not his skills as a doctor, had cured his daughter.

Clement, Euodia, Epaphroditus, Syntyche and the others gathered to see the two men off. Marcellus shook Luke's hand warmly. "Despite what you say, doctor, I still want to thank you for coming to my daughter's aid. If you say God healed her, then I thank you both for it."

Lydia embraced Timothy. "We will all miss you," she said. Then she hugged the tall physician. "And will you give Paul my—"

Luke completed her sentence. "Your best wishes," he said as he looked deeply into her eyes, "and your Christian love."

She smiled up at him. "Yes," she said, "give him that."

The men picked up their traveling packs and went up the road as the group watched. They stood at the top of the hill and waved. Then they were gone, following the Egnation Way along the river toward Thessalonica.

Marcellus looked down at Lydia and saw the tears in her eyes, her breasts heaving as though she were about to burst into tears. The small group of Christians melted away. Orcas and his family went home, Clement and Papie went back to the dyeing vats, and Euodia took Doronius into the house for his breakfast. Only Lydia and Marcellus remained standing outside.

He put his hand on her shoulder and pulled her close to him. "I have waited patiently for your answer, Lydia," he told her.

She looked into his handsome face, feeling mixed emotions course through her body. She swallowed hard and nodded. "I have thought a great deal about it, Marcellus. And I have prayed about it."

"And have you come to a conclusion?"

She took his hands in hers and looked up into his eyes. "Yes, I have, Marcellus. I will marry you—if you become a Christian."

Paul was delighted with the attitude of the Jews in Berea. In the synagogue they had listened without opposition, asking many questions concerning where in the Scriptures the coming of Jesus had been foretold. Then they had removed their scrolls from the box behind the blue curtain of the altar and saw for themselves that what Paul said was true.

These Jews of Berea were scholars, reserving their judgment until they had examined the facts for themselves. And when they saw everything Paul had claimed was indeed in the Scriptures, they willingly believed that Jesus was the long-awaited Messiah.

"At last," Paul beamed to Silas, "we have found fertile ground for our work." But what Paul did not know was that one of the men of the Berean synagogue who had earnestly believed in Jesus was at that moment traveling to Thessalonica. There he would tell those of the Thessalonian synagogue about the man Paul and his wonderful message of the Messiah. That well-meaning man would trigger the leaders to send a group of angry men to Berea to oppose Paul and try to stop the word from being preached in Berea.

Paul's ministry had attracted some of the most prominent Gentiles of Berea to hear him. He now spoke not only in the synagogue but in the marketplace. In the evenings he taught those who had heard his message during the day and had believed and had wanted to learn more of Jesus.

A place was found near the city where a stream had created a small pond deep enough to immerse those who desired to be baptized into the new faith. The two missionaries were well pleased with the success of their work in such a short time in Berea, not aware it would be cut short by the Jews of Thessalonica who were even now assembling men and preparing to come to Berea.

Marcellus looked incredulously at Lydia. "You will marry me only if I become a Christian?" he asked. His face registered both surprise and anger. "What difference does it make what my religion is? If you love me, you will marry me, Christian or not!"

She tried to calm his outburst. "You don't understand," she told him. "I cannot marry a man who worships . . . idols!"

"Idols? You call our gods mere idols? All my life I have been brought up with reverence to the gods of Rome. Now you ask me suddenly to abandon what I have been taught all my life and worship this . . . this invisible God of the Hebrews? Lydia, I can't do such a thing!"

"But you saw the power of our God. Your daughter lives! Isn't that proof enough of our God?"

He turned away from her. "I don't know what to think. Lucretia says it was a sorcerer's trick. She thinks Luke gave Tia a drug which caused her to appear dead for a brief period of time. Then, when you prayed to this God of yours, it appeared a miracle had taken place."

Lydia's face turned white. "Marcellus! How could you believe such a thing? It was no trick! Do you really believe I would do such a thing?"

He took a deep breath. "I no longer know what to believe. I gave you time to answer me, Lydia. Now you must do the same. I must think about your condition. When I have decided, I shall let you know."

She watched him mount his horse and ride off. Her eyes were again full of tears and she wanted to cry. Only the voice of Euodia calling from the house prevented it.

"Come quickly, Lydia! Something is wrong with Doronius!"

She rushed into the house to find Euodia sitting on the floor cradling Doronius in her arms. His body lay limp and still in her arms, his breath coming in gasps.

"My baby! What happened to him?"

"I don't know," sobbed Euodia. "One moment he was fine, eating his breakfast and the next he collapsed. Lydia, I am afraid he is very ill!"

Lydia took him from Euodia. "Run and get Clement and Papie. Tell one of them to go after Luke and bring him back. He can't be too far down the road. Quickly!"

As soon as he learned what had happened, Epaphroditus sprinted up the hill and down the Egnation Way toward the bridge that carried it across the river toward Thessalonica. At first he ran swiftly, but when his breath began to become labored, he settled into a trot, pacing himself for the miles it might take before he caught up with Timothy and the physician.

As he climbed a steep hill on the far side of the river, a pain knifed into his side. "Jesus, help me!" he prayed as he clutched his side and ran on. A few moments later the pain subsided and he got his second wind.

Then, as he came over a rise, he saw them, two figures in the distance on the road. Summoning all his strength, he quickened his pace, and five minutes later he was within hailing distance of them. But he had no breath left with which to call out. By chance, Timothy happened to look back, and his brow furrowed as he recognized Papie running after them.

He caught hold of Luke's arm. "Look back there! Epaphroditus is coming!" They turned and began walking back to meet him. The young man was near collapse when they came together. He dropped to the road and panted out the message. Immediately Luke started back. Timothy would stay with Papie until he had recovered sufficiently to return.

Luke could not run the way the young man had. He paced himself and trotted, and soon he crossed the bridge and came around the bend where the house by the river came into view. He sprinted the last few hundred yards and entered to find Lydia still holding the child, applying cold cloths to his small head.

His practiced eye went quickly over the child as he took him from Lydia. He undressed him and completed his examination. He saw the red staining the child's lower garments and his face grew tense. "Dear Jesus, help this child. There is nothing I can do for him!"

He carried Doronius to his bed, the limp body becoming ashen. He is bleeding internally, Luke thought. A blood vessel must have ruptured!

Luke turned to Lydia, Clement and Euodia who stood behind him in the child's room. "We must pray for him," he told them. "There is nothing I can do. It is in God's hands!"

Fervently they joined in prayer, asking God to heal Doronius, to perform a miracle the way He had when Tia lay dead. They knelt beside the small bed, Clement's hands upon his tiny head. Luke could hear the rasping breath. Then it stopped.

With tears running down his cheeks, he felt for a pulse. There was none. The child lay still and pale. Luke walked to the window of the room. "Please, Father. Raise him up as you did Tia. In the name of your Son, Jesus, we ask this."

Still there was no sound of breathing, no movement from the still, small form on the bed. Luke looked at the group who knelt in prayer about the bed. They were all new Christians, all expecting to see a miracle. They were praying, asking the same God who had raised Tia from the dead. They were sure He would do the same for this child, Lydia's beloved son.

Luke listened and watched. When he was certain there would be no miracle in answer to their prayers, he moved slowly to Lydia's side and put his hand upon her shoulder as she knelt by the bed. With a voice choked with emotion, he told her what he must. "He is gone, Lydia. He is with Jesus now."

Syntyche had been sent into town to tell Marcellus that Lydia's child had been taken ill. Lydia did not know exactly why she had sent for him, but she wanted him with her even though there was nothing he could do.

The girl found him in the agora presiding over a case. When she tried to approach him, she was stopped by a lictor. She called out to the tribune and he heard her, and seeing the desperate look on her face he beckoned for her to come forward.

Quickly she told him that Doronius had been taken seriously ill, and he immediately went to his horse and galloped off toward the river. When Timothy and Epaphroditus arrived, Luke met them at the door and told them the boy was dead. They went inside at once to comfort Lydia. They found her sitting beside the small bed, holding the tiny, cold hand of her dead son, staring out into vacant space.

"Lydia, I—" Timothy started to say, but Euodia touched his arm.

"She can't hear you," Euodia told him. "She has gone into shock."

Marcellus had ridden at breakneck speed through the streets and out the Egnation Way to the house on the river. Within his heart was a strange fear, a bewildering sensation of impending disaster. As he galloped under the stone arch and rounded the bend in the road, he saw the rambling house by the Gangites. It stood with an almost deserted look. He could see no one moving about the grounds and there was an utter stillness in the air.

He reined his horse and dismounted. Luke stood in the doorway. "What has happened?" he asked impatiently of the doctor.

Luke seemed to have suddenly aged. His face was pale and his eyes were haggard and red. "Doronius is dead," Luke said.

Marcellus stood beside Luke, knowing not what to say, what to do. Luke placed his hand on the tribune's shoulder. "Go in to her," he told Marcellus. "She needs you."

He found her in the room, still sitting beside the bed, her hand clutching the still fingers of her dead child. He knelt beside her.

"Lydia, I—I—" He put his arms around her and pulled her head to his chest. "I don't know what to say to you," he whispered to her. He swallowed hard, and in a wavering voice he continued, "Lydia, look at me. What should I say? I am sorry, so very sorry. I don't understand this any more than you do. But life is a fleeting thing, a fragile thing." He stroked her hair. "Cry, Lydia. Cry it out. Lydia, can you hear me? Cry it out!"

At last it came. From deep down inside of her came the wail, rising slowly from her throat until it filled the room. Marcellus held her tightly as her body trembled violently, the cry of primordial heartbreak issuing from her very soul, a cry that mothers have cried from the first eve of creation.

When he at last was able to lead her from the room, Clement and Euodia wrapped the small body in the finest cloth from the storeroom. Timothy and Epaphroditus dug a grave by the bank of the river, at the spot where he had often played.

When all was ready, Marcellus brought her to the river bank. Clement offered prayers as the child's body was lowered into the rich, moist earth beside the river. Lydia stood looking as the earth was replaced over the remains of her son. She stood very still, staring at the tiny bundle as the black earth covered it and until she could no longer see it.

Marcellus led her back to the house. Luke persuaded her to drink a glass of wine, into which he had dissolved a powder. When the sedative began to take effect, Euodia put her to bed and sat alongside the bed all night, her own grief overpowered by her concern for the young lady she loved.

The men sat silently in the atrium. Luke had insisted they drink a little wine. All were absorbed deeply in their own private thoughts. "I think it best if I stay here awhile longer," Luke told Timothy. "You go on ahead and join Paul and Silas. I will come later when I can."

Early the next morning Timothy left again, heading alone down the Egnation Way, dreading what he must relate to Paul when he arrived in Thessalonica.

When Marcellus returned home, he told his sister what happened, that Lydia's son had suddenly died. And in her eyes he thought he saw a faint glimmer of sympathy.

— Chapter Thirteen —

Timothy arrived in Thessalonica and inquired where he could find Jason's house. He followed the directions and found the right street. As he walked along the stone wall hiding the house, he saw scratched into one of the stones the sign of a fish. Confident that he had located Jason's house, he entered the courtyard and knocked at the door.

Jason greeted him warmly and had food and drink brought into the atrium. Then, as Timothy refreshed himself, Jason related what had happened to Paul and Silas and gave him the instructions Paul had left.

The following morning, after a good night's sleep in one of Jason's comfortable guest rooms, Timothy again set off to proceed to Berea and meet Paul at the synagogue there. Two days later he arrived and found the synagogue. When he inquired about Paul, the man knew all about the stranger who had come with the exciting news concerning the Messiah. He conducted Timothy to the house where Paul and Silas were staying.

"Timothy," Paul exclaimed as he embraced him. "It is so good to see you. But where is Luke? Didn't he come with you?"

Quickly Paul was brought up to date about all that had happened in Philippi and Luke's decision to remain there a while longer. Paul nodded in agreement. "That was wise," he said. "Luke can always be counted on to do the right thing."

Timothy told Paul about how hard Lydia was taking the death of her son and the apostle's eyes filled with tears. "I should have been with her," he said. "She is a fine woman. I wish I could comfort her in her sorrow."

Timothy had other news as well. Jason had been informed that the leaders of the synagogue in Thessalonica were aware that Paul was now preaching in Berea. He was not sure what they intended to do but was certain that something was in the wind. His fears were not long in being realized, for a delegation of Jews from Thessalonica were only a day behind Timothy on the road to Berea. When they arrived they went directly to the synagogue and told them how dangerous Paul's preaching was.

"This man is the same sort that caused the trouble in Rome," they said, "and you know what happened there. Our people were banished from Italy and suffered much hardship as a result of a few troublemakers. This man Paul is even more dangerous than they were. He preaches another king beside Caesar.

"His claims of this man, Jesus, being our Messiah are absurd. Think now, brothers, if Messiah has come, are we now free? No, we find ourselves no better off than before. Surely if this Jesus had been the Anointed One, He would have liberated His people from the yoke of the Romans. Jesus is not Messiah! Paul is a liar! Heed our advice and rid yourselves of him before he brings destruction down on all our heads."

As the leaders of the synagogue in Berea listened, fear gripped them. They agreed they had better do something about Paul before it was too late.

Lydia had placed fresh flowers on the grave of her son. Now she sat on the bank of the river and watched the current and the drifting clouds, oblivious to everything except the deep and agonizing hurt she felt and the blackness of the depth of gloom into which she had plunged.

She had spoken little since Doronius's death. Everyone had tried to comfort her, but even Luke had been unsuccessful in bringing her out of the deep depression. Lydia had stopped attending the services in her house in the evenings, now led by Clement. When Orcas and the others came, she left the house and came to sit by Doronius's grave.

"Leave her alone," Clement had advised. "She will get over it in time."

Luke agreed. "Time can be the greatest healer of such things. But I am concerned about her. She will not eat and her face is drawn. She is losing weight. I fear for her health if this continues much longer."

"She was like this for a while after she had her miscarriage back in Thyatira," Euodia told Luke. "Then one morning she came down to breakfast and was suddenly her old self again. Give her time. She is a strong person. She will get over this."

But Lydia did not get over it. Her black mood continued, and for weeks she refused to eat more than a few mouthfuls of food each day, and then only to please Euodia who coaxed her. No longer was she interested in dyeing cloth. Day after day she sat by the river, looking at the small plot of ground that held her son, oblivious to all that went on around her.

Marcellus had not seen her for several days. His duties had taken him out of Philippi, and he was hopeful as he rode down the hill toward the house that she might be better. He looked anxiously at Euodia as he reined his horse, but she shrugged her shoulders, nodding toward the river. He tied the horse and walked toward the Gangites.

If she was conscious of his approach, she did not show it. He sat beside her on the grass and idly picked up a handful of stones and tossed them one by one into the river. He watched the ever widening circles they made as they plunked down into the still water near the bank. On the far side a fish jumped, catching a low flying insect in mid air.

For a long time he sat silently next to her. Finally his hand touched her arm and he stroked it gently. "You can't go on this way, Lydia."

She turned her head and looked at him for the first time, her face reflecting what she felt inside herself. "Lydia," he said in a low voice, his hand reaching out and touching her face, "Lydia, you can't change what has happened. You have to go on living. What you're doing now can't alter what has happened. It won't bring him back."

He saw the pleading in her eyes, the hopelessness, the terrifying bewilderment. When she spoke, her voice was as a child's, faced with an unthinkable problem. "Why?" she asked him. "Why? First my father, then my husband! And now my child! Why, Marcellus? Why?"

He felt an intense compassion for her as he tried to answer. "I don't know, Lydia. There are some questions for which there are no answers."

He pulled her close to him and pressed his cheek against hers, feeling the bittersweet taste of her tears. "Lydia, I love you. I want to marry you. If I have to become a Christian to have you, then I shall become a Christian."

She was sobbing now, quietly, in his arms. He could feel the emotions drain from her body to his.

"It doesn't matter," she told him between sobs. "It just doesn't matter anymore. Nothing does!"

As soon as they entered the synagogue, Paul knew what was going to happen. He immediately recognized several of the men from the synagogue at Thessalonica, men who had opposed him vehemently there. The service began and Paul prayed silently that the Holy Spirit would guide his words and actions. The leader announced that Paul of Tarsus had again asked to address the assembly, and Paul stood up and walked to the front to speak.

"Men and brethren," he began, "you have heard me relate how God has shown me the error of my persecution of Jesus who was crucified at Jerusalem. It was that same Jesus whom I met on the road to the city of Damascus in a blinding light. It was this same Jesus whom God raised up after three days in the grave—"

"Liar!" came a cry from the crowd.

"Blasphemy!"

"This man has no truth in him!"

Paul closed his eyes tightly. His human instinct was to confront the men who had so rudely interrupted him, using his skill as an orator to still them and send them cowering from the building. But the Holy Spirit stilled his tongue and he took their abuse in silence.

"This man preaches treason," a man shouted. "He was found doing the same in our city and the judges ordered him arrested."

Several of the men of Berea who had believed what Paul said tried to restore order, but they were shouted down by the superior numbers of the men from Thessalonica who had come to cause Paul trouble.

Paul motioned to Silas and Timothy, and they quickly left by a rear door. "I must leave this city," Paul told them. "The Holy Spirit has ordered me to do so. But you two must stay and continue the work quietly. I am the target of their attack. When I leave there will be no more trouble. When you have done all you can here, meet me in Athens, where the Holy Spirit has instructed me to go."

Within the hour Paul left Berea. With him went several of the Jews who had believed and were anxious to hear more. All the way to Athens as they walked, Paul taught them of Jesus and also what they must do to organize a church and nourish those who had been baptized into the new faith.

When they reached the beautiful city of Athens, Paul gave them a message to deliver to Silas and Timothy back in Berea.

"Tell then," he said, "to come to me here with all haste after their work is done there. I shall await them here."

With each passing day, Euodia had expected Lydia to throw off her deep depression and regain her former spirit. But Lydia still sat most of the time, staring into empty space, refusing food and all attempts to engage her in meaningful conversation.

Marcellus came to see her almost every day, but even his arrival did not seem to change her mood. She consented to walk to the river, silent and withdrawn, by his side. She did not object when he took her hand, but it was limp and unresponsive.

As they sat by the river, Marcellus tried in vain to get her to talk. Occasionally she breathed a deep sigh, but she rarely spoke a word. But even this was a sign of encouragement to Marcellus, for she no longer sobbed the desperate sobs of the first days of her grief.

"The river is beautiful, isn't it?" he asked.

Lydia did not move nor look at it. "Yes," she said, her voice flat and without enthusiasm.

"Lydia," he said gently, "you said it did not matter whether I became a Christian. What did that mean?"

When she did not answer he moved closer and placed his arm about her. "Lydia," he asked again, "what did you mean? Will you marry me? Will you be my wife?"

He felt her stiffen under his touch. She looked straight ahead, not even blinking her eyes. Then her lips moved, slowly, "Nothing at all matters anymore," she said. "Nothing at all."

"Not even me, Lydia?"

There was no reply. He sat beside her for a while, feeling the hurt within him. It's not fair, he told himself. It's just not fair. Slowly he arose and stood looking down at her. "Lydia, I can't bear to see you like this. I want you for my wife, but I can't marry empty flesh. Nor can I stand by and watch you torment yourself over something that has happened in the past. I can understand how you feel. If I lost my daughter, I would also grieve. But, Lydia, those who are alive must go on living."

His hand stroked her hair, feeling its softness, wanting her, needing her. "I'm going, Lydia. I have to go on living. If you come to your senses and want to see me, send for me. But I won't, I can't come back while you are like this."

She was vaguely aware that he had left and she was again alone with her grief. She preferred to be alone, to feel the throbbing ache within her breast, the hollow waves of emptiness that coursed through her body.

Her mind pulsated with the same question. Over and over it came, always the same. Why? Why had God done this to her? This God she had believed in so fervently. This God who had sent His own Son into the world to die. Could this Father, this God of love, do such a thing to her? Had she been deceived by Paul's words?

Paul had described this God as a loving heavenly Father, one who cared for people. I wish Paul had never come here, she suddenly thought. I wish he had never come from Asia into Macedonia with his pretty tales of a caring and loving God and a Savior who gave His life so that all might live. Doronius had not lived!

She longed to hold her son once more in her arms, to feel the soft, smooth skin of his young body, to see again the sparkle in his bright eyes, to hear the sound of his voice as he called to her. But never again would she see him running toward her or taste the sweetness of his kiss. And this was more than she could bear.

Slowly she arose. The water's edge was but a few feet away. That was the only answer she could find, to submerge her pain in the cool water of the Gangites, to let the current carry away her grief. It would take but an instant and all of the sorrow would be gone. Oblivion! To sleep! To have peaceful sleep for eternity!

She took a step toward the bank, then another. She paused at the edge. No more pain! No more to feel the deep hurting inside her breast! No more emptiness!

She dove from the bank into the swift current and felt for an instant the chill of the water as it swept over her.

Paul had never seen a city as beautiful as Athens. Everywhere great marble buildings graced the wide streets and avenues while statues of perfect sculpture gleamed in the bright sunlight. Libraries and auditoriums, baths and all sorts of public buildings were in profusion. Everywhere also were temples and shrines to seemingly hundreds of gods and goddesses, and to Paul these were an abomination.

He longed to bring the knowledge of the true God, the Living God, to these people of Athens and someday perhaps see the pagan temples abandoned and torn down.

He found lodgings near the synagogue where he would await the arrival of Silas and Timothy. He spent the days until the Jewish Sabbath seeing the sights of the city and acquainting himself with the streets and sections of this large Greek city. On the Sabbath he went to the synagogue. As usual, the president of the synagogue asked if any visitors had a message for the congregation and Paul arose to speak. But his message was not well received, and not one person was convinced of what he told them.

Paul left the synagogue and went into the streets, preaching to the crowds in the agora about the Living God who had sent His Son to die for the salvation of all people. To the citizens of Athens, it was not uncommon for someone to stand in the marketplace and speak. While Paul was speaking, others were doing the same, and the crowd had a choice of which man to listen to. This was the primary source of entertainment for the Athenians, and they were eager to hear anything new or unusual that such a speaker might bring to them.

Many people listened to Paul, the same as they listened to the other speakers. Some men even argued with him in the manner they argued with the philosophers, but none took his message seriously. To them, Paul was just another man extolling the virtues of another god. What was one more god to them? They already had hundreds.

If Paul had counted the number of temples in the city he would have found over 3,000. Everywhere were altars and statues where the citizens offered sacrifices. The acrid odor of incense filled the air. On just one street were temples dedicated to Minerva, Venus and Diana, and altars to War, Victory, Fame, Modesty and Pity. This had to be, Paul thought, the most idolatrous city in the world.

It was no wonder, Paul had to admit, that his message was not received by these people who were so totally caught up in the rites and worship of their pagan gods. His story of a loving, caring God who was willing to sacrifice His own Son for them had little impression in the midst of all the incredible mythology of the Greek religions.

But on one day as Paul spoke in the marketplace, a group of

learned men, philosophers of the Stoic and Epicurean schools of thought, came to listen to him. "This babbler seems to set forth strange gods," one of them said. "Let us hear what he has to say."

The man turned to Paul. "What is this new doctrine you speak of? You seem to bring new things to our ears. Now tell us what they mean."

But it was entirely too noisy in the agora for Paul to speak properly to these men. They led him up a hill known as the Acropolis and halfway to the top found a rocky semicircle called the Hill of Mars. It was here that Paul faced this learned group and began to speak.

"Men of Athens," he began. "I perceive that you are unusually religious, for as I passed along your streets I saw the gods you worship. But I also saw an altar inscribed with these words, 'To an Unknown God.' Now it is this God which I proclaim to you whom you worship in ignorance."

Instantly their attention and interest was aroused, and they leaned forward to hear what he had to say.

"God, who made the world and all that it contains, since He is Lord of the heavens and of earth, does not live in temples of stone fashioned by the hands of men, nor can He be served by sacrifices from men's hands. He does not need such things, as He is the giver of life and breath to men.

"And since He made all nations of one blood and fixed the times and seasons and determined where they should dwell, and since He ordained that they should seek God, who is not far away from any of us, and since we live and move and have our existence in Him, we ought not to think of Him as a figure carved in marble or cast of silver or gold. For even some of your own poets have said we are his offspring."

The men nodded in agreement, very pleased with what he had said so far. It was evident to them that Paul was a learned man, and despite being a Jew, he even knew the words of their own poets.

"In the past God has excused the ignorance of men, but now He commands them everywhere to repent and to cease from such things. For God has fixed a day when He will call all the world to account and will judge all mankind by His Son, Jesus Christ; and the proof that God is able to do this is the fact that He raised Jesus from the dead."

From the rear of the men seated about Paul came a laugh. "You say a man was raised from the dead?"

"What kind of foolishness is this?" cried another man. "Next he will tell us that eggs lay chickens."

There was a roar of laughter from the men. "This man speaks nonsense! I will hear no more of it."

The men drifted away. A few, with better manners than the rest, told Paul they would hear him again on another day, but Paul knew they did not mean it. He had faced opposition from many sources during his years as a missionary, but this was the sort of opposition he was not prepared to meet. They considered him a source of amusement, and their ridicule silenced him in a way that stones and insults could not have. Dejected, he left Mars Hill feeling a failure and went back to his lodgings.

As Marcellus passed by the house on the way to his horse, Luke and Epaphroditus were just coming out of the door. "Where is Lydia?" Luke asked.

"She is still sitting by the river," Marcellus shot back as he swung into his saddle. "If she comes to her senses, let me know."

"You didn't leave her alone by the river, did you?" asked Luke, his voice containing a trace of alarm.

"Yes, she is just sitting there, interested in nothing. I'm tired of carrying on a one-sided conversation." He rode off up the hill.

Luke and Papie exchanged glances. It had been a rule among them never to leave Lydia alone, especially by the river. Luke had cautioned that a person in the state of depression she was in may try to end his life. Always, even when Lydia thought she was alone, someone was watching her. Both men started running at once toward the river. Epaphroditus, being much younger, reached the bank before Luke.

"Luke," he cried, "she's not here!"

A few seconds later the physician reached the river. His eyes went immediately downstream. "There!" he shouted, "I see something just below the water!"

"It's her!" Epaphroditus screamed. He shook off his sandals and plunged into the water, his dive carrying him downstream. His strong arms cut the water as he stroked toward the object, and he dived below the surface as he neared it. His hands caught hold of clothing and he fought the current to bring what he had seized to the surface.

Luke ran down the bank and was opposite to where the young man surfaced. He also leaped into the water, and when Epaphroditus's head bobbed up, Luke was in the water beside him. Together they pulled her to shore. Luke examined the still form that lay on the grassy bank. She was not breathing, he observed.

"Luke, she isn't dead, is she?"

"Help me turn her over," Luke commanded and they rolled Lydia onto her stomach. Luke's practiced hands found the proper position, and he leaned forward, putting his weight on her back. Then he quickly released, and heard a gurgling sound come from her throat. Again and again he pressed and released, forcing water from her lungs. Papie stood by, feeling so helpless as he watched anxiously for a sign of life.

"She can't be dead," he exclaimed. "She just can't be!"

It seemed to Lydia that all of the sounds of the world had suddenly ceased. She found herself gliding effortlessly through what appeared to be a long tunnel. Then, from its blackness, she saw a light, and she emerged into the most beautiful meadow she had ever seen. The grass was greener, the flowers brighter, the sunshine, if you could call it that, was more brilliant, for the light appeared to come from no specific direction but just to shine in everything.

She found herself walking effortlessly through the grass. In the distance was a river, and as she approached she could see something on the far bank. A man stood there, a man such as she had never seen before. His face and body glowed, radiating a white light, yet the light was soft and did not hurt her eyes. On His face was a smile, and although she had never before seen Him, she felt as though she had known Him all her life.

Then she saw someone standing next to this man, holding His hand. Her heart quickened as she saw that it was Doronius, his tiny face a picture of happiness and contentment. He clung to the man standing beside him as though he never wanted to let go. Lydia saw that the river was shallow. She could wade easily across to them. Forward she went and was about to step into the water when the man on the far bank raised His hand and shook His head. From His gesture she knew she could not cross to the other side.

But suddenly her heart knew a fullness, a peace and joy she had never known before. Slowly she turned and walked back in the direction she had come. Yet it was not in sadness but with a strange feeling of ecstasy that she left her son standing on the river bank. Then she was in the tunnel again, falling, down and down through the darkness until . . . .

She opened her eyes. A slight groan left her lips as she felt the weight press against her back. Then it was gone, only to come again as Luke tried to revive her.

"Oh," she cried, "Doronius! You are safe and happy with Jesus!"

Luke smiled down at her. "You had us worried, Lydia. There for a while I thought you'd never breathe again."

Lydia looked up into the faces of Luke and Epaphroditus. The sky was blue again and the white clouds appeared as puffs of Egyptian cotton against it. They helped her to her feet and walked her back to the house to bed. As she slept, Luke kept vigil beside her bed.

When Lydia awoke she was ravenously hungry. Euodia brought her food and she ate all of it quickly. When she had finished she looked up at the grins on the faces of Luke, Papie and Euodia.

"What are you all grinning about?" she asked. "Haven't you ever seen a person eat before?"

The old Lydia was back. Gone was the gloom, the deep depression, the utter despair she had wallowed in for so long. She remembered the vision of Doronius standing beside Jesus and could recall even the smallest detail of it, of the meadow, the flowers, the river and, most importantly, the face of the Lord. It was many days before she could bring herself to tell anyone about the vision, as though keeping it to herself would enable her to retain the feeling of peace and joy she experienced with it.

Her family was more than content just to have her back to normal. Euodia went about her work singing. Clement and Epaphroditus whistled. Luke grinned as he checked her pulse then, satisfied, told her that Marcellus wanted to see her.

Lydia shook her head. "Not today. I don't know when, but right now I have no wish to complicate my life. I have all I need right here, right now."

Paul sat with his head in his hands, in deep despair. "Lord," he prayed, "I have failed you here. There are so many who need to hear the truth, who need You. Send your Holy Spirit to open their eyes and ears and soften their hearts so that they might believe, and in believing be saved, for this is a wicked and perverse city."

Just then a tap came on the door of his room. Paul opened it to find a small group of men and women. One of the men, older than the others and very distinguished looking, spoke. "I am Dionysius," he told Paul. "I am a member of the Athenian Supreme Court. I have come with these people to hear more of this new doctrine which you preach about God."

Paul heartily welcomed them into his rooms, thanking God for this sign that his ministry had not been in vain in Athens. For hours they sat and listened as Paul told them about Jesus who had given His life to give salvation to those who believe on His name.

This time there were no rude jokes or laughter. These people had come in sincerity to listen, and they believed. From this small group the church of Athens was formed. Their meetings were held at the home of one of the women, named Damaris, who through her gentle nature and loving spirit brought many more into the kingdom of God.

After several weeks, Silas and Timothy had not yet come, and Paul again grew restless. Had something happened to them? He was tempted to return to Thessalonica to search for them, but the Holy Spirit advised him otherwise. Instead of going himself, he sent one of the new Athenian Christians to Thessalonica to inqure as to the state of things, along with a message that Paul was going on to Corinth and they were to meet him there.

He went to the port city of Piraeus where he found a ship bound for Corinth, the capital of that part of Greece known as Achaia. With his money running out, he wondered what fate awaited him in Corinth, but the knowledge that the Holy Spirit was always with him sustained him.

When he arrived, his money was almost gone, and he decided to try to find work at his old trade of tent making. Finding the street where the makers of tents were located, he entered a shop owned by a man named Aquila, a Jewish refugee from Rome who had arrived in Corinth with his wife only a few weeks before. Paul not only found work in the shop of these kind people but also lodgings in their home. They were devout Jews, and Paul took his time, sharing with them little by little his experiences and his faith in the Messiah who had already come. Slowly they opened their minds and hearts to the new religion and finally became believers and were baptized.

In the Corinthian synagogue, Paul was introduced as a Jew who had actually been in the temple in Jerusalem and who had studied with the renowned Gamaliel. But when Paul spoke, he did so with caution and with less forcefulness than he had spoken with before. A wave of discouragement had come upon him after what had happened in other Greek cities, and Paul was not his old self at all.

Corinth was an ancient city, older even than Athens. It was also the home city of the goddess Venus, called Aphrodite, the goddess of love. Aphrodite's temple was served by over 1,000 religious prostitutes, and it was considered an act of devotion to this goddess to engage one of these and to commit the act within the temple confines.

Corinth had become world famous for its brothels and houses of fleshly pleasure. Indeed, seamen from around the world who visited this port spread tales of the variety and quantity of carnal houses to be found there, making Corinth a symbol of sin throughout the Roman world.

After several weeks, Silas and Timothy arrived in Corinth, and Paul's spirits soared when they told him that the churches at Philippi, Berea, Thessalonica and Athens were standing fast in their faith. His heart was deeply warmed when they related how these congregations prayed daily for him and for his work. Silas handed him a purse, a collection taken spontaneously in all the congregations to bring to him as a gesture of their love and support. The money, Silas told him, was so that he could devote his full time to preaching and not have to earn his living making tents.

Paul's work had not been in vain in Macedonia or Achaia. The churches were not only holding their own but were growing. The seeds he had planted in Europe were bearing fruit, and his heart beat faster as he thought of each one he had converted and brought into the kingdom of God. Since Aquila's house could not hold the additional men, Paul, Silas and Timothy rented rooms next door to the synagogue with a man named Justus.

Paul knew he faced a difficult battle in Corinth, for the city was full of the forces of Satan. Then, just when he needed a spiritual lift, a vision of the Lord appeared to him, just like the vision Joshua had seen over a thousand years before. *Be not afraid,* the Lord told Paul, *but speak, and hold not your peace; for I am with you, and no man shall set on you to hurt you; for I have many people in this city.*

Paul also remembered his confrontation with the Lord on the road to Damascus and recalled what Jesus had said to Ananias: *He is a chosen vessel unto me, to bear my name before the Gentiles, and kings, and the children of Israel: for I will show him how great things he must suffer for my name's sake.*

Paul went into the synagogue for the last time. With renewed vigor he spoke, proving that Jesus was the Son of God, sent to bring redemption and salvation to sinners, and that God had raised Him up after He had been crucified.

But the Jews in the synagogue refused to believe him, and

cursed him and blasphemed the name of Jesus. Their hearts had been hardened, and no amount of argument would turn them to Christ.

Paul faced the snarling congregation. "Your blood is upon your heads," he told them. "From henceforth I will go to the Gentiles."

— Chapter Fourteen —

Lydia had thrown herself into her work and the business prospered. Now she was in a position to dye more cloth than Stetius could use. "I will have to do what my father did," Lydia told Clement. "I'll have to travel to other cities and find more customers."

"But you can't travel alone," Clement insisted. "It's too dangerous for a woman to travel alone."

"But I went alone to Mytilene to make arrangements to buy the cloth and dye," she protested.

"That was only one trip. And we were all worried about you then. But constant travel is far different. Sooner or later there would be someone to take advantage of you, a woman traveling alone."

"But you forget," Lydia smiled. "Now there is always someone with me."

"Someone with you?" asked Clement. "And who is that?"

"Why Jesus, of course," she replied, and Clement was embarrassed that he had forgotten.

She decided to go first to the cities nearest Philippi and to restrict her travel, for the present at least, to places where she could travel by ship. For all the perils of the sea, it was still far safer than traveling across the wild stretches of uninhabited land where robbers and worse terrorized the travelers.

"Thessalonica," she said. "I shall go to Thessalonica and try to establish customers there."

Clement insisted that he go with her as far as Neapolis, where she would board a ship for Thessalonica. Lydia prepared her samples of cloth, swatches that would tell a potential customer her goods were of the finest quality and truest colors. The next morning they set out for the port city and arrived there in the late afternoon. While Clement took care of the donkey, Lydia engaged rooms at the inn. A ship was leaving the next morning for Thessalonica and Lydia bought passage on it.

As the small ship sailed slowly out of the harbor, Lydia waved at Clement standing on the quay. Her heart felt light and the fresh sea breeze was good as she filled her lungs with it. It was good to get away from Philippi for a while, she thought. She wondered whether she should have stopped to see Marcellus before she left, or at least sent him a note. But it was too late now. The coastline moved rapidly by and the quay was now out of sight.

In Corinth, Paul's heart was so stirred by the good news that had been brought to him by Silas about the churches that he decided to write them a letter. He took out his quill and ink pot and parchment. Quickly he wrote, commending the faithful at Thessalonica on their steadfastness in the face of persecution.

It was a letter of loving advice, cautioning them to grow in grace and to walk in the light of God's truth. They were to abound more and more in the richness of their testimony, for one day the Lord would return and gather them into His presence, both the believers who were living and those who had passed on.

"I charge you that this epistle be read to all the holy brothers," wrote Paul, and he ended his letter with the words, "The grace of our Lord Jesus Christ be with you, Amen."

He entrusted the letter to one of the Corinthian Christians to carry to the church at Thessalonica. This man sailed that day on a ship that carried him northward.

When Lydia landed at Thessalonica she found the city vaguely familiar. Her father had taken her with him as a child on his rounds to call on his customers and here she recalled familiar landmarks. The captain of the ship recommended an inn several blocks from the waterfront, and Lydia hired a porter to carry her bags there.

Her room was airy and spacious, although her view was restricted by a temple across the street. She lay down on the comfortable bed and relaxed, planning again in her mind what she would say when she called on the merchants who might buy her cloth. But there was something else, even more important, to do. There had been no news of Paul since he had left to come to this city from Philippi and she intended to find the house of Paul's cousin Jason. Paul may still be here, she hoped.

Early the next morning, armed with directions from the innkeeper, she set out to find Jason's house. The directions were good, and in less than an hour she stood before a splendid house surrounded by a wall whose gate showed signs of recent repair. Her eyes brightened when she saw the outline of a fish inscribed on a stone next to the gate. So Paul had at least been successful in converting his cousin to Christianity, she thought.

A servant answered her rap on the door, and when she inquired about Jason she mentioned that she was a friend of Paul's. The man smiled and showed her to a large atrium where she was offered refreshment while she waited for the master of the house to come to her.

"I am Jason," said the man who entered. "I understand you are a friend of Paul's. Tell me, how is he and where has he gone?"

Her face fell. "I was hoping you could tell me the same thing," she answered. "I have not seen him since he left Philippi to come here."

They sat and sipped cool fruit juice as Jason related what had happened when Paul had come to Thessalonica. Her concern for his safety grew as Jason told her some of the Jews whom Paul had angered in this city had pursued him to Berea. "And so," Jason said, "that is all I know. But do not worry, he is well able to take care of himself. And God will protect him."

Lydia told him the reasons she had come to Thessalonica, to find new customers for her cloth. His interest was immediately aroused. "I have friends in the business of selling cloth," he told her. "Here, let me write a note for you to take to them. If your goods are as good as you claim, you will have no trouble in establishing business here."

They exchanged news of how the churches at Philippi and Thessalonica were faring. Both were amazed at how fast they were both growing, even in the face of ridicule and persecution. Lydia promised to return the next evening and speak to the group that met at Jason's house, then left to see the merchants to whom he had written the introductory letters.

Her first call found the merchant not in, and the attendants could not tell her when he was expected. But the next visit was with a fine gentleman who read Jason's letter with interest and welcomed her to his shop. "I remember your father," he told her. "He was an honest man and a master at dyeing cloth, especially of silk. I could not do business with him because my brother-in-law was also in the business, but he has passed on now. I see no reason why we cannot do business together."

He was impressed by the quality of Lydia's samples and exclaimed enthusiastically over the purple silks. "I have not seen such quality in a long time," he admitted. "Indeed, I shall be most happy to buy these fine fabrics from you, dear lady."

He gave her a substantial order for woolens and silks. As she was about to leave he told her, "I have not been satisfied with my supplier. He came to this city only a short time ago, and since he was a local tradesman I gave him my business. But his quality is not good and his word is worth less than nothing. He promises delivery and all I get are excuses. I am glad you have come."

As Lydia left the shop, a man watched her. He had seen her enter and recognized her. Now, as she left, he followed at a discreet distance until she entered the inn where she was staying. Then he entered the courtyard of the inn and sat down at a table. He ordered wine from the serving girl and made himself comfortable to wait until Lydia went out again to follow her.

So, thought Vestus, the gods have given me a chance to avenge myself. So you have come to Thessalonica to sell your cloth, eh? Well, Lydia, my fine lady, you have no tribune here to protect you. I shall deal with you with no interference.

The ship on which Uncas, the man who carried Paul's letter, had traveled made excellent time from Corinth. The winds had been most favorable and had carried the ship along with good speed. It was now in the headwaters of the Thermaic Gulf. Tomorrow it would land at Thessalonica and Uncas would take the letter to Jason's house, following the directions he had been given by Paul.

Uncas was a young man of twenty-two with a strong and muscular body. He had been a wrestler after the Greek style, and he prided himself in keeping his body fit. He was employed by his uncle in the leather trade, and in his traveling bags were samples of the leather goods that had been made in his uncle's shop in Corinth. He was proud to carry the letter from Paul, and it was strapped to his body beneath his traveling robes in a small, waterproof bag along with his money for the trip.

He had gone to hear Paul speak at the urging of his uncle who had become a believer. As Paul's voice had filled the room, Uncas had recognized the sound of truth and had also believed. He had been baptized into the new faith the next day. Eagerly he had come to Paul when he heard someone was needed to carry the letter to the church at Thessalonica. His trip was to have been a month later, but when his uncle heard of Paul's need of a bearer, he agreed for Uncas to make the trip at once.

Now Uncas lay on his sleeping robes on the deck of the ship, the sea around him illuminated by the full moon as the trim craft cut easily through the waters of the gulf. He was anxious to deliver the letter and to fulfill his mission for Paul. But now he sighed deeply and yawned as the gentle motion of the ship put him to sleep.

Vestus saw the sun go down and the moon peek above the horizon. He arose and stretched his legs. It was obvious that she was going no place else today. He paid for his food and wine and decided to come back early the next morning. He would follow her all day, all night if necessary. He was curious as to where she would go, and he knew that sometime, sooner or later, she would give him the opportunity he waited for. Sooner or later she would be alone on some deserted street.

In Corinth there were two men who would play a great part in Paul's ministry. One was Junius Gallio, the Roman proconsul of Achaia. Gallio was quite typical of the Roman officials who governed the provinces that made up the empire. He was very willing to let the local people settle their own differences as long as this presented no threat to Rome and as long as their taxes were paid on time and in full. Gallio was, in addition, an even-tempered man who administered Roman justice fairly.

The other man in Corinth was named Sosthenes, a Greek Jew who was the leader of the Corinthian synagogue. He and the other Jewish leaders deeply resented Paul's success in converting Gentiles to the new faith and were incensed at Paul's anger when his message was rejected by the Jews of the synagogue.

Sosthenes aroused a group of people in the agora, men who hung out in the marketplace because they had nothing better to do with their time, and incited them to attack Paul while he preached in the streets. This mob, under the direction of Sosthenes, dragged Paul before the Roman proconsul, Gallio, who was hearing complaints in the courtroom.

But Sosthenes had not thought out his plan very well, and when Paul stood before Gallio with the angry mob at his back, the Jewish leader was totally unprepared when the proconsul asked, "What charges have you brought against this man?"

Sosthenes suddenly realized he had no charges that would be of interest to the Romans. All he could charge Paul with was, "This man persuades men to worship God contrary to the law."

The Roman governor scowled at Sosthenes. "And what else has he done?"

Sosthenes shuffled from one foot to another. He scratched his head, pulled at his beard, and finally answered, "Well, nothing, your Excellency, but—"

Shaking his head, Gallio rose from his chair. "I refuse to have anything to do with this affair," he said sternly. "I am here to judge lawlessness, crime and wrongdoing, not to decide questions of words and names and matters of Jewish law. These things you must settle among yourselves."

He motioned to the guards and they drove the mob from the courtroom, Sosthenes among them. But a large crowd of Greeks had assembled outside and had witnessed the affair. This crowd had resented Sosthenes's attempt to have an innocent man punished. As Sosthenes came out of the courtroom, this crowd seized him and beat him whie Gallio stroked his chin and watched them, content that the Jewish leader was getting exactly what he deserved.

The captain of the Roman guard looked questioningly at the proconsul, trying to see whether Gallio wanted him to step in and stop the crowd. But Gallio shook his head at the captain and turned again to watch, obviously enjoying the turnaround of events. He would have no more phony complaints from the synagogue leaders, he wagered. And after that Paul was left strictly alone by the Jews of Corinth and could walk in safety anywhere in the city without fear.

This incident was soon spread over the entire city and Paul became a public figure overnight. Greeks who would never have stopped to listen to his preaching now flocked to hear him. And some of those who listened came to believe and were baptized into the faith. This single incident probably did as much to add members to the new Corinthian church as anything that happened in the city.

Vestus had arisen before dawn and was waiting outside the inn where Lydia was staying. At last his patience was rewarded, and she emerged from the inn and walked toward the agora. He followed her at a safe distance, keeping to the side of the buildings so that it would not be obvious to her that she was being followed. She entered a shop, one that was very familiar to Vestus.

"My customer!" he swore. "She is stealing my customers here!"

He waited outside as Lydia was shown in to the owner of the shop. As Lydia displayed her samples, the owner's eyes were wide as he recognized the quality of her cloth. Soon she had been given a small order with the promise of a much larger one if her delivered goods were as good as the samples he had seen.

She left the shop and continued down the street, with Vestus again following. Now he did not have to hide, for the streets were crowded and he could track her movements from just a few paces behind. She shopped at a food vendor and ate lunch, then continued on. She entered another shop, again a seller of cloth. When she handed the proprietor the letter from Jason, he welcomed her warmly. She spent almost the whole afternoon in this shop while Vestus fumed outside.

This time when she left she headed toward the most exclusive section of the city. Vestus wondered what a mere seller of dyed cloth would be doing in this elite section of Thessalonica.

She stopped at the gate to Jason's house and was let in by a servant. Vestus waited a moment and then walked slowly past the house. Who lived here, he wondered? Who could she possibly know who lived in such a mansion?

An old woman, obviously a day laborer hired by a rich woman to do cleaning, emerged from the gate of the house next door. Vestus approached her and smiled. "Madam," he asked, "is this the house of Renaldius, the prominent judge?"

She looked at him and then the house he indicated. "Oh, no," she said, "that's the home of Jason, the merchant."

He thanked her and the woman went on up the street. Vestus sat beneath a tree in the shrubbery where he could observe the gate of the house of Jason the merchant, without being seen.

When the sun went down and Lydia had not come out, he got restless. But then he saw other people, both men and women, enter the house, admitted by the same servant who had opened the gate for Lydia. In half an hour, he counted twenty-three people who had entered the house, most of them very plainly dressed and certainly not of the social status of the wealthy merchant who owned this fine property. Why had people of this sort been invited to a rich man's home, he wondered. There was certainly something very strange going on here.

Now it was quite dark. The wall of the house was close to a tree, a tree that could be easily climbed. He looked carefully up and down the street and found it deserted. He reached up and grabbed a low branch and swung himself up into the tree, then dropped down on the inside of the wall. He stood very still for several moments, then satisfied that he had not been observed, he slowly approached the house.

It was almost dark when the ship carefully docked at the mole in the harbor of Thessalonica. Uncas was one of the first to leave the ship. He stopped at a waterfront tavern to ask directions to Jason's house and set off with Paul's letter still secure in his leather traveling wallet. Within half an hour, just as it was dark, he found the right street and searched for the sign of the fish that had been scratched on the stone by the gate.

In the moonlight he saw it and rapped loudly on the gate. A moment later the door of the house opened and a servant came to the locked gate to see who was calling so late.

"My name is Uncas. I bear a letter from Paul in Corinth," he told the man. He was immediately let in and was taken into the atrium of the house, where the other Christians were holding services. Vestus had been hiding in the shrubbery near the door and heard what Uncas had told the servant.

"Paul!" he exclaimed to himself. "That's the man who caused so much trouble here not long ago. And come to think of it, Jason was himself implicated in some way with it."

Vestus waited until they had gone inside, then crawled to an open window where he could hear what was going on in the house.

"Sir," the servant announced, "this man is from Corinth. He bears a message from Paul."

Instantly everyone began to talk at once. "Paul! How is he?"

"Is Paul well?"

"What is going on in Corinth?"

Jason held up his hand. "Please," he said, "let us see what the message has to tell us. Then I am sure this young man will be happy to answer any questions."

Jason opened the seal on Paul's letter and began to read. "Paul and Silas and Timothy to the church at Thessalonica, which is in God, the Father, and in the Lord Jesus Christ: grace be unto you and peace . . . ."

The room was completely quiet as Jason read them the letter, each person hanging onto every word the apostle had written. Lydia could almost hear Paul speaking. She closed her eyes and visualized him, as though he were actually in the room; the words were so much like him, so very familiar to her.

Jason read on. "For if we believe that Jesus died and rose again, even to them which sleep in Jesus will God bring with him. For we say to you by word of the Lord, that we which are alive and remain until the coming of the Lord shall not prevent them which are asleep. For the Lord himself will descend from heaven with a shout, with the voice of the archangel, with the trumpet of God: and the dead in Christ shall rise first.

"Then we which are alive and remain alive shall be caught up together with them in the clouds, to meet the Lord in the air; and so shall we ever be with the Lord."

Jason finished reading the letter and lowered the parchment.

The room was still, each person absorbing the impact of the apostle's letter.

"Praise the Lord!" one man exclaimed. "He is coming for us soon."

"Any day now," agreed another.

"Why do you say that?" asked a woman.

"Why? Because Paul has told us so. He says that those of us who remain alive will be caught up to meet Jesus in the air. That means us, those who live now. Jesus will come again while we still live!"

"Yes," agreed another man, "that's what Paul has told us. It's plain enough."

"And he will break the yoke of Roman bondage! Hallelujah! Our King is coming to free us!"

Vestus took all of this in. When they spoke of Jesus coming, he did not know what they were talking about, but when they spoke of the yoke of Rome being broken and their King coming to free them, his eyes grew wide.

"This is a subversive organization!" he exclaimed. "These Christians are plotting revolution!"

Suddenly what he had overheard took on a new aspect. The Romans would pay for this type of information. They would pay well for it. And at the same time he would have his revenge on Lydia, for subversives did not live long under Roman rule.

He found a place at the wall where the branches of the tree made it possible to climb over. Once on the other side, he hurried off. The chief magistrate should be very interested in this, he thought as he broke into a trot.

Lydia spoke up. "Paul says that this letter should be read to all the brethren," she said. "There are brethren in Philippi who must hear it as well. We should make copies. I shall take one back with me. Others should be sent to Berea and Athens."

"You are right, Lydia. Here, I'll get the writing materials and we shall make copies for the congregations in the other cities."

Those at the meeting who were literate helped to copy the letter. They worked long into the night. Finally, when copies had been made for all the churches, they went home.

"It would not be safe for you to go back alone to the inn," Jason told her.

"I shall accompany her," Uncas volunteered. "I am much too excited to sleep anyway."

Lydia gratefully accepted. This would also give her an opportunity to ask Uncas many questions concerning Paul which she could not do when the others were present. They left Jason's house together and set off, Lydia asking him questions almost at once. Uncas related all he knew as they made their way back to the inn where Lydia was staying.

Vestus banged on the door of the house. Not a light showed, and it was obvious that the occupants had long since retired for the night. Again he knocked, this time harder. Finally he saw a lamp at the window and a sleepy servant appeared. "What do you want at this hour?" the man demanded.

"I must see the chief magistrate at once!"

"His Excellency has retired for the night," the servant said in an irritated voice.

"But this is important. A matter of great importance."

The servant hesitated. "He does not like to be awakened," he said. "Can't it wait until morning?"

"Go and wake him. Tell him there is a plot against Caesar. I must see him at once!"

The servant moved away from the window and Vestus could see the light of the lamp moving through the hall. A few moments later he heard the sound of the latch being lifted and the door opened.

"What is this about a plot against Caesar?" a bleary-eyed man demanded.

"I overheard it myself," Vestus replied. "And as a loyal citizen I came to you at once."

"All right, then, come in. But this had better be true. I do not like to be awakened in the middle of the night to be made a fool of."

Vestus followed the chief magistrate to the atrium. "Now what is this plot? Tell me quickly!"

"The Christians, sir. They had a meeting tonight at the home of Jason, the merchant. I heard them say that their King was coming to free them from the yoke of Rome."

"Christians? What are Christians?"

"I know little about them myself, your Excellency. But they are led by that man, Paul. The one who caused trouble here not long ago."

"Oh, that man again! Is he back in Thessalonica?"

"No, sir, but he sent a letter back. He is in Corinth. It was brought by one of the conspirators. I heard it read to them. It was full of subversion."

"Jason's house, you say?"

"Yes, Excellency."

"And this letter, what did it say exactly?"

"It said that this king, a man called Jesus, would very soon come and free them, remove the Roman rule."

"And what else?"

"Most of it was obviously in some sort of code, known only to the Christians. It sounded like foolishness to me but they were very excited about it."

"What is your name, man?"

"Vestus, sir. I deal in dyed fabrics. Fine cloth, perhaps you have heard of—"

"This is very interesting, Pestus. I would like to read this letter for myself."

"Vestus, sir. And I can lead you to the very house of the conspirators, sir. I am a loyal cit—"

"Good! You, there, go fetch the captain of the guard. Have him bring a company of men at once," the chief magistrate ordered a servant.

Then he turned back to Vestus. "Well, Pestus. We shall surround this house and arrest these people. I want to see this subversive letter. And if what you say is true, there should be a reward in it for you, Pestus."

"Vestus, sir. And thank you very much. I'm just trying to be a good citizen."

"Yes. I'm sure you are. And when the soldiers come you will guide them to this house."

"Yes, sir. I will be glad to do that."

Within the hour a company of soldiers had arrived with an officer in charge. Vestus took them to Jason's house and they climbed the wall and surrounded it. Then the captain beat on the door until a servant opened it.

With the point of his sword at the surprised servant's throat the officer forced him back inside the doorway. "Move back inside, man, and be quick about it. You men search the house!"

The soldiers swarmed inside. The occupants were all taken into the atrium where the captain waited. The soldiers searched the house from top to bottom.

"What's the meaning of this?" Jason demanded.

"You should know, old man," the captain replied. "Anyone who plots against Caesar should not ask a question like that."

"What? Plot against Caesar? Me? I know nothing about that!"

"Quiet. You will have your chance to speak. Before the chief magistrate."

Uncas had seen Lydia safely to the door of her room at the inn and had retraced his steps back to Jason's house where he had been invited to stay while he was in Thessalonica. His eyes widened as he saw the soldiers around the house. "What's going on here?" he asked a guard.

"A raid," the soldier told him. "There's a group of rebels in there who are plotting against Caesar. That's all I know."

Uncas turned and walked away. When he was out of the guard's sight he broke into a run, back to the inn and Lydia's room.

"Lydia! Wake up! It's Uncas."

When she opened the door and saw his face she knew immediately something was terribly wrong. "What is it? What's happened?"

"Quick! You have to get out of here. Get your things and come with me."

Lydia hurriedly packed her clothing and Uncas carried her traveling bag as they left the inn. "Down by the mole," he said. "If there is a ship out tomorrow, you must be on it." He told her what he had found on his return to Jason's house.

"A plot against Caesar?" she gasped. "I don't understand!"

"Neither do I, but we can't take any chances. You have to get out of the city. The servants will probably name everyone who was at the house last night. The soldiers will come to the inn looking for you."

"What about you, Uncas? You must come with me to Philippi. I have a friend there, a tribune. If they come to Philippi looking for us, he'll straighten this out. You can't possibly do anyone here any good. Come to Philippi with me."

He thought for a moment. "I suppose you're right. There isn't anything I can do here for them. Perhaps it would be better if I went with you. After things quiet down maybe I can come back and try to do something."

They found a dark cranny on the docks and waited until morning, hoping to find a ship leaving for Neapolis.

Uncas had been right. One of the servants, terrified by the soldiers, told the captain the names of those who had been at the meeting. The officer found the parchment with Paul's letter and with this in his possession, he led Jason and the others to the house of the chief magistrate.

Soldiers were dispatched to round up those named by the terrified servant. Vestus, with a smirk, gave the captain the whereabouts of a lady named Lydia who was one of the chief conspirators. She was at the inn, he told the officer.

Jason was brought alone before the magistrate while his family and servants waited outside. With his wrists chained together, he faced the chief magistrate. "What is this all about?" he demanded to know. "I am a loyal and law-abiding citizen. I have friends in high places. What is the meaning of this?"

"Here is the letter, sir," the captain said, handing the parchment to the magistrate.

"Good. You, there. Be still while I read this! Captain, bring that lamp closer so I can see."

He read the letter from Paul while Jason looked on. Vestus sat smirking in the corner of the room. When the magistrate had finished, he looked up, first at Jason, then at Vestus.

He turned to the officer who had led the search party. "Were any weapons found in the house?"

"No, sir," the officer replied.

"And the others who were at this—ah, meeting, what are their occupations?"

"The servant gave me the details, sir. All that information is right here." He handed the magistrate his report.

The chief magistrate studied the report. "Hmmm. One carpenter, one worker in metal, two men who collect the city's trash, one scullery maid—" He turned to Vestus, his eyes flaming. "You, there, Pestus, or whatever your name is—do these people sound like the types who could overthrow Rome? Remove Caesar from the throne? And this letter from the man named Paul! It is full of utter nonsense! This king, this man who you said is coming back to free them from Roman rule, he died at Jerusalem. A dead man a threat to the emperor? Rubbish!"

He ignored Jason now, his fury directed at Vestus, who backed farther into the corner of the room as the chief magistrate inched forward toward him. "And this King Jesus, the one you said these people were expecting to come back! How? Flying through the clouds! That's how! What foolishness! What utter nonsense! And they all expect to be whisked away in the clouds with Him. And with dead men who come from their graves!"

The chief magistrate clenched his fists. "Guard, seize that man. Take him out and beat him! Teach him not to wake me up in the middle of the night with . . . with poppycock tales such as this!"

"No, wait your Excellency! You don't understand! I was only doing my duty as—"

"Guard!"

Vestus was dragged from the room, screaming his protests. The chief magistrate turned back to Jason. "As there is no law I can find against being insane, I will have to release you. I don't understand what this is all about, but if I were you I would not hold meetings of idiots in my house again. Is that clear?"

"Yes, your Excellency. Perfectly clear."

242

"Then get out of here. Guard, release him and let him go."

Jason and his family and the others who had been arrested went home. As they left they could hear Vestus screaming in the night as the soldiers administered the beating. When it was finally over, Vestus, bleeding and exhausted, crawled home.

"But I'll get even for this," he swore through blood-caked lips. "You, Lydia! I'll get you for this, even if it takes the rest of my life."

As dawn broke and the tide changed, a ship left the harbor. On board were Lydia and Uncas. They had no way of knowing the outcome of the previous night, and it was not until a letter arrived from Jason some weeks later that they could relax and forget the incident.

— Chapter Fifteen —

"Marcellus came here while you were away," Clement told her. "He was very worried that you had gone to Thessalonica by yourself. And he was hurt that you hadn't told him or even said goodbye to him."

Lydia sighed. "I should have. It was thoughtless of me not to have seen him before I left."

"He said to let him know when you returned. He said someone has been trying to find you. Someone you will want to see."

"Oh? Is that all he said? He didn't tell you who it was?"

"No. That's all he'd tell me. You really should go and see him. Or at least let him know you're back."

"You're right, Clement. Would you ask Papie to take him a message for me?"

Lydia wrote a short note to the tribune, and Epaphroditus carried it into town and found Marcellus. "Lydia said to give you this," he told him.

Marcellus hastily read the note, then looked up at Epaphroditus. "Tell your mistress I shall call on her tomorrow afternoon and that there will be someone with me." Papie nodded and returned home. He relayed the message to Lydia.

She frowned. "I wonder what all the secrecy is about. I wonder who he's bringing to see me. Or who in the world would be looking for me."

Early the next afternoon Marcellus rode down the hill. Behind him came an expensive carriage, obviously owned by someone of great means. It was pulled by a matched set of fine, black horses, their coats shining in the sun, and around their necks were harnesses set with golden decorations in the shapes of flowers.

Marcellus dismounted and came forward to greet Lydia who stood by the door. "It's good to see you again," he said rather formally. "I hope you are yourself again and that the gods have answered my prayers for your health." He took her hand and held it a moment before kissing it.

By now the carriage had come to a stop and the door had opened. Out came a young man dressed in the finest of clothing. He walked to where the tribune and Lydia stood and bowed slightly to them.

"Lydia," Marcellus said, "may I present Alsatio Herteles, the man who sold your late husband the gold mine."

Lydia glared at the man who stood before her. "You—you are the man who defrauded my husband?"

He stepped back a pace at her anger and held up his hands. "Madam, I did not defraud anyone! What I sold to your husband was truly what it was understood to be."

"But you told him it was a gold mine! A rich gold mine!"

"That is true. It was. It still is."

"But we found no gold. Only a worthless substance called fool's gold."

"And where is this supposedly worthless substance? May I see it?"

"I no longer have it. It was left at the assayer's office. It was not worth carrying away."

Herteles shook his head. "I would certainly like to have seen it."

Clement had joined the group. "Wait, Lydia. The first nugget Nadius found. I still have it. We decided to keep it as a memento."

Herteles smiled. "Then may I see this nugget? I want very much to look at what that assayer called 'fool's gold.' "

Clement went to get the nugget and Herteles turned to Lydia. "Since I sold the property to your husband I have been away, to Rome and other places. I have just returned, and when I inquired about your husband I learned that he had been killed in an accident at the mine. Then Marcellus told me about what had happened. I am truly sorry, madam. Please believe me, I would defraud no man."

Clement returned and handed the nugget to Herteles. He examined it closely. "This," he said, "is pure gold."

"But the assayer—"

"He is the one who defrauded you, madam. After he told you it was worthless, what did he do with the so-called 'fool's gold'?"

"Why, he swept it into a container. To throw out, I presumed."

"And then he quickly left the city. I have already checked into that. He is the one who defrauded you. He has your fortune."

"Then the mine—it is still worth a great deal of money?"

"A great deal, madam. You could still work it and recover a fortune in gold. It would take more work now that the shaft has collapsed. It would have to be dug out again."

Lydia shook her head. "No. I could never do that. I couldn't bear to look at it again."

"Then you could sell it. In fact, I am willing to pay you three times what your husband paid me for it. I can easily sell it again."

Lydia thought. After a moment she faced Herteles. "That is very generous of you. You are indeed an honest man. A fine man. But I do not want three times the amount. If you will just give me back what Nadius paid you for it, I will sell it back. I want no profit on that sad memory."

"But Lydia," Clement interrupted.

"No. I have made up my mind."

Herteles nodded. "Very well. I shall have the papers drawn up. Tomorrow I'll return with the money."

Herteles boarded his carriage and signaled the driver to ride off. Marcellus turned to Lydia and smiled. "You are an unusual woman, Lydia. A very unusual woman."

"God has been good to me, Marcellus. My business prospers. I have people I love around me. And with the money from the mine I shall purchase this house. With what is left over, I shall expand my business. I need nothing else."

He shook his head sadly. "Nothing else, Lydia?"

"I included you in those around me, Marcellus."

He kissed her gently on the forehead. "I'm glad you did. Then you will not object if I come tonight to call on you?"

She smiled up at him. "If you didn't, I would be very disappointed."

"Then until tonight," he said as he mounted his horse and rode up the dirt trail to the Egnation Way. She watched him, waving as he turned at the top, her heart feeling strange, almost the way it did when she was but a young girl. She turned and skipped back into the house. "Euodia," she called. "Please get my new gown ready. I want to look my very best tonight."

After the message from Jason had been received in Philippi and it was safe to return, Uncas left. Luke, anxious to rejoin Paul and with his presence no longer needed in Philippi, went with him. The congregation at Philippi bade him a sad farewell, but they understood that he must be with Paul, for the apostle suffered from a recurring illness and Luke should be there to take care of him.

The two men went to Neapolis and boarded a ship that would eventually take them to Corinth. As the ship pulled away from the quay, Luke wondered whether he would again see his friends in Philippi, for he sensed the danger in the way ahead, not from the sea but from the ignorance in men's minds and their preference for the darkness of the world rather than the light of God's truth.

Syntyche watched Epaphroditus as he lifted the heavy bucket of dye and poured the contents into the vat. His young muscles rippled in the sunlight, his skin smooth and tanned, and she felt the same skipping of her heart every time she saw him. She had lived in Lydia's house since Orcas and his family had moved out of Philippi to the forests north of the city where he could cut wood. Lydia had helped her fix up the small room next to the storage shed where the dyes and cloth were kept, and she was happier now than she had ever been in her life.

Lydia had even sent Clement to talk with the brothers who had owned her when the demon possessed her. The offer that Lydia made to them was gladly accepted, for she had been useless to them since Paul had exorcised the demon. Then Lydia had set her free and had welcomed her into the household of Christians, telling her that no person should own another.

All had treated her kindly, all except Euodia, that is. It was not that the older woman had been unkind, it was that Euodia had ignored her completely, speaking to her only when it was absolutely necessary to give her instructions about what to do in the kitchen.

But regardless of how anyone treated her, she would have put up with anything just to be near him, this young man about her own age with whom she had fallen deeply in love.

Epaphroditus, however, was completely unaware of this. He had not even noticed that she made sure he received the choicest part of the meat or the most succulent of the vegetables when she served them at meals. But someone else had noticed it, for it had not escaped the watchful eyes of his mother, Euodia. And Euodia bit her lips as the anger rose within her.

Euodia had gone to Lydia about her. She had told Lydia that the girl was no good, that she had never been any good, and that she would never, ever be any good. But Lydia had laughed at her fears and had told her Syntyche was welcome to stay as long as she pleased in her house. Euodia never complained again to Lydia, but the longer the former slave girl was in the house, the more she disliked her. It was not that the girl actually had done anything, but her mother's fear was that her son would fall in love with her, since she was the only girl of his age he came in contact with.

It is a physiological fact that boys mature more slowly than girls, but mature they do. Every boy eventually reaches a stage in life where girls become more than just companions who are different. And eventually this happened to Epaphroditus. One day Syntyche was only a member of the group of people who lived in the same house, but as day dawned the next day, he made a startling discovery, a most disturbing and unexplainable discovery.

On that day, when Syntyche brought him cool water from the well as he worked, and as she smiled at him, he felt a queasy emotion inside himself. He did not know what it was, but it was there. And unlike all the days prior to this one—when she had done the same thing and he had thanked her and gone back to work—this day he looked at her in a much different way as she went back to the house. He noticed how attractive she was, how pretty her golden hair looked, and her blue eyes. Odd, he thought, that he had not noticed these things before.

With the money that Herteles paid her for the mine, Lydia bought the house and the property that ran to the river. That evening as she and Marcellus strolled the banks, she had a fresh feeling in her heart.

"It's good to walk on one's own land," she laughed. "This earth and grass are the same as yesterday, but somehow they feel different today. Today the land is mine, and it is beautiful."

"It's good to hear you laugh again, Lydia. I was afraid there for a while I never would."

She took his arm and looked up at him. "I treated you badly, didn't I? I guess I treated everyone badly. I'm sorry, Marcellus."

They walked in silence for a few moments. Then he pulled her around so that she faced him and kissed her. "Lydia, when are we going to be married?"

She pulled away and looked across the river. A swan paddled along close to the far bank, graceful in the water, his beak dipping into the lily pads to catch the small fish there. In the distance there was a dull flash of lightning as a storm swept along the horizon. When she turned again to face him her eyes were misty.

"If I do marry, Marcellus, there would be no one but you I would rather marry. But right now, I can't."

He breathed deeply and closed his eyes. "And why not?"

"I can't explain it. At least so you would understand. But for now I know it is the right thing."

"This new religion has a lot to do with it, doesn't it?"

She took his hand and patted it gently. "Oh, Marcellus! If you could only see things the way I do now. If you could only know the joy I have now, the certain knowledge that God is with me, always. And that He cares about me and about you and all people. Not only those who believe, but all people."

"I don't want to discuss religion, Lydia. I didn't come here for that. I don't believe in the gods made of wood or carved in stone. That's nonsense for the superstitious. But this invisible God you believe in, I can't bring myself to believe in Him either."

He looked imploringly into her eyes. "Lydia, if there really were a God, then why would He permit such injustice in the world? Why would men kill each other in senseless wars? Why would babies die? If there really were an all-caring, all-knowing, all-powerful God, why would He allow such things?"

She shook her head sadly. "I can't answer those questions, Marcellus. But that doesn't mean He isn't real."

"Then why, Lydia, did He allow your own son to die?" And as soon as he had spoken, he was sorry. He saw the flash of hurt in her eyes as the memories came flooding back. "I'm sorry, Lydia. I shouldn't have asked that."

When she answered, her eyes blazed with a fire he had never seen before. "My son is not dead. He lives. He lives with Jesus and he will live forever."

He looked at her, not really believing what he had heard. "Lydia! Lydia! That man Paul has cast a spell on you! How can you believe such things?"

"I believe them because they are true. I have seen Doronius, Marcellus. I have seen him in the arms of Jesus. And someday I shall be with him. In heaven. For eternity."

"But Lydia!"

"And you, Marcellus, unless you can someday bring yourself to also believe, you will spend eternity in hell!"

He recoiled from her words. "You can't be serious." He looked at her, studied her face. "Lydia, you must be crazy. You are talking nonsense."

"If I am crazy, then I wish this whole world were just as mad! For unless all men turn to God, the true God, and His Son Jesus, they are also doomed, just as you are doomed to an eternity in hell!"

He turned. "I'm leaving. I won't stand here and listen to this nonsense any longer. I can't accept these things you speak of. I am a Roman. A Roman tribune. I was raised on Roman gods. For as much as they are, which I must admit isn't much, at least they do not condemn others to hell for not believing in themselves."

He walked quickly toward the house and mounted his horse. Lydia ran after him shouting, "Marcellus! Wait! You don't understand! It is not God condemning you. You are condemning yourself!"

But he had not heard. He was off in a cloud of dust up the hill and her words echoed back empty and alone.

"They think *what?*" demanded Paul.

Uncas shrugged his shoulders and answered. "They think the Lord is coming back right away. In a matter of a few days or weeks at the most."

"And where did they get that? Certainly I never told them that!"

"I'm sure you didn't mean to give them that impression," Uncas told him, "but they got that idea from your letter to them. Many at Thessalonica have stopped work. They are living on their savings or on the hospitality of a few who will let them."

Paul rubbed his chin. How, he wondered, could the Thessalonians have gotten so far off the track? He would have to straighten them out in a hurry. But he could not leave Corinth, at least not right now. He would have to write another letter to them, one that would set them straight on the coming of the Lord, for no man knew that day. And get them working again, earning their living. He called for writing materials and dictated.

When Timothy had written what Paul told him, Paul took the pen himself and wrote the closing. Then he read aloud what he had included in the letter, the second to the Thessalonian church.

"Let no man deceive you by any means: for that day shall not come, except there be a falling away first, and that man of sin be revealed, the son of perdition . . . ."

He nodded his head as he continued. "For even when we were with you, this we commanded you, that if any would not work, neither should he eat."

Paul finished reading and signed the letter. He had already arranged for one of the Corinthian Christians to carry it to Thessalonica. As the bearer set out, Paul prayed that his message would set straight the unfortunate misconceptions that had arisen. He also knew that all of the young churches would tend to go astray now that he could no longer be with them to personally guide them. He must train men, he concluded, men to be set as pastors over these young churches, men whom he had trained himself.

"Timothy," he announced, "I think it is nearly time for you to take over much of this work."

Syntyche had not planned it but when the opportunity came, she took advantage of it. He had left the house to walk to the river where the cool evening breeze caught the scent of the trees and wafted them along on the moonlit air. She slipped unnoticed out of the house behind him and took the shortcut to the river. She stood close to the trunk of the old acacia tree, and he almost bumped into her as he came around it.

"Oh, I'm sorry! I didn't see you there," he said. The near collision left him standing very close to her, closer than he had ever been before.

"That's all right," she replied, her voice low. "There's room for both of us here."

He was conscious of goose bumps running down his back. "Ah, it's sure dark here," Epaphroditus said. He felt the touch of her arm against his own and he thought how strange it felt, warm and smooth and soft. The scent of her hair was strong as he felt her presence next to him.

"I hope I didn't frighten you, Syntyche. I mean, coming out of the dark and all. I—I, ah . . . ."

"No," she laughed, "you didn't frighten me at all." Her voice sounded strangely like music to his ears, melodic and sweet. Funny, he thought, how he had never noticed that before.

"Papie, look! See how the moon shimmers as it is reflected on the river. Isn't it beautiful? I love to come here at night like this to look at it."

But his eyes were on her in the moonlight, not the river. "Yes, beautiful. The most beautiful thing I've ever seen."

She moved and he felt her hand upon his arm. The tingle went up through his muscles and continued through his shoulder, and he felt it all over his young body. "Come on," she urged, "let's walk along the bank."

They walked along the river, and once where the bank was slippery she lost her footing and fell against him. He put out his arms and caught her. The softness of her young body was next to his, his arms holding her.

"Syntyche, I—"

He did not exactly know how the next thing happened, but their lips were suddenly together and he tasted the sweetest taste he had ever experienced. He drew away his head. "Oh, Syntyche! I'm sorry. I didn't mean to—"

"I'm not," she said and her lips were again pressed against his. Papie's arms tightened around her and they slipped down together on the grass. Her hands were caressing the back of his neck.

"Syntyche," he murmured.

"What, my darling?"

"No—nothing." Now it was Epaphroditus who pressed his mouth to her's, and he kissed her long and passionately. He had lost all track of time. Finally it was Syntyche who had to break away and warn him, both of them actually. "They might miss us back at the house," she said. "We'd better go back."

Reluctantly he let her go and they walked back, hand in hand, until they were close to the house. "Good night," she said and kissed him once more. She entered the door to her room next to the storeroom, and he went into the main house. As he came in, Clement's voice asked, "Is that you, Papie?"

He swallowed hard. "Yes. I'm going to bed now." But as he lay on his pallet, he could not sleep, still tasting her lips, smelling the sweetness of her hair and feeling the tenderness of her skin against his own. Finally, almost to morning, sleep came and he dreamed of her.

Aquila had never felt at home in Corinth. The carnal nature of the city was a constant source of irritation to him since he and his wife had fled persecution in Rome and had settled here. One day he approached Paul. "Priscilla and I feel we should leave this city and establish ourselves elsewhere."

Paul was astonished at this. "But where would you go?"

"Ephesus, perhaps. We have relatives there."

Paul nodded. "I can understand your leaving, my friend. This city is full of sin and corruption. But you will be sorely missed."

"And we shall miss all of you," Aquila replied. "But we really feel this is the time for us to move on. There will come a time when we shall be no longer welcome here, as it was in Rome. Soon we shall be too old to make a change. I believe we would find Ephesus to our liking. Of course, there are many Christians there. We would still have the fellowship of believers."

Paul stroked his chin. "I have long desired to return to Asia and visit the churches there. I would also like to travel once more to Jerusalem. The brothers should be informed of how things are going here in Europe. They may be angry with me for coming here without their permission, but they could not deny God's blessing has been on the work here."

"Then come with us," Aquila said. "You could travel as far as Ephesus with us at least."

"I must pray about it," Paul replied. "Then I can give you my answer, old friend."

In the weeks that followed, Epaphroditus and Syntyche tried to find every opportunity to be alone together. This was not possible every night, for the congregation of Christians met several times each week, and they were both expected to be present at these meetings.

For the past several days, it had not been possible to see each other, and they grew more anxious to be in each other's arms. The chance came during the day when Clement had to go into town and left Papie alone at the vats.

Syntyche carried the freshly filled water jars from the well and took it behind the house to the vats where he was working. "I've brought you a cool drink," she said. A second later, after they had both looked around to make certain no one could see them, they were in each other's arms.

"Oh, Papie," she sighed. "I love you so much." Their lips were together, long and lingering, their arms entwined about each other's body.

Then, from behind, came the unmistakable voice of Euodia. "And how long has this been going on?" she demanded. "You there! Get away from my son!"

"Mother! We were just—"

"I have eyes! I can see what you were doing! I'll deal with you later. But you, young lady—let go of my son! And stay away from him. I won't have some gutter slut like you seducing him!"

"Mother! You can't call her that!"

"Don't tell me what I can call her! She's trash. And I won't let her get her filthy hands on you!"

Syntyche was sobbing. Epaphroditus put his arms around her and held her close. "Now listen to me, Mother. We have done nothing wrong. That is, unless falling in love is wrong. I love Syntyche and she loves me, and you can't call her names. I won't let you!"

Euodia put her hands on her hips and her eyes were fire. "So you have already cast a spell on him? I won't let you get away with this! Get out of here! Now! And don't come back!"

"Wait, Syntyche! She can't do this. This isn't her house."

Euodia shook her fist and screamed at them. "If this harlot doesn't go, then I shall! We'll see whose house this is. Just wait!"

Euodia turned and walked hurriedly toward the main house. "Lydia! Lydia! I must see you right away!"

Lydia listened to the older woman tell her story and make her demands. As Euodia fussed and fumed, it was all Lydia could do to keep from laughing. What the young people had done did not seem the capital offense Euodia was making it out to be. She let Euodia talk herself out, then spoke. "Clement is the leader of our church and Epaphroditus's father. We shall wait until he gets back. He will have to make any decision about sending Syntyche away. She is a sister in Christ and I won't turn her out."

"Sister in Christ?" wailed Euodia. "She is of Satan! She has seduced my son!"

Lydia tried to conceal her smile. "I don't believe your son needed much encouragement," she chuckled. "He is a man now, and men do notice the opposite sex when that time in life comes."

"I will not live in the same house with her," Euodia insisted.

Lydia faced her with a serious look. "You will do exactly what your husband tells you to do," she told Euodia sternly. "He is the head of your household and you will obey him. That was Paul's instructions, not mine. The husband is the head of the wife."

Euodia sat in silence, fuming, until Clement returned.

Paul read the letter from Lydia, which the bearer had delivered to him, telling him of the news from the church at Philippi. The man also had delivered to Paul a purse containing a substantial sum of money. This was what had been left after she bought the property by the river and made some improvements in her vats and equipment. He noted with pleasure that the church there was growing, not only in numbers but in maturity.

He sat back and thought about the churches in Europe. Not only was the congregation at Philippi doing well but the churches in the other cities were also. Timothy and Silas were quite capable now and he could rest easy in the thought of leaving them to take care of the growing young churches.

He had prayed about leaving, about going on to visit Ephesus and the other Asian cities, then traveling on to Jerusalem to confer with the Apostles there. He would also make a full report to the church at Antioch, which had sent him out originally as a missionary. Yes, he decided. When Aquila and Priscilla booked passage for Ephesus, he would travel with them.

"Now wait a moment," Clement told them. "You can't all talk at once." He held up his hand and finally the group was silent. "Now, let me hear what Euodia has to say. Then I'll listen to the rest of you."

Euodia took a deep breath and scowled at Syntyche. "I found them together, kissing. And I don't know what else. Your son,

Clement, was carrying on with this—this no-good girl. I just won't have it! Either she leaves this house or I do!"

Clement held up his hand again. "Now let me get this straight. You saw them kissing. Did you see—actually see—them doing anything else?"

"Well, no. But where there's smoke, there's fire. She's seducing him. He's so young and he knows nothing about the wiles of loose women."

Again Clement's hand went up. "Wait, now! The fact is that you saw them kissing. Nothing else. Right?"

"Yes, but—"

"Thank you, Euodia. That's all for now. Epaphroditus, would you please tell me what has been going on? What is between you and Syntyche?"

The young man's face was flushed and his embarrassment was obvious. "There's not very much to tell. We love each other. We want to get married and we—"

"Over my dead body!" shouted his mother.

"Euodia! Please be quiet!" Clement turned back to his son. "Go on."

"That's about it, Father. We haven't done anything wrong. We were just kissing. Is that wrong?"

"Not that I can see," Clement replied, looking in his wife's direction.

"But there's more than that," Euodia interrupted again. "That girl slept with those two drunken brothers who owned her. Everyone knows all about that! I can't allow my son to marry a—"

"Euodia, shut up!" Clement said firmly. "Now, my dear wife, I want to test your memory. Do you remember, back before we were married, when we walked through the forest one evening and sat watching the sunset near the lake? And do you remember what—"

"Clement! Don't you dare tell anyone about that!"

"I won't, my dear, if you keep your mouth shut and listen to what I have to say. Now to continue. Syntyche, would you like to say anything?"

"Yes, sir. What Epaphroditus has told you is true. We love each other and we want to be married. We did nothing wrong. And as for what I did—what I was forced to do when I was a slave—that also is true. But when Paul came and I heard him speak and became a Christian, he told me God would no longer remember what had happened before. He said I was a new person—a new creation he called it—in Jesus Christ. If God no longer remembers, I don't see why all of you can't forget, as well."

She looked around at them and her eyes finally came to rest on Epaphroditus. "But I don't want to cause trouble. Not for you, not for Lydia, not even for you, Euodia. It would be best for everyone if I left. By morning I'll be gone."

She brushed a tear from her eye and looked at Lydia. "I want to thank all of you, and especially you, Lydia. I never had a family, not one that I can remember anyway. And you—you all have been—" She could not finish the sentence. Her breast heaved as she sobbed, her face buried in her hands. Suddenly she stood up and ran from the room.

"Wait, Syntyche! Wait for me!" Epaphroditus shouted after her. In a flash he burst out of the room to follow her.

Clement shook his head. "Now, wife, I want to talk to you. What that child said about being a new creation is right. She is a new creature in Christ. What she was forced to do before is, well, over and done with. Now listen carefully to me, Euodia. Do you want to lose your son? Because that's exactly what's going to happen. Either you accept Syntyche for what she is today, a sweet and innocent young lady, or don't and lose Papie. The choice is yours."

Her eyes were wide as Clement's words sank in. "I don't want to lose Papie," she cried. "I don't want to lose my son!"

"Then withdraw your statement about the girl. Go on. One or the other. You can't have both."

She suddenly went to her husband and buried her head in his chest. "Oh, Clement! What a fool I've been! If God can forgive and forget, then I should be able to do the same! Please go after them. Tell her I'm sorry."

"You must do that yourself," Clement told her. "I'll go with you, but you must tell her yourself."

He took his wife's hand and together they went to find the young couple, to give their blessing to their plans to marry.

Paul, Aquila and Priscilla said goodbye to Silas and Timothy and the Christians at Corinth as they boarded the ship that would take them to Ephesus. They left Cenchrea, Corinth's port, and sailed without incident across the sea to Asia. Although the trip was pleasant, Paul was anxious to visit the church, and as soon as they had landed he had them off and on the way to the synagogue.

It was the Sabbath and the building was crowded when Paul got up to preach Jesus as the Messiah who had fulfilled all of the Scriptures. He was surprised when the Jews did not oppose him but searched the Scriptures themselves to see that what he was saying was actually true. In fact, this Jewish congregation begged Paul to stay with them, but when the ship sailed the next day he was again on board. He told Aquila he would return, entrusting him and Priscilla to carry on the work at Ephesus with the Christians who already lived there.

The ship sailed, this time bound for Caesarea, the closest port to Jerusalem. When Paul arrived at the Holy City, the streets were crowded with pilgrims, for it was feast time and many Jews had come from all over Judea to be at the temple for it.

Paul met with James and Peter and explained to them what he was doing with the Gentiles in Greece. He received their blessing on his work, much to his surprise and left Jerusalem with a new peace and determination in his heart.

He went from there to Antioch, staying through the winter and spring and well into summer. If he were going to return to Ephesus and from there back to Macedonia and Achaea, he would soon have to start, for the winter meant the passes through the mountains would be blocked with snow. The church at Antioch was sorry to see him go, but they understood his mission. Providing funds for his journey, they wished him well as he left with a farewell dinner the night before.

Little did the faithful of Antioch realize they would see his face no more. Events were forcing the issue, and the apostle was making his last journey through Derbe, Lystra and Iconium. But to Paul, it was a marvelous experience, for in each of these cities were Christian churches, and he could see the results of his years of work bearing much fruit. Souls were being added each month in these churches, adding to the growing congregations of believers, and Paul thanked God for allowing him to see it.

His journey ended at Ephesus, where he was to spend several years.

— Chapter Sixteen —

PHILIPPI, A.D. 54

The news of the death of the Emperor Claudius had reached Philippi. The new Caesar was a young man named Nero, the son of Claudius's wife, Agrippina, who had been adopted by the emperor after much urging by the sly and ruthless Agrippina. Rumors said that the emperor's death was by rather unusual circumstances, some even hinted he had been poisoned by his wife. But there were always rumors abounding and no one in Philippi really cared. This city was far too removed from Rome for this to make any difference.

Clement looked with pride on his two-year-old granddaughter, born to Epaphroditus and Syntyche. He wished Euodia would truly take her daughter-in-law to heart, but the uneasy truce that existed between them was, he conceded, better than open hostility.

In the last few years Lydia's business had flourished beyond her wildest expectation. Her purple cloth was now shipped on a regular basis to all of the cities of Macedonia and Achaia. But when Clement looked at her, his heart was filled with admiration and respect and, at the same time, sorrow. She was still a relatively young woman, grown more attractive with the years, yet he could see that in spite of her protests of being happy she was a lonely and unfulfilled woman.

Marcellus still came to see her regularly and a deep friendship had developed between them. But was friendship enough, Clement wondered? There were times when he looked at her and she was deep in thought.

He could see the hurt in her eyes and the longing for things she could not have. Time had scarred over the wound caused by the loss of her son, but there remained beneath that scar a void, an emptiness, a never-to-be-completed chapter of her life. Clement noticed that when the infrequent news of Paul reached Philippi, she listened with more than the usual interest, and her questions of the traveler who had brought the news were direct and caring. Was he well? Had he suffered any more attacks of his malady? Was he getting enough rest? Questions that to Clement's observant mind were above and beyond the curiosity of even a close friend. His heart ached for this girl whom he had long regarded as more of a daughter than an employer and friend. For Clement knew that if Lydia's heart had been set on Paul, its desires could never be fulfilled.

The church at Philippi had grown. In fact, there was even a branch. Orcas, the former jailer, had converted so many of his friends and his relatives that it had been feasable to establish another church in the community north of the city where they all lived. Under Orcas's care, this was growing still larger and getting ready to spin off still another church. Clement's heart was filled with joy when he saw what the Holy Spirit had accomplished in so little time.

Paul could also look back on what had been accomplished in the few short years of his missionary work. The church at Antioch was strong, so strong, in fact, that it had enabled him to begin his missionary work. Now other churches were doing the same, sending out men to evangelize areas where the word had not yet been taken. Ephesus had sent men to the eastern portions of the land that bordered the Aegean Sea, and many new centers of Christianity had been established.

The churches of Europe were not yet that strong but were growing. The one at Corinth had given Paul much concern, for they had drifted away from the principles he had taught them, setting up factions within their church and following false doctrines. He had written them two letters and had visited them briefly to attempt to straighten out their problems.

Paul's greatest source of pride was the men he had trained to carry on the work. Silas and Timothy had long since been entrusted with major responsibilities, and both had performed well. Apollos, who had been converted by Aquila, was a very successful missionary.

Now young men such as Erastus and Titus were being trained along with Gaius and Aristarchus. It would be through men such as these that the work would be carried on if anything happened to him, Paul was sure.

Luke, the ever faithful physician, stayed with him. In fact, Paul had just recovered from a very serious illness, and it was the care and treatment of Luke that had pulled him through.

But it was not all smooth sailing for the new religion. The church at Ephesus was going through a time of persecution, primarily from the guild of silversmiths who made statues of Diana, the goddess of the city. The impact of the church had seriously affected their business, and they had struck back at the Christians. Gaius and Aristarchus had been seized and dragged into the open theater where a large crowd had gathered.

"Great is Diana of the Ephesians!" the crowd had shouted, and some of them were about to beat the two young men. Some Jews who had witnessed this and who desired to get rid of Paul, encouraged the crowd to go and arrest Paul and bring him there also.

Paul, as soon as he had heard what had happened to his two disciples, tried to get to the arena but was held back by his friends who feared for his life. A Roman official sped to the scene of the riot and addressed the crowd. "Men of Ephesus," he said, "all the world knows that our city is the humble slave of the great Diana, whose image fell from Jupiter. But these men you have dragged here are not thieves, attempting to steal the treasures of her temple, and they have not spoken against our great goddess."

The Roman pointed to Demetrius, the leader of the silversmiths. "Now if Demetrius or any other thinks he has a grievance against any person, the courts are open and the judges are even now sitting. Anyone may take his case before them and be judged in a proper manner.

"But I warn you that such an uproar as this is illegal and may bring down the punishment of Rome. This is a riot, and we will be held accountable. I advise you to go home quickly and think over what I have said."

The threat of the Roman official sobered the crowd. Gaius and Aristarchus were released, and the mob dispersed. But the anger of the silversmiths remained and they were still dangerous to the Christians. That night Paul addressed the congregation of the Ephesian church. "I think it better for all of you, and for the cause of Jesus in this city, that I leave. Since I am the one against whom most of the hatred is held, the situation will be more quickly resolved if I am not here."

The next morning Paul and Luke left, making their way on the road to Troas. Paul hoped to find Titus there, returning from Corinth where Paul had sent him to deliver his second letter to that church. But when the two men arrived at Troas, Titus was nowhere to be found. On the next available ship, Paul and Luke sailed to Neapolis to visit Philippi.

"Lydia! Come quickly! Paul is here!"

She heard Papie's excited voice, and the news made her heart skip a beat. Paul had come back. He was here at last. She had waited so long for this moment, but now that it had arrived, a hundred fears raced through her mind.

How did she look? Should she put on another tunic? Was her hair all right? She wanted to look her very best when he saw her, especially after all these years.

"Lydia! Come on! Paul and Luke are coming down the road." Papie's shouts filled the house again. This time she arose and went to the door. Euodia and Syntyche were already outside, hurrying up the hill to meet them. Clement had come running from the vats. Epaphroditus held his daughter, grinning from ear to ear. "Oh, Lydia! They're here! They're really here!"

She walked slowly to the edge of the road and waited for them. She saw the two women who had raced up the hill embrace the visitors. Clement ran past her, hurrying up the road to hug them also. Then they had come down the hill and Lydia could see his face. Oh, she sighed, he has aged! The years have taken their toll of him. But the eyes! They were still the same, and it was his eyes she looked into as they embraced.

"Lydia! Lydia! How good it is to see you again," Paul said. "Lydia, my child, you are still beautiful!"

Child, she thought? Did he think her a child? Then he released her and grasped Papie's hand. "How you have grown," he beamed. "And who is this charming young lady?"

Epaphroditus held up his daughter and grinned. "This is my daughter, Paula. I hope you do not mind. We named her after you."

"Mind!" Paul roared. "I am delighted!" He took the girl in his arms. "Yes, she looks like Syntyche. She is a beautiful child. I am happy for you both."

Lydia embraced Luke. The wise physician had not missed the look on her face when she had welcomed Paul. "Oh, Luke," she whispered in his ear. "He looks so bad. He has aged so much."

"He has been very ill, Lydia, and as usual works entirely too hard. He has pushed himself to the limit—past it really."

She caught a deep breath. "He's not going to die, is he?"

The physician chuckled. "No, not yet, at least. God will not allow that to happen until his work has been completed."

They all went into the house, and wine was brought out to toast the return of the apostle and Luke to Philippi. Paul wanted to know how every member of the church was. Papie was sent to notify Orcas and his congregation that Paul had returned. The evening brought hordes of people to Lydia's house as all of the Christians came together to welcome him back.

Late that night Luke tugged at Paul's sleeve. "You really ought to rest," he told him. "Lie down for a while."

"Rest? What for? I shall have an eternity to rest! Right now I want to know what is happening in the church here. Rest can wait!"

They talked past midnight and into the wee hours of the morning. Paul was elated as he saw the converts the original members had made. Orcas told him of plans to begin a new church a few miles from where the one he now pastored was located. They sang and talked and prayed until near sunrise. Finally Luke was able to get the exhausted apostle to bed.

Unable to sleep himself, Luke walked down toward the river. He was suddenly aware of a figure beside him. "I can't sleep either," Lydia told him. They sat together on the grass at the riverbank. "It's been a long time," Luke reflected. "Almost three years."

"I know," Lydia agreed. "I counted every day of it."

"And how is the Roman tribune, Marcellus?"

"He is fine. And Tia, the child you treated, is a grown-up little lady now. And very pretty."

"I am glad. She was a dear child. I am very glad for Marcellus's sake that God saw fit to restore her to life."

"I wish Marcellus realized that it was the hand of God. He still will not budge. If only he would find Jesus and the true God. He is not happy. I know what a difference it would make in his life."

"And you are still trying to convert him?"

"He refuses to listen to me. If I as much as mention Jesus he gets angry."

Luke shook his head. "That is a shame. I like Marcellus."

"He is really a good man at heart, Luke. It's just that his background as a Roman—and a rich one at that—and all of his training make it hard for him to change."

"Then you remain friends, that's good. But don't give up on him, Lydia. Pray for his soul."

"I do. Every night. He still loves me. Every few months he asks me again to marry him. But I can't, Luke. As fond of him as I am, I can't marry him."

Luke studied her eyes in the early morning light. "Do you know what I think, Lydia? I think your heart still belongs to Paul."

She lowered her head. "I didn't think it showed."

"You know it's impossible, don't you?"

"Yes, I know that. But I can't help myself. My head tells me to forget him, but my heart won't let me. Does that make any sense to you?"

"Yes, but it doesn't ease your pain any. Paul will never marry, Lydia. He isn't in one place long enough even to consider it. He is married to his work, his mission."

They walked slowly back to the house as the morning's first rooster crowed. "Yes, I know that. Get some sleep, Luke. And, Luke . . . ."

"Yes?"

"He doesn't suspect, does he?"

He smiled and took her hand. "No, Lydia. He doesn't suspect. And I shall never tell him."

She lay in her bed, but sleep refused to come. Just to be near him was something, she thought. She must be content with that.

Marcellus had heard that Paul and Luke were back in Philippi. He wanted to see the doctor again, for he had grown fond of the wise physician when Luke had stayed in Philippi previously. But Marcellus had reservations about meeting Paul. For some reason he could not explain, the thought of meeting him brought on a strange feeling, something very close to fear. Why, he asked himself, should I be anxious about confronting that man?

But he had come and now stood at the door to Lydia's house, and she had taken his arm and was leading him inside. "I know Luke has been wanting to see you again," she told him. "And I want to introduce you to Paul."

Inside, Luke greeted him warmly, and they chatted for a few moments, mostly about Tia, how she was and how she had grown and what she was doing. But the whole time Marcellus's eyes were searching the room, trying to find the man he dreaded to meet. Finally Lydia came back into the room, and he heard her voice. "Come, Paul. I want you to meet Marcellus." Then, suddenly they were face to face.

A rough and powerful hand grasped his own. "I am Paul of Tarsus," a dynamic voice told him. "I have heard much about you from Lydia. I am grateful for what you have done for her."

Marcellus took in the man who stood before him. He was not tall but his body was muscular and heavy. His face was framed by what was once reddish brown hair but was now streaked with gray. His features were large, his face far from handsome. But his eyes! As Marcellus gazed into them it were as though he peered into the very depths of eternity.

Finally he nodded and returned Paul's greeting. "I am Lucius Marcellus," he said. "Lydia has also told me much about you." Their hands pumped and the tribune felt the strength in Paul's hand, not as much of a physical strength as something else, something far beyond mere physical strength. When Paul released his hand, it still tingled and he felt a wave of almost electric vibration course through his arm. "I feel as though I already know you," Marcellus told him.

"Good. Then let us talk," Paul smiled. The tribune felt the magnetism of the man, a strange force that made Paul's presence in the room felt above all others. Paul led him to chairs, and they sat facing each other.

Marcellus had vowed he would not be drawn into a religious discussion. He had made that vow before he had come to Lydia's house. But he heard himself now say to Paul, "This new religion you preach—being a Roman I do not understand it." He tried to recall the words back but he could not. Why, he asked himself, were the first words he had spoken the very thing he had sworn not to discuss?

Paul studied him for a moment before replying. Then, with a half smile on his lips, Paul had said, "Why, tribune, I find that hard to believe. Romans are a very religious people. And as to not understanding it because you are a Roman, I find that stranger still. You see, I am also a Roman. I have been a citizen of Rome since my birth. Yet I find no trouble in comprehending it."

"You are a Roman citizen?"

"And my father before me," Paul answered. "And his father before him."

Marcellus squirmed in the chair. "Perhaps I should have stated it in a different way. I find the idea of there being only one God rather difficult to grasp."

Paul smiled fully now. "But you were born of but one natural father, were you not?"

"Of course, but—"

"Then how does the concept of there being only one Creator cause you difficulty? Can you imagine what a complete hodgepodge would have resulted if a dozen gods had been involved in the creation of the world? What a mess there would have been!"

Paul laughed and continued, and Marcellus had the feeling that he had walked into a trap of his own making. "What of the sun? One god would have wanted it to rise in the west and set in the east. Another desired perhaps that it come up in the south and go down in the north. We would be living in chaos!"

Marcellus tried to find a way out. "I never considered it before," he admitted. "But you tell of this one God having a single Son and sending Him to earth. You also say this Son is equal to God. How can this be? Is that not two gods?"

"I can see your dilemma," Paul said. "But consider it this way. You are standing on a high cliff overlooking the sea. Far out a wave arises and approaches the shore. Faster and faster, higher and higher, it comes until it crashes upon the beach. Then it is gone. Back to the sea."

Marcellus nodded. "Yes. I can picture that. But what—"

"Then tell me this, is the wave separate from the sea or is it a part of the sea?"

Marcellus considered his answer. He had the feeling he was being trapped again. "Well," he finally said, "I guess the wave is part of the sea."

"You are correct. The wave arises and for a short time has an existence separate from the sea, but it still remains a part of the sea. Then, when its separate and distinct existence is over, it returns to the sea. Is that not right?"

"Yes."

"That is what the Son of God is, a wave sent from heaven, having a separate existence from God, the Father, but always being part of God. He came to earth for a brief existence as a man, then, when His role was over and fulfilled, returned to heaven and is indistinguishable from God. He himself said, 'I and my Father are one.' "

Marcellus's brow wrinkled as he thought about what Paul had explained. It did make sense now that Paul had told it in that fashion. For an instant he was on the verge of accepting it, but something within would not let go; it seized his heart with a stony grip and held firm. His old doubts returned; he could not forsake his Roman teachings for this new concept.

"I shall have to think further on this," he told Paul.

The apostle looked into his eyes for a moment, knowing that the tribune had almost come over the line that separated the unbeliever from the Christian—almost, but not quite. Paul turned away sadly. He had many times before brought men to the point where Marcellus had been, only to see them turn aside at the last moment and return to the ideas of ignorance and darkness. Perhaps some day Marcellus would cross that line, but not today. Today he had let his old nature overcome the urging of the Holy Spirit.

For the next month Paul made his headquarters at Lydia's house, but almost every day he ventured out, some days into the city to preach in the agora. But more often he went into the countryside, into the hills around Philippi. There, to plain and simple people, he brought the message of Jesus Christ and salvation. And many of these simple people, farmers, shepherds, woodcutters, ordinary people, believed and were baptized into the faith.

Each night at Lydia's house when Paul would speak and teach, Lydia sat by his feet, holding in her heart the words he spoke to those who had come to hear him. But Marcellus did not come again while Paul stayed in Philippi, for he was afraid he might not be able to resist the power of the man from Tarsus and his message of the Son of God.

Paul could not remain long in Philippi. A month later he announced his decision to go south, to visit the churches at Thessalonica, Berea, Athens and Corinth, where there was still trouble. Titus, who had delivered his last letter to that church, had arrived in Philippi. He had brought both good and bad news. The letter had achieved some success, for the church had heeded Paul's advice and had changed. As Paul had suggested in his letter, they had punished the man who had lived openly in sin among them. But the church was now divided into two groups, those who were for Paul and those who doubted his apostleship and criticized him. He must go there in person and deal with this division.

He went south, following the route he had taken years before, and visited the churches that had been established. He reached Corinth just before winter set in and immediately began to deal with the division within the church. Those who opposed Paul became even more intense in their hatred of him now that he was there in person. He was safe as long as he remained within the city, for they could not touch him there. They waited for Paul to leave Corinth. Then, as he left, they would strike and rid the world of this man.

Lydia's days were full. Her business took most of her time now, and the remainder was spent with her family and with Marcellus. He visited often now that Paul had gone, and he resented the time she must be away from Philippi in her business trips. He was especially upset when he learned she was planning a trip to Corinth. Her explanation was that this was only a natural expansion of her trade, but how much her desire to see Paul again entered into this decision she would not admit, even to herself.

She sailed from Neapolis, and as the ship finally entered the port of Cenchraea, her pulse quickened with the realization that she would soon see him again. She took a carriage the short distance to Corinth from the port and arranged for rooms at the inn not far from the house where Paul and Luke were staying. Once settled in, she sent a message to Paul by a bearer telling him she was there.

Several hours later she answered a knock at the door of her room to find a young man. "I am Tertius," he told her, "a friend and disciple of Paul's. He wishes you to come to his home for dinner, if it is convenient."

"Oh, yes," she smiled. "Please come in. I won't be but a few moments."

When she was ready, Tertius escorted her to a large house near the Jewish synagogue. "And how has Paul been?" she asked him as they walked.

"Quite well. Busy, as usual. He is now writing a long letter to the Christians in Rome. Although he has not visited them, he feels a heavy burden for the church there. I have had the honor to be his secretary in this. I write down what he dictates. His eyes are not good, as you surely know."

"Yes. He has suffered much from the eye disease. Luke is still with him, isn't he?"

"Yes, constantly. I believe Luke is afraid to leave his side, for fear of the return of his old malady, the fever."

"Luke is a true friend. And Timothy, is he also here?"

"No. Timothy is serving several churches. Paul has great confidence in him. I hope he will have the same in me some day."

Lydia smiled at the sober young man. "I am sure he will, Tertius."

They arrived at the house. "Here we are, madam. Let me open the door for you." He rapped twice, then once. A bolt slid back inside and he opened the door. Lydia wondered about this. Was Paul in danger? If not, then why these precautions?

Then Paul's booming voice filled the room. "How good to see you!" His strong arms were about her and he hugged her tightly, pecking her cheek with a fatherly kiss. Too soon for Lydia he released her and held her at arm's length. "And still as pretty as ever. Come, my dear, sit down and tell us all about our brothers and sisters at Philippi. How is little Paula? She should be—let's see—three or is it four years old now?"

"She will be four next month," Lydia told him. "All send their regards and their love. To you and Luke, as well. But where is he?"

"He will be back soon. He has gone off into the woods to replenish his supply of medicinal herbs. He should return shortly."

"And have you resolved the problems here in Corinth? I know they were worrying you when you were with us in Philippi."

Paul smiled but there was little mirth in it. "Some problems cannot be resolved. Not in this life, at least. Luke says I have become the most famous man in the empire. He is joking, of course, but the fact is that there are many my preaching offends. Many would like to see me silenced. Some would have me beaten, a few would prefer me dead. But this is all to be expected. I am not afraid of them. If God is for me, who can stand against me?"

"But you must be careful."

"Oh, I am. Careful to ask God's protection, my dear. You see, nothing can possibly happen to me without God's permission. My life is perfectly safe. I have not yet accomplished all that our Lord had given me to do. Until that time, I have nothing at all to fear, not from man, not from Satan. But I would willingly give my life if it would better serve God to do so."

"There have been several plots against him," Tertius told her. "Even now we have been informed of an attempt on his life when he leaves Corinth next week to travel to Cenchrea."

Lydia's voice was filled with apprehension. "Then you must not go!"

"He will not listen," said Tertius. "All of us, Luke, Timothy and many others, have warned him against making this trip to Jerusalem, but he will not listen to us. Perhaps he will pay more attention to you."

"Please, Paul," she begged. "You must not place your life in jeopardy. You must not go!"

Paul only smiled at her. "What I must do, I must do," he said.

Lydia quickly took care of the business she had in Corinth and spent as much time as possible with Paul. Noticing that the members of Paul's household had paid little attention to housekeeping, she moved from the inn to the room Timothy had occupied until recently. With buckets, mop and scrub brush, Lydia began to put the house in order. The members of the household appreciated this, but what they appreciated even more was the respite from Luke's cooking as Lydia took over that chore as well.

The days flew quickly by, and the day came when Paul and Luke were to leave and journey to Cenchrea by carriage to board the ship for Jerusalem. For the past several months, Paul's house had been watched by two men who took turns sitting in the window of the house across the street. When the carriage arrived that morning and was boarded, this did not go unnoticed by the men across the street.

"It's him," one of the men exclaimed to the other. "And Luke is with him. Quickly, pass the word."

In front of Paul's house, two figures, covered by long traveling robes, waved goodbye to the small group who stood outside the house.

"Farewell Paul," one of the group said. "May God be with you."

"Please come back quickly, Paul. Goodbye, Luke."

"Safe journey, Paul."

They entered and the carriage driver flipped his whip. The team of horses trotted away, down the street and onto the road that led to Cenchrea. It was still early morning and little traffic was on the road. The horses steadied their gait and the miles sped by. Halfway from Corinth to the port the carriage rounded a curve in the desolate and lonely stretch of road. Suddenly the driver saw the road ahead blocked by men on horseback and reined to a halt.

"You, there! Get out of the way and let me pass!" the driver shouted.

One of the horsemen seized the bridle of the lead horse of the carriage. "We want to see one of your passengers," he told the driver.

The carriage was surrounded by the men on horses. One of them opened the door. "Get out!" he commanded. The two figures in traveling robes came out of the carriage.

"What is the meaning of this?" demanded Luke.

"We want the other one," a man said.

The other figure slipped the hood of the robe down. "And what may I do for you gentlemen?" Lydia politely asked them.

The men stared at her. "Where's Paul?" they shouted.

"Paul?" Lydia smiled sweetly. "I know nothing of Paul. I am just a businesswoman returning home," she told them. "I know nothing of any man named Paul."

The astonished men on horses backed their mounts away. They turned and rode briskly back the road from Corinth. But in the meantime Paul and Tertius had already left the city on the northern road, bound for Philippi where Paul would meet Luke. They stayed with Christians all along the journey, and Paul arrived in Philippi a month later than the physician and Lydia.

"And you should have seen their faces," Lydia laughed as she told Paul about the incident on the road to Cenchrea.

"I thought one of them was about to have a seizure, he was so mad," Luke chuckled. "His face was red as fire and he was choking on his words."

With Paul and Tertius were four other young men, one from each of the churches of the towns they had visited on the way to Philippi. Paul asked Clement to name one young man from his church who would go to Jerusalem with him. Each would carry a purse, his church's offering to the mother church in Jerusalem. Paul was anxious for the Jerusalem elders, especially James and Peter, to see for themselves the fine young men of the churches Paul had begun in Europe and who would carry on his work in the future.

They rested for several days, then Paul urged them on, to travel to Neapolis to take ship to Judea. As they were ready to leave, Clement took Paul's hand. "I have a strange feeling about this trip," he told Paul. "I sense that great danger awaits you in Jerusalem. May God protect you."

They boarded a ship at Neapolis bound first for Troas. Paul preached to the Christians there until the ship was ready to sail again. From Troas it went on to Miletus, some twenty-five miles south of Ephesus. Many of the faithful walked that distance to see Paul again and hear his words.

Again they took to the sea, stopping briefly at Rhodes, then to Patara in Lycia. This ship would take them no further and the party boarded another bound for Tyre and then Ptolemais, where they would leave and continue their journey by land. When they left the vessel, they traveled the coastal road to Caesarea where Philip the evangelist lived. His hospitality was welcomed after their long and tiring journey.

Also at Philip's home was the aged prophet, Agabus, the man who had foretold the great famine in the days of Claudius Caesar. As the prophet looked at Paul, his expression changed. He took from Paul the long, linen girdle he wore and tied Paul's hands and feet with it.

"Thus says the Spirit," Agabus intoned, "in this same way shall the Jews of Jerusalem bind the man who owns this girdle and deliver him into the hands of the Romans."

"Paul!" they all shouted, "do not go! Take the warning of the prophet and stay away from Jerusalem!"

But Paul held up his hands. "I am ready not only to be bound but even to die at Jerusalem for Jesus' sake."

They could not dissuade him. The next morning he set off for Jerusalem with Luke and the six young men. They were joined in the trip by a man named Mnason, a Christian, who owned a house in Jerusalem and who invited Paul and the others to find shelter while they were in the Holy City.

— Chapter Seventeen —

JERUSALEM, A.D. 57

Paul had delivered the offerings of the European churches to James at the mother church in Jerusalem. The Lord's brother was astonished at the size of this offering and the devotion of the newly established churches. He was surprised as he talked with the young men Paul had brought with him, for they had a maturity of faith far in advance of their years. Paul told him that all of these young men had been Jews who were converted and that they had also brought their own tithes and offerings for the temple.

James agreed with Paul that this would go far to convince the Jews of Judea that the Christians had not totally forgotten their ties with the old Hebrew faith and the temple of God. When they presented their tithes to the high priest, this should help to heal the rift between the Jews and Christians of the city.

Paul and the young men would have to go through the rites of purification before they could enter the courts to present their offerings. As soon as their discussions with James were over, Paul and his disciples from the European churches began this rite, and when it was completed they entered the temple.

But present in the temple were certain Jews of Asia who had known Paul when he had preached in their cities, and they consulted with one another to see how they could deal with the man they all hated passionately.

The young men who were with Paul were unknown to these Jews of Asia and they suspected them of being Gentiles, for Paul had made it known when they refused to believe him that he would take his message to the Gentiles. They cried out that Paul was profaning the temple by bringing Gentiles into the holy courts, and the cry was taken up by many of the Jerusalem Jews within the courts.

"Men of Israel, help! This man has defiled the temple by bringing Gentiles into it!"

A crowd quickly gathered around Paul. "This man teaches all men everywhere against the law and the temple!"

The mob seized Paul. Some of them beat him with their fists and some with sticks. They dragged him outside into the street. "We have caught a traitor to Israel!" someone shouted.

"Death to the traitor!" came a cry.

"Kill him!" the mob demanded.

Roman troops were always stationed just outside the temple walls, for riots were not unusual in this tempestuous city, and they came quickly at the sound of this disturbance. At the sight of the soldiers the crowd fell back. As it was evident that Paul was the object of the crowd's fury, the soldiers assumed he was a criminal they had caught.

"Seize him!" ordered the Roman decurion, and his men took hold of Paul roughly and put chains about his arms. "Bring him along!" the sergeant ordered, and the soldiers pulled Paul along the street toward the Antonia Tower and its prison.

The crowd followed and Paul was dragged to the steps of the stone fortress near the temple. The captain of the Roman garrison came out when he heard the sound of the crowd and stood at the top of the steps.

"What has this man done?" demanded Lysias, the Roman captain.

Everyone began to shout at once and the captian could not make sense from what was said. He motioned for his men to bring Paul into the tower where criminals were held awaiting trial. But as they pushed Paul through the crowd and up the steps, the mob surged forward beating Paul. When he reached the top of the steps, Paul managed to say to Lysias, "I am a Jew of Tarsus, a citizen of no mean city. I beg you to let me speak to this crowd."

Lysias was amazed at Paul's calmness in the face of danger, and he nodded permission for Paul to address the crowd. Paul raised his hand and his boldness quieted them.

"Men, brethren and fathers, hear my defense which I make to you now . . . ." The crowd was astonished, for Paul spoke to them in Hebrew, their own beloved language and not Greek, which they would have expected. He was obviously a man of learning.

"I am a Jew, born in Tarsus of Cilicia, but was brought up in this city in the school of Gamaliel. I was as zealous for God as all of you are today."

He had captured their interest and attention, for the school of Gamaliel was most prestigious. They would listen to this man. Paul continued, telling them he had at first persecuted Christians. But then, on the road to the city of Damascus, he had met this same Jesus face to face and had been convinced of his error. This same Jesus he had persecuted was actually the Messiah, the Son of God.

He told them he had been sent to preach to the Gentiles. At this they shouted at him again and surged forward, trying to get up the steps at him. "Away with him!" they screamed. "He is not fit to live!"

Lysias, not understanding Hebrew, was totally unaware of what Paul had said. He ordered his men to take Paul inside and flog him, for he still thought him a criminal. But inside, as an officer bound him to the flogging post, Paul asked, "Is it lawful to scourge a man who is a Roman citizen and is yet uncondemned?"

The officer immediately ordered his men to stop, for it was against Roman law to do this, as Paul well knew. He went to his captain and told him that Paul claimed to be a Roman citizen. Lysias returned with the officer and questioned Paul.

"Tell me," he demanded, "are you a Roman?"

"I am," Paul replied.

"Loose him," ordered the Roman captain. He had almost committed a serious mistake, for Roman law protected its citizens scrupulously against false arrest and floggings when the citizen had not been tried fairly under the law. The captain studied the man before him. "I had to pay a large sum of money to be made a citizen of Rome," he told Paul.

"But I have been a citizen from birth," Paul said.

The soldiers brought Paul his clothing and helped him put on his robe and cloak, then took him to a cell. He fully expected to be released as soon as the crowd outside had dispersed.

But he was not set free, for the Jews had filed charges against him and demanded that he be brought before the Sanhedrin. The next day Paul was escorted by the soldiers to the Hall of Polished Stones where the Jewish court sat. Again some people in the street tried to lay hands on him, but the soldiers rescued him and he was brought into the court.

Paul tried to speak in his own behalf but the crowd in the room would not let him. Again they tried to beat him, and finally the soldiers had to shield him with their own bodies. Since it was apparent the mob would not permit the Sanhedrin to hear his case, they took him back to the Antonia Tower.

Paul lay on his straw pallet in his cell that night. He had just fallen asleep when he saw a vision of the Lord standing before him.

Be of good cheer, Paul. As you have testified of me in Jerusalem, so must you bear witness of me in Rome.

It had been nine months since Paul and the young men left Philippi. There had been no news of them and Lydia was concerned. Many had warned him of the danger that awaited him at Jerusalem. Then one day one of the men who had accompanied Paul arrived, and from the look on his face, Lydia knew the news was not good.

"He has been arrested," Simetrius told her. "He is being held by the Romans at Caesarea."

"At least he is still alive," Lydia breathed. "Thank God!"

"He is well enough. But there were at least three plots against his life by the Jews of Jerusalem. But Paul says not to worry. He has seen a vision where the Lord told him he would bear witness in Rome."

"Rome? How will Paul get to Rome when he is a prisoner in Caesarea?"

"I don't know, Lydia. But Paul is certain he will go there. He asks all the churches to pray that the Lord's will be done."

"We shall certainly do that. But is he well? Is Luke with him?"

"Yes. Luke will not leave his side. And Tertius remains with him also. The rest of us Paul has sent back to the churches here. We are to carry on the work."

When Simetrius had departed, back to the church at Thessalonica, Lydia lay on her bed and thought. Paul would need money. So would the others who were with him. She suddenly sat up in bed. "Euodia! Get my clothes together. I am going to Jerusalem."

When she told Clement of her plans, he shook his head vigorously. "It is entirely too late in the year. No ships will be venturing out with winter coming."

"But perhaps one might," Lydia reasoned. "I want to get there as quickly as possible. He may be in need."

"You will have to wait until spring. Winter storms are treacherous. No ship's captain with good sense would venture out and risk them."

Lydia took a deep breath. "I'll go to Neapolis anyway. Just in case. If no ships will sail I can't help it, but I want to see for myself."

"Then I'll go as far as Neapolis with you," Clement told her. "But you will be disappointed. No ships will be venturing that far."

The next day Lydia and Clement rode to Neapolis in a hired carriage. They went directly to the quay and inquired of any ship going to Caesarea. It was late in the day and they had found none so far. "You see, Lydia, it is no use. Let's go home."

"There are still a few ships at the far end of the quay we haven't tried. I won't go back until I have asked all of them."

They approached the next ship at the dock and Lydia hailed a crewman. The man called the captain and Lydia asked him, "Will you be sailing anywhere in the direction of Judea?"

The man laughed. "Judea? Not at this time of year. But there is a fool up there who is going as far as Paphos on Cyprus."

"Where's his ship?" Lydia inquired. "I'd like to speak to him."

They followed his directions, and Clement went aboard to find the captain while Lydia waited on the quay. As soon as Clement had boarded this ship, he didn't like the looks of it. The timbers were rotted and the whole ship gave the impression of a lack of maintenance. But he found the captain and they went ashore to talk with Lydia.

"I want to go to Judea," Lydia told him. "I understand this ship will sail for Cyprus. Will you take me as a passenger? I might find a ship there to take me the rest of the way."

The captain peered at her through bloodshot eyes. It was apparent he had been sleeping off the effects of too much wine when Clement woke him. "This is no passenger ship, lady."

"I don't care about that. I want to go to Cyprus with you. Will you take me?"

"Lady, if you want to go to Cyprus, I'll take you. But there's no facilities on board for women. And no guarantee you'll find a ship in Paphos going to Judea."

"I understand that. When do you sail?"

"Day after tomorrow. If the weather's good."

"I'll be ready," Lydia told him. "And I'll be on board when you sail."

Antonius Felix, the Roman procurator of Judea, had been born a slave. But possessing a natural aptitude for survival and getting ahead, he had managed to win his freedom. Then, after looking over the men of Rome who were on the upward move, he had attached himself to Claudius, then only a minor official in the tax office. But Claudius was in the blood line of the caesars and Felix had bet on the right man. After Caligula was murdered by the praetorian guard, Claudius was made emperor and Felix's gamble had paid off.

For many years he was chief aide and personal confidant to the emperor, but when he saw events shaping up in Rome that were unfavorable, he called in hs debts and was made procurator of Judea. In addition, he had married a young woman of royal blood, a princess of Jewish aristocracy. Drusilla, not yet twenty years old, had been raised in the decadent and permissive society of Rome.

She cared nothing at all about her own people, the Jews, or for the Jewish religion.

Lysias had sent Paul to Caesarea under strong guard, for he had been warned of an attempt on Paul's life. With him went a letter written by Lysias to Felix to explain why he was sending the prisoner to him. When Felix read this, his curiosity was aroused. The Jewish leaders came to Caesarea, bringing with them a lawyer named Tertullus, to plead their case against Paul. But the charges they brought were so patently absurd that the proconsul knew immediately that Paul was an innocent man. But to satisfy the Jews he reserved judgment and kept Paul a prisoner in Caesarea.

Paul was not confined in a cell but allowed to come and go as he pleased in the company of a soldier to whom he was chained. His friends were freely allowed to visit him. Felix, never one to overlook an opportunity, kept Paul in the hope that one side or the other would offer him a sizeable bribe either to release or convict the man.

Lydia rented a room at the inn near the waterfront to await the sailing of the ship. Clement tried to reason with her, but his pleas were to no avail. "This is madness, Lydia. I don't like the looks of the ship, the captain or the crew, to say nothing of the weather. Please forget this folly. At least wait until spring."

But Lydia would not listen to him. Clement did not know what to do. He was convinced that her decision would mean disaster. Perhaps she would listen to Marcellus, he thought. If he returned to Philippi right away, he would have time to bring Marcellus back before the ship sailed.

Leaving Lydia at the inn but not revealing his plans, he raced back to Philippi and found the tribune in the agora.

"Clement," Marcellus said, "what brings you here?"

"It's Lydia. She is setting out for Judea to see Paul. I can't change her mind. The ship sails the day after tomorrow. It has a drunken captain, a motley crew and planking that certainly could never weather a storm. Can you go back to Neapolis with me? Maybe you can talk some sense into her."

Marcellus listened in disbelief. "It would be suicide for her to sail! Of course I'll go with you." It was too late that evening to ride to the port. Since Lydia would not be leaving for two days, the men started out early the following morning.

Marcellus's carriage picked up Clement. As soon as he had closed the door, the driver flicked his whip and they were off at a gallop toward Neapolis.

Lydia answered the knock on her door to find a seaman. "The captain says to come right now if you want to sail with us. We changed plans. We're sailing today instead of tomorrow."

She threw her belongings into her traveling bag and returned to the ship with the man. After her bag had been stowed aboard, the plank that served as a gangway was removed and they cast off the lines.

"What's happened to make you change plans so suddenly?" Lydia asked the captain.

He frowned at her question. "Tide's right," he said, but the look on his face indicated there was more to it than that.

As Lydia walked about the small ship, the stench from below offended her nostrils. She unfolded a blanket next to the rail and sat down while the ship was rowed out into open water where the sails could be raised.

"They certainly seem to be in a great hurry," Lydia said to herself. In a few minutes they cleared the breakwater, and the dirty and torn sails were raised. As the wind filled them she saw the familiar skyline of the port disappear. She had sailed from

Neapolis many times, several trips to Mytilene due east and many times southward to Thessalonica and the Greek cities beyond.

They were almost out of sight when Lydia saw something glint in the early sun, something on the dock. It looked like the metal of a Roman soldier's breastplate. Then she could make out other men running on the quay. They did indeed appear to be soldiers. She wondered what they were doing on the dock.

Back on the quay the centurion looked at the ship fading in the distance. He had been too late to keep the ship from sailing. The men who had robbed and killed the merchant had escaped. The report he had received indicated the captain and several of the crew of that ship had done this. He shook his fist at the small, dingy blotch on the horizon.

Lydia's first cause for concern came when the ship turned to follow the coast southward instead of out into the open sea toward the islands of the Aegean. Perhaps the captain was taking this course to catch some hidden current. But as the day wore on and they still made way to the south, she really began to worry.

"Captain," he asked, "why are we heading south?" The man looked at her, surprised that she could recognize the direction. "We should be heading east toward Samothrace."

He smiled at her with his black, rotted teeth and turned away without answering. Lydia sat back down on the blanket. Perhaps Clement had been right, she thought. Something was definitely wrong. When it began to grow dark, she wrapped her robes around herself as she lay on the breezy deck and tried to ignore the brazen looks of the crewmen as they passed her.

Just before the blackness of night fell, the ship pulled into a cove to anchor for the night. Cooking fires had been lit on the afterdeck, and she smelled meat roasting on spits over these fires. At least she would not go hungry, she thought.

But no one came to bring her dinner and she was not asked to go aft where the crew was already enjoying the meal. Then the captain lurched out of the darkness and she saw him reach something toward her.

"Here you are, Darlin'. We'll eat our dinner together and get good and friendly. Real chummy, you might say. And later on tonight, we'll get even closer, if you know what I mean!"

As she took the roasted joint of meat from him her eyes were wide with fear as she realized his intentions.

"She isn't here," Clement told Marcellus. "The innkeeper said she left early this morning with a seaman."

"Then we must hurry to the docks. By the gods! I hope that ship hasn't left yet!" Marcellus said as they left the inn. But when they reached the quay where the ship had been moored, it was empty.

"You there!" Clement called to a seaman on the dock. "When did the ship that was tied up here leave?"

"This morning, sir," the sailor answered, and seeing a Roman officer was with him, he went on. "The authorities are very interested in that ship. Soldiers came just as it was going over the horizon."

Marcellus and Clement exchanged glances. "Was a young lady on board when it sailed?"

"Oh, yes. She boarded just as they was casting off. A fine lady. Dressed real nice."

"Come on," Marcellus said, "we have to find the military commander here." They hurried away into the downtown area of the city to the office of the Roman commander of the troops stationed in Neapolis.

Two hours later Clement was on his way back to Philippi. With Lydia gone it was his responsibility to run the business. They had found the Roman troop commander and had learned that the captain and crew of the ship had murdered a man in the city and had robbed him. The commander was horrified when he was told that a woman had sailed as a passenger on the ship. And when Marcellus informed him that the woman was his fiancée, he put his troops at the tribune's disposal.

There had been a Roman ship in the harbor, a small fast ship. An hour later Marcellus was on board with a complement of troops and cast off to try to overtake the killer's ship.

At the quay, just before they had cast off the lines, a merchant captain told them the captain had stated he was heading for Cyprus. The captain of the Roman ship doubted this, however. "These kind always tell people they are heading for one destination, then set a course the opposite direction."

"Then where do you think they've gone?" asked Marcellus.

"My guess is south. There are many hidden coves along the coast to the south. Many of these pirates use them to hide away in."

They headed south and Marcellus hoped the Roman captain's guess was correct. If not, they would never find the ship—or Lydia. The breeze filled the sails as the small ship jumped through the blue waters, skirting the coastline as closely as possible. A watch was set and the Roman crewmen strained their eyes for any glimpse of a ship in the many coves and inlets they passed.

"If they've entered an inlet that curves back, we'll never see them," the captain told Marcellus. "But we have no choice. It would take us a year to enter and search every one of them."

When darkness began to fall the captain of the Roman ship wanted to put into one of the small bays for the night. "We can't search for them in the dark," he said. "And if they're in a cove, we would pass it without even knowing. They are probably at anchor right now as well. We have a better chance of finding them in the morning."

So they entered a small inlet and dropped anchor for the night. The Romans lit their cooking fires and fed the crew. Marcellus was not hungry. He stood at the rail, staring out into the darkness.

"I'll find you, Lydia. If it takes the rest of my life, I'll find you."

As the first ray of the morning light struck the mast of the pirate ship, Lydia stirred slightly and moaned. She tried to open her eyes but only one of them responded, the other swollen shut where the captain had struck her with his fist.

At first she could not remember where she was. But then the horrible events of the night flooded into her mind and she prayed they were not real but a terrible nightmare. Then she felt the ache in her body and realized they had not been a ghastly dream. They had been real.

She pulled on what was left of her torn clothing and tried to sit up. Every bone ached, every muscle was sore where she had fought desperately. Her face felt swollen and she tasted dried blood in her mouth.

From above on deck she heard the voice of the captain. "Hoist the anchor!" She felt the movement of the ship getting underway, moving out of the cove where they had spent the night. Suddenly she realized she would never set foot on land again. They would use her, use her body, until they had to come into some port. Then she would be killed, thrown overboard for sharks to devour. What a fool she had been! Why hadn't she listened to Clement?

Lydia lay back in the darkness and closed her eyes. Fervently she prayed, "Dear Lord Jesus, please get me out of this. Somehow, get me out of this. I want to live."

The Roman ship had also been underway since first light, following the coastline southward. Marcellus and the captain stood on the steering deck while the watch kept lookout for the sign of any vessel. Then came a cry from a forward crewman.

"Sail! Sail!" All eyes strained to catch sight of it.

The Roman captain pointed. "There! There it is. Dead ahead." He was pointing to an almost invisible spot on the horizon. They watched as the white spot grew larger. A man in the crow's nest shouted down.

"She's heading this way!"

As the ships approached close enough for recognition, the captain shook his head. "That's a merchantman. Too large to be the pirate."

Marcellus watched the ship pass. His heart sank. It was an honest trader on her way north. The crews exchanged waves as they passed within a few hundred yards.

The hours droned on and the sun climbed higher in the sky. The captain turned to the tribune. "There's always the chance the pirate stayed in a cove and we passed him. We may be too far south now."

"Or," replied Marcellus, "that he didn't come south at all."

"That's a possibility as well," the captain admitted.

"What do you advise, captain?"

The Roman officer stroked his chin. "From the description we got of the ship, I'd say we'd overhaul them by noon if they're still south of us. If by then we don't spot them, I think we should head back up the coast. If they're behind us, we'll find them."

"I'll abide by your judgment, captain," Marcellus told him.

The sun rose higher in the sky. No more ships were seen by the watch. When the sun stood directly above them, the captain turned to the tribune. "We should turn back," he said. "My original guess was probably wrong. I'm sorry."

"You did your best, captain. You used your best judgment."

The order to come about was given and the ship began to swing. Now they would have to tack against the wind. Marcellus felt a deep sense of frustration. Why had this happened? To Lydia? A sweet and decent woman who had never harmed anyone. It was not fair! She didn't deserve this!

The salt from the spray of the sea was mingled with the salt from the tears which ran down his cheeks. He would never see her again, he realized. They would kill her, they would throw her body to the sharks. But first they would— He shuddered as he thought about what had probably already happened to her. And he could do nothing, nothing at all!

He raised his eyes to the clouds, fluffy and white as they drifted along against the deep blue of the Aegean sky. Then, from deep inside himself, he felt a surge of emotion.

"God," he said, "if you are real, then why did you let this happen?" He heard his words hurled back to him in the breeze. He wiped the tears from his eyes with the back of his hand, then clenched his hand into a fist and shook it at the sky.

"If you are really there," he shouted, "if you are really God, then do something! Lydia believes in you! If you are the all-powerful God that Paul believes in, then save her! Show that you are God! I beg of you."

Then he was sobbing as he stood by the rail. The Roman captain saw this and his heart went out to the tribune. He would feel the same if it had been his own fiancée who had been taken by pirates. He wished he knew what to do, what to say. But he could think of nothing that would help. He walked quietly away, giving the tribune privacy for his grief.

The ship had completed the turn and was tacking out to sea. High on the mast a crewman wiped his eyes and stared hard. Was it really something on the horizon? He waited until he was certain his eyes were not playing tricks. Then it grew larger. A sail.

"Sail," he shouted. "Sail, there, sir."

At about the same time a lookout on the pirate ship called out a warning. "Ship ahead!"

The captain scanned the horizon and picked it up, a small spot of white against the blue. "Port your helm," he told the steersman. "I want some running room. Bring us out farther from shore." Then he called to the man on deck. "Can you make her out yet?"

The crewman squinted. "I think she's a trader. Maybe a Roman militia, though. Can't tell for sure, but she's small."

The pirate captain nodded. He would hold his course and wait for identification. If this ship were coming from the north he would have been worried, but this was heading toward him from the south. It could hardly be anyone looking for his ship. But it would pay to be careful anyway.

"I can make her out now," the crow's-nest shouted. "She's a Roman."

"Get that woman below," he ordered. "I don't want her on deck screaming. Put her back down in the hold."

A crewman seized her and forced her down a hatch. She fell roughly on top of crates and boxes. At first her eyes could make nothing out, but as she became accustomed to the darkness she could see barrels, jars and all sorts of containers in the hold. She found a small empty spot and lay down there.

"Lord," she prayed, "help me. Dear Jesus, help me."

Marcellus could see the ship plainly now. It fitted the description they had been given on the quay at Neapolis. He buckled on the sword he had been given, feeling the hilt, cool and firm, in the scabbard. The captain explained to him what he intended to do. They would pass the ship, as close as possible, to inspect it. Then he would swing around and with the wind again at his back, he would catch the slower ship. Grappling hooks would be used to pull the ships close together and the Roman soldiers, now hidden below deck, would storm the pirate.

The ships grew closer. The Roman captain stood on the steering deck, looking as unconcerned as possible. As they passed, he waved to the captain of the other ship, a friendly greeting which was returned. Then, just as the Roman ship cleared the stern of the pirate, the captain gave the order. "Port your helm. Bring us around. Deck crew, full sail. Boarding party, stand by to throw grappling hooks. Archers, stand ready!"

They were less than two hundred yards behind the pirate now and gaining, standing slightly to starboard of her. Then they were alongside and the heavy hooks were thrown, catching the rigging and rails of the ship.

Aboard the pirate, the crew tried desperately to cut loose the ropes fastened to the hooks before the ships could be pulled together. The Roman archers were ready for this and set loose a torrent of arrows upon the deck of the pirate. The lines were drawn tight and the ships were locked together.

Marcellus stood at the rail with the boarding party. "Board!" came the order. Marcellus leaped across the short span between the ships and landed squarely on the pirate's deck. He was conscious of other Romans landing beside him. His sword was drawn and he charged forward, toward a group of crewmen huddled behind the rigging as protection against the archers. He saw a man straight ahead and his sword thrust out. He felt it strike home and heard the grunt of the man as he went down.

Marcellus looked about. The deck was covered with Roman soldiers, thrusting, hacking at the pirates. It was all over in a moment. Marcellus seized a pirate crewman by the neck. "The woman!" he demanded. "Where is she?"

The man's eyes bulged as Marcellus's grip tightened around his throat. "There," he gulped, "down in the hold."

Marcellus flung open the hatch cover. "Lydia!" he shouted. "Are you in there?"

For a few seconds there was no answer. Then from the bowels of the ship came a voice. "Yes. I'm down here." Her voice was weak, almost a moan. Quickly he vaulted down through the hatch and into the hold.

"Lydia! Where are you?"

"Here. Oh, thank God! Is that you, Marcellus?"

He held her in his arms, tenderly. "Oh, my darling."

His lips tasted the blood on her face as he kissed her. "Oh, Marcellus, how did you get here? How did you ever find me?"

"Don't worry about that now," he whispered in her ear. "All that matters is that you're alive."

She was sobbing now in his arms. "They—they did horrible things to me. They beat me. They made me—"

He pressed her close. "Shhhhh! Don't even think about it. All that matters is that you're alive and I've found you. And never again will I let you leave me. Not for a single day. Do you hear me?"

She hugged him tighter now, feeling the warmth of his body and letting his love ease the pain she felt deep down inside.

— Chapter Eighteen —

JERUSALEM, A.D. 59

Paul had spent two years in Caesarea while he awaited trial before Felix. His ministry was almost at a standstill during this time, and only the thought of the young men he had trained to carry on his work sustained him. His friends begged Felix to release him but were refused. The Jewish leaders also had come to the Roman proconsul. They had demanded Paul's execution. They, too, were refused.

Money had arrived from Lydia and from the churches in Asia and Europe, providing well for him during his confinement. But Paul grew tired of waiting. The Lord had promised him he would bear witness in Rome, and he was anxious to get on with it.

One day extraordinary news arrived. Antonius Felix had been recalled to Rome to stand before Nero, the young emperor, and answer charges of mismanagement of the affairs of the province. A new Roman governor was on the way, a man named Festus. Perhaps now, thought Paul, something will happen and I shall go to Rome.

Festus arrived in Caesarea but spent only a few days there before he was off to Jerusalem. He was anxious to meet the Jewish leaders and to determine for himself the source of trouble in this rebellious province. When he arrived and met with them, he fully expected to hear complaints against Roman rule and

Roman taxes. He was totally surprised when their chief complaint was about a prisoner in Caesarea named Paul, a man he had never even heard of.

Festus was eager to please the Jewish leaders and he promised, "As soon as I return to Caesarea, I shall look into this matter and bring it to a quick resolution."

They had asked that Paul be brought back to Jerusalem to stand trial before the Sanhedrin, but Festus surmised something else was in their minds. Indeed it was, for they had planned to murder Paul as soon as he entered the city.

"It is not the custom of Romans," he told them, "to punish any man until he has received a fair and honest trial. Come back with me to Caesarea and I shall hear what you charge against him before I decide what to do with him."

The next day they accompanied Festus to Caesarea and Paul was brought before his accusers. Festus listened to the charges, his brow knotted. They all seemed to do with religion and not with any crime against Rome. Finally he turned to Paul and asked, "Are you willing to go to Jerusalem and stand before me there?"

Paul answered quickly. "Against the Jews I have done no wrong, as you very well know. But if I have sinned against Roman law and have done anything that deserves death, I am ready to die. But if none of these things is true with which they accuse me, no man can give me up to them, for I appeal to Caesar."

Festus was amazed. He knew no Roman citizen could be denied that right—to appeal to Caesar. After a quick conference with his advisers, he faced Paul again. "If you have appealed to Caesar, then to Caesar you shall go."

Paul was led back to prison and Festus turned to Agrippa with a puzzled look on his face. "This man might have been set free if he had not appealed to Caesar," Agrippa said to Festus.

Several days later Paul was given over to the custody of a centurion named Julius, and with a company of soldiers and other prisoners bound for Rome, he was taken aboard a ship sailing for the port of Myra on the Lycian coast.

On the same ship went Luke and Aristarchus as paid passengers. At Myra they changed ships, boarding a grain ship bound for Italy. Luke stayed with Paul while Aristarchus was persuaded to return home to give word to the churches of Europe of what was happening with Paul.

The years had passed quickly for Lydia. For several months after her ordeal with the pirates she had become morose and withdrawn, but the attention of her family and the love of Marcellus had restored her. Epaphroditus had now taken over the operation of the business, freeing his father to work full time pastoring the growing church. Reports came every few months from Judea on Paul. At every service at the house by the river, prayers were said for Paul and his safety.

It was during just such a meeting that Aristarchus arrived at the house with the news that Paul was even then on his way to Rome. The church, not certain what this would mean, thanked God for Paul's safety and that his hope of witnessing for the Lord in Rome was about to come true.

"It is certain that when he appears before Caesar he will be released," Aristarchus told them. "Even the centurion who is taking him to Rome knows Paul is not guilty of any crime. Soon he will be with us again."

Lydia was thrilled at the good news. It had been so long since she had seen him, heard his voice, touched his arm. Certainly by spring he would be in Philippi again.

But Lydia's hopes were not to be. The ship bound for Italy was shipwrecked in a storm and Paul, Luke and the rest of the passengers spent the winter on the island of Malta. Then, when finally they arrived in Rome, Paul remained in Roman custody to await his hearing before Nero. It was to be two years before Nero found it convenient to hear his case.

"But Lydia," Epaphroditus insisted, "there is no reason I cannot go. Byrtra can easily take charge dyeing the cloth and there are others who can handle the things I have done. Besides, it will be for only a short time."

Lydia looked into his pleading eyes. Yes, she thought, you are really the one who should take the money to Paul in Rome. If I cannot go myself, then you should go, no matter what it means to us here. She turned to him, taking his strong, young hands in hers. "Very well. Go. And God go with you."

The next week found Papie saying farewell to his wife, daughter, family and friends and beginning the journey to Rome. From the port of Neapolis he boarded the ship, the purse from the church tucked safely away beneath his traveling robes. He watched the shoreline recede, then turned his face to the sea. His heart beat faster as his adventure began, one that nearly resulted in his death.

When Epaphroditus arrived in Rome he found he was not the only young man who had come to the aging apostle's side. Timothy, Mark, Tychicus, Demas, Thophimus, Titus and Epaphras were there in addition to the ever faithful physician, Luke. The purse he brought enabled the group to rent a large house, and Paul was free to come and go as he pleased, as long as he was chained to one of the praetorian guards who watched him night and day.

Soon Epaphroditus was caught up in the evangelistic spirit of the group, and he accompanied them as they preached on street corners and in the marketplaces of the city. Then, when he had gained sufficient confidence, he began to preach himself and found he enjoyed it. From early morning until late at night he went, speaking to anyone who would listen. Luke cautioned him to take better care of himself, but his words of advice went unheeded.

Papie's tall, lean body became thinner and his face was gaunt from lack of rest. One evening as he preached, a storm struck, drenching him to the skin. But as long as one person stayed to hear him, he would not go home and get out of the cold rain. Late that night he arrived back at the house, his face ashen and his eyes glassy.

"I . . . I don't feel well," he said and collapsed into Luke's arms.

"Hurry," the physician shouted to Timothy. "Help me get him into bed." Luke felt his head. "He's burning up with fever!"

All night Luke attended him as his fever raged. The cold cloths and the potions did not help. The group joined in prayer for their seriously ill comrade, but still he drifted closer and closer to death.

But he lived through the night and the next day. For over a week he lay between life and death. Then the prayers and Luke's medicine began to effect an improvement in his condition. This was slow, painfully slow, and he lay for two months too weak to arise from his bed.

Finally he recovered and the group rejoiced. Even the praetorian guards were glad to see this pleasant young man up and around again. One of them came to Luke and told him, "If I had been that sick, I would have lain in the barracks and died. My fellow soldiers would not have given me the care you gave to him."

Luke smiled at the big soldier. "Our Lord commanded us to love one another," he told him.

The soldier nodded. "And it would be a far better world if all men obeyed that commandment. I think I am beginning to believe in this God of yours."

"No, Papie," Paul told him, "I think it better that you return to Philippi. In fact, I have long desired to write a letter to the church there and you will be able to take it for me."

"But Paul, I wish to serve the Lord. Please let me stay in Rome with you."

Paul shook his head and smiled. "Do you think you will serve Him less back with the church at Philippi? And with your family? When the letter is finished, I ask you to take it to your father for me. Will you do this? Remember, God uses men right where they are. And right now you belong in Philippi."

Epaphroditus lowered his eyes, disappointed. "Yes. I will do whatever you ask."

Paul called for Timothy to bring the ink pot and quill and began to dictate the letter that would later be known as Paul's Epistle to the Philippians. "Paul and Timothy, the servants of Jesus Christ, to all the saints in Christ Jesus which are in Philippi . . . ."

On he wrote, extolling the faithful to remain firm in their belief, cautioning them against false teachings, thanking them for the gifts, and explaining to them that Epaphroditus had been seriously ill as a result of his zeal in preaching the Word of the Lord. Paul praised Papie highly in his letter and told the church at Philippi to receive him in high honor for the work he had done in Rome.

Then Paul remembered what Epaphroditus had told him about the ill feelings that his mother had for his wife and he wrote, "I beseech Euodia and Syntyche, that they be of the same mind in the Lord. And I entreat you also, help those women who labored with me in the gospel and with Clement also, and with others of my fellow laborers, whose names are in the book of life."

Paul finished dictating the letter and signed it. When it was sealed, he handed it to Epaphroditus. He grasped the young man's hand. "Now go, and may God be with you, Papie." Paul's eyes misted over as he embraced him. "And give my love to Lydia. Thank her for me in the name of the Lord for all she has done."

Paul threw himself into the task of strengthening the growing church at Rome, which even now had penetrated the very household of Nero. Through the praetorian guards who had first come to respect Paul, then to love him, and finally to accept Jesus as their Savior, other members of Caesar's house came to Paul to hear and to believe.

For the first year of his stay in Rome, Paul saw tremendous advance not only in the Roman church but in all of the congregations. But the following year, A.D. 62, brought horrible news. James had been murdered in Jerusalem, thrown from the highest pinnacle of the temple by the high priests, then clubbed by those in the street until his life was gone from his body. When this news came, it brought a change in Paul. He knew now that there would be little time left to accomplish his mission before a horrible persecution would fall on them.

"So much to be done," he sighed, "and so little time to do it."

Luke tried to comfort Paul. "Why do you say that? Much has already been done."

"I feel in my bones, Luke, that bloody times are just ahead. I am weary, so weary, old friend. It has been a long race. But in the time left there is much which must be done before I can cross the finish line and lay down to rest."

He called for Timothy to bring the ink and quill again. He felt an urgent need to communicate with the churches, to warn them of the coming hard times, to exhort them to stay steadfast in their faith. He wrote to the churches at Colossae and Ephesus, and sent a personal letter to a man named Philemon in whose home the Colossian church met.

Paul dispatched Titus and Timothy to deliver these letters and to remain to minister to those churches. Again Luke tried to slow him down, for the pace was beginning to take its toll on the apostle. "No, my friend, soon there will be time to rest." He looked seriously at the kind physician. "Soon there will be none of us left. Others must be ready to take our place. Trouble me not with your advice to rest, old friend. I know you mean well, but there is too much remaining to be done. The work cannot wait."

And Paul did not spare himself. During that year he worked even harder, as the squirrel who senses winter upon him races to store sufficient food for the time when the snows make all work impossible.

Then in A.D. 63 the word came that Nero would hear Paul's case. Dressed in the best clothing he owned, Paul was taken to the hall where Caesar would listen to the charges against Paul and Paul's defense against them.

In the marble splendor of the hall he waited, chained to his guard. Other Roman citizens were there who had appealed to Caesar. But the personification of Roman justice was late, and Nero kept them waiting for hours.

At last the trumpet sounded the approach of the emperor and all within the hall of justice rose in respect. Paul saw Nero for the first time, a young man yet in his twenties but bloated by dissipation until he resembled an obese and disgusting clown.

Paul's case was not the first to be called, and he listened with interest as Nero heard them. He was dismayed at the verdicts that the dispenser of justice handed down, for there seemed to be no correlation between the evidence and the judgment. One man had been very obviously guilty, but Nero found him innocent. Two others had been obviously innocent, and the emperor's verdict was guilty. Despite the fact that these two had been charged with minor crimes, Nero had them put to death.

Then it was Paul who was called to the front, and he walked to the emperor's chair and stood before Nero. The emperor did not even glance at him as the charges were read, but when he heard they had been brought by Jews he sneered, for Jews had been held in suspicion since Claudius had banished them from Italy.

The court officer read a letter from Festus which had accompanied Paul. The Roman proconsul was generous in his praise of the prisoner, explaining that he had thought the man innocent but had to send him to Rome because Paul had appealed to Caesar.

Then for the first time, Nero looked at Paul. The emperor's light blue eyes gazed deeply into the dark, intense eyes of the apostle.

"Are you one of those—what do you call them—Christians?"

Paul's voice was loud and clear. "I am," he stated proudly.

Still Nero's eyes were locked with Paul's. For the emperor, it was as though he was looking into the very depths of eternity. For a full minute Nero could neither move his eyes nor speak. He tried to force his wrist to move, to turn his hand with the thumb downward as a sign of the verdict of death. But Nero could not move his hand. Beads of perspiration broke out on his forehead and he felt a chill run down his spine.

Then, finally, he broke away from Paul's eyes. Arising quickly, he threw his cloak around himself and strode from the marble hall.

"Release this man," he told the court officer. "I shall hear no more cases today."

Paul heard the sound of the guard unlocking the chains, and they fell, clanking, to the stones of the floor. He sighed deeply. He was free at last. Free to carry on the work of the Lord! Free! Free! Free at last!

— Chapter Nineteen —

"You must get out of Italy," Luke told him. "Nero could change his mind at any moment."

Paul sat in his chair and thought. "I have felt the Holy Spirit calling me to Spain," he replied. "I have done here what I could. We shall go to Spain."

And to Spain they went, although the stay there was to be very brief. Then Paul and Luke took ship back to where the ministry had started, the churches in Asia which needed all the encouragement they could get in order to survive the ordeal that was certain to come.

News of Paul's release arrived in Philippi and Lydia was ecstatic. "Are you sure?" she asked. "He is really free? And he is in Ephesus and plans to come here soon?"

Clement laughed. "Yes, I am sure. The messenger arrived just an hour ago. Paul is free and will come to Philippi soon. Now calm down, Lydia. He won't be here for at least a month."

Lydia threw her arms about the older man. She buried her head in his strong shoulder and cried softly. "Oh, Clement. How I long to see him! I can't wait another month. I just can't wait!"

"Of course you can," Clement consoled her. His big hand stroked her hair. "It has been years now, Lydia. You can wait another month. Now that you know he is free and safe, another month will pass quickly."

"I hope so. I must go and tell Marcellus. Will you arrange a carriage for me? I must tell him the good news."

Lydia changed her dress and hurried to the waiting carriage. She urged the driver to greater speed as they went up the hill and onto the stone-paved Egnation Way into the city of Philippi. At the entrance to Marcellus's house Lydia jumped down from the carriage and rushed to the door. Soon she stood before the tribune, her face shining with happiness as she excitedly gave him the news of Paul's release.

Then her eyes saw the look on Marcellus's face. "What's the matter? You don't seem to share my joy."

He took her hand in his, his face grave. "It's not that, Lydia. I'm glad to hear of Paul's release. But today I received another piece of news. Rome has burned, almost all of it completely to the ground. And Lydia, they are blaming it on the Christians!"

And indeed Rome had burned, almost all of it destroyed. This city had grown from a small town to a population center teeming with over two million inhabitants. To house many of them the city had grown not only outward but upward. Wooden second and third stories had been added to original first-floor structures, some of these jutting out across the narrow streets making the thoroughfares almost tunnels with the wooden upper levels of the buildings nearly touching as they leaned across the streets.

Many of Rome's public buildings had been constructed of marble, but every roof was fashioned of wood. The huge amphitheaters contained seats made of wood, as did the theaters and coliseums. Rome was a tinder box, a huge unlit bonfire, ready for a spark to ignite it.

On the night of July 18, A.D. 64, the spark was struck. The fire started in the dry wooden bleachers of the Circus Maximus, and in minutes the entire structure was engulfed in flame. Then the fire jumped from the blazing arena to the houses nearby.

Augustus Caesar had foreseen the danger that fire presented to Rome, and during his reign he had divided the city into fourteen wards and 250 precincts, each with a contingent of the city's seven cohorts of professional firemen to protect it. When the blaze started in the Circus Maximus, these firemen responded but were unable to contain the fire, which seemed to explode about them.

In a short time, as the fire quickly spread, the streets were jammed with people racing to escape the inferno and preventing additional firemen from other districts from reaching the scene.

The fire produced a whirlwind of superheated air, roaring about it like a cyclone, throwing pieces of burning debris in an ever widening circle and starting new fires wherever they struck. Soon almost all of the city was ablaze.

Nero had been away when the fire broke out, visiting his country estate. When the sky suddenly was illuminated by the bright red glow, he knew immediately what was happening. Nero rushed to Rome in his carriage, but it was impossible to get through the tidal wave of people, wagons, carts and horses of those fleeing the holocaust. Realizing it was hopeless to try to enter the city, he returned to his estate.

The fire raged for eight days before it burned itself out. In that time it had destroyed two-thirds of Rome. Of the city's fourteen wards, ten were in ashes. Gone were the magnificent buildings, the theaters, arenas, baths, libraries, shops, streets of beautiful colonnades, the marketplaces. Gone also were the homes of most of Rome's two million inhabitants, all that they owned consumed by the fire's monstrous appetite.

A tragedy of this magnitude needed a scapegoat. At first a

rumor spread that it had been Nero, himself, who had started the fire. The people were furious, frustrated, needing something or someone on which to vent their fury. Nero could not let that someone be himself. He supplied a scapegoat. The Christians, Nero claimed, had started the fire.

A month later Paul and Luke arrived by ship at Ephesus. His plans were first to visit the church at Colossae and then to return to Ephesus for a prolonged stay. But waiting for him at Ephesus was Timothy with horrifying news.

"Come with me," Timothy told him. "You must talk with a man who has just returned from Rome. They are killing every Christian they can find. Men, women and children. You must hear this man for yourself."

They went with Timothy at once. The man told them what was happening at Rome, and Paul's face grew ashen with horror. "Nero has ordered the death of every Christian. They are being rounded up like sheep for slaughter, all of them. Men and women, children, infants, all are being taken to the arenas to be massacred by gladiators for the amusement of the crowds. Some are taken to the palace and Nero has them smeared with pitch. Then they are lit to serve as torches to light his estate at night."

The man was sobbing now as he continued. "As many of us as possible have escaped into the countryside. Some have found sanctuary in the catacombs of the burial yards. A few, such as myself, have managed to get to a port and leave the country by ship. We had to bribe the captain to take us in. It cost me all I had but at least I am alive."

He broke down completely now, burying his head in his hands as he sobbed. "My family! My parents did not get away! They were caught up in the holocaust and killed by Nero's soldiers in the street. What is to become of us? We have nowhere to hide! They will wipe us off the face of the earth!"

Paul took the man by the shoulder and shook him. "Now listen to me! No man can lay a hand upon you if it is contrary to the will of God! I want you to travel to the church at Philadelphia and warn them of the coming persecution. Tell them what is happening in Rome, but also tell them not to fear. God will protect them from this evil. But if they are destined to die, let it be with the name of Jesus on their lips."

The man drew himself together and looked into Paul's eyes. "I shall do as you say." He left them and prepared to travel to the church at Philadelphia, inland from Ephesus. Paul, Luke and Timothy took the road to Colossae.

"Oh, Lord," Paul prayed, "give me the strength to finish my work. There is so little time left in which to accomplish it."

"But, Lydia," Marcellus pleaded, "it would be easier for me to protect you if you were my wife."

She took his hand in her own. "You still don't understand. Now it is even more impossible for me to marry you than before. I would certainly not place you in jeopardy for my beliefs. And you can't realize, Marcellus, that it really doesn't matter what happens to me? It is my soul that's important, not by body. Caesar may destroy my body but he cannot touch my soul."

"Stop talking nonsense, Lydia! Your life's in danger! As are those of Euodia and Clement, and Epaphroditus and his whole family. Soon the order will come, then the soldiers. But if you were my wife, they would not dare to harm you, or the others of your family. Can't you see that?"

"I understand what you are saying and I appreciate your concern, but it doesn't matter. It really doesn't. Jesus has overcome death, not only for himself, but for all who believe in

Him. I wish I could make you understand, and change your mind so that you could share the rewards of heaven with us."

He shook his head. "No, I don't understand. I don't understand you at all. But I will do what I can when the time comes to protect you."

Paul had boarded the ship at Ephesus and it now stood at the dock in Troas. He was impatient to be at sea again, anxious to get to Philippi. He must prepare the church there for what was certain to come. Timothy had been left at Ephesus while he and Luke had gone on to visit the churches in Europe.

Paul had stopped briefly at the home of Carpas, where the church of Troas met. He had warned them to stay as quiet and inconspicuous as possible until the wrath of the Romans had been spent and it was again safe to openly preach the message of Jesus.

Now the captain gave the order and the boat was rowed out from the quay into the current. The sails were raised and they were underway, bound for Neapolis. Paul's thoughts returned to Timothy and he remembered many things he had meant to say to him, to warn him of. He must write a letter to Timothy, he resolved, as soon as he reached Philippi.

The order had gone out from Rome to the captains of the provinces. On Nero's order, the leaders of the sect that called themselves Christians were to be arrested as enemies of Caesar. No trials were necessary for them. They were to be executed. A list of names of known Christian leaders was attached. At the top of the list was the name of Paul of Tarsus.

The road down the hill was wonderfully familiar as Paul and Luke trudged out of Philippi toward the house on the river.

They had gotten almost to the door before anyone saw them coming.

"Praise God!" exclaimed Euodia. "It's Paul and Luke!"

Epaphroditus heard his mother's shout from the back of the house at the dyeing vats. He hurried to wipe his hands, stained yellow from the dye, and ran to them. "Paul! Paul!" he cried with joy.

Lydia heard them from inside the house where she and Clement had been going over the business accounts. She felt a sensation of mixed emotions sweep over her, a feeling of both exquisite happiness, but at the same time a terrible feeling of impending disaster.

Clement rushed immediately from the room and threw his big arms about them. But Lydia had remained seated at her desk, her heart pounding, almost afraid to move, not daring to look at him or to be seen by him. She heard the shouts and the laughter from the outside as she sat, then finally she brushed back her hair and stood up. She straightened her dress and walked to the doorway.

From the door she could see him, and his appearance startled her. His face was now deeply lined, the once thick reddish-brown hair now almost pure white. The stocky, strong frame was now thin and stooped. He raised his eyes to meet hers, and she saw that the eyes had remained the same—dark, deep, burning with an inward fire.

Her fear was instantly gone and she ran toward him. In a second she was in his arms, her head buried in his chest.

"Oh, Paul!" she cried softly. "Oh, Paul! Welcome home!"

It was now too dangerous for the Christians to meet in Lydia's house. They assembled where the Jews used to meet, down at the bank of the river, under the stars and the trees. As they came together there on this night, Paul spoke to them.

"My brothers and sisters in Christ Jesus," he said, "I stand before you not in defeat but in victory. We cannot be defeated by men, not when we are the family of God.

"Though they take our lives, they cannot take our souls. Though they kill our bodies, they cannot kill our spirits. Remain steadfast in the faith, firm in the knowledge that we belong to Christ who has overcome death on the cross. To live is to suffer, but to die for the name of our Lord is to gain all things.

"Yet you must remain alive to carry on the work that the Holy Spirit has begun, to continue to bring the words of life to those who have not heard of the sacrifice our Savior made for all men. And so I urge you to hide yourselves from the swords of the enemy, to flee before the spears of Caesar and the arrows of the soldiers.

"Live and continue the good fight until our Lord comes again in power and glory to judge those who oppress His people."

Paul took a loaf of bread and broke it into pieces, passing them among the men and women who stood in the darkness of the grove of trees beside the river.

"Jesus, on the night He was betrayed, took bread and blessed it and broke it. He told His disciples, 'This is my body, broken for you. Take and eat it in remembrance of me.' "

Paul held up a cup. "Then after supper He took the cup and blessed it and said, 'This is my blood which is shed for many. Whenever you drink it, do it in remembrance of me.' "

Paul passed the cup and each sipped it and passed it on. And each person there felt within his heart that something very special was happening, something very deep and mysterious. And each one sensed the great responsibility Paul was passing into their hands. They must keep alive the church of Jesus Christ no matter what happened, no matter what befell them. The work must go on, the church must survive, the truth must be passed on.

And they must take the gospel, the good news, of Jesus Christ to the uttermost parts of the world.

Paul stood in silence for a few moments after they had finished, praying that each one present would face the future, no matter what that future might be, with the strength only the Lord could provide.

Then he told them, "I must go. There are others I must minister to for the last time. Pray for me, as I will pray for you. And the grace and peace of our Lord Jesus be with you, now and forevermore."

Slowly, silently, they left the river bank and returned to their homes in the darkness. Paul, Luke, Clement and Lydia stood together by the river until all had gone. Then a voice came out of the darkness.

"Paul! Paul of Tarsus!" Lydia recognized Marcellus's voice.

"I am here," Paul answered.

"You must go quickly. Soldiers are on their way here even now to arrest you. Over there by the trees are two horses tied. You and Luke must go now, quickly."

They had found the horses where Marcellus told them they would be. Quickly they moved through the trees and out onto the Egnation Way on the road to Thessalonica. "Someone must have seen us come to Philippi," Paul said, as they crossed the stone bridge over the Gangites.

"I thought there was one man who looked hard at you when we got off the ship at Neapolis," Luke replied.

They made certain that they entered Thessalonica under cover of darkness and made their way to Jason's house on foot, leaving the horses in a thicket on the outskirts of the city. But when they stood before the house they realized that they were still in great danger. The gate into the courtyard had been smashed and the windows of the house broken out. The courtyard was covered with debris that had been torn from the interior of the once-splendid home—furniture, dishes, shattered vases and draperies torn to shreds.

A man passed as they stood looking, and Paul spoke to him. "Friend, what has happened here? Does not Jason, the merchant still live here?"

The man shook his head and frowned. "No. He was an enemy of Caesar, curse his soul. He and his whole household were executed more than a week ago. They were members of that band called Christians."

The man went his way and Paul and Luke looked at each other in shock and sadness. So the persecution had reached as far as Thessalonica! But did some of the church escape? Did they still remain?

The answer was not long in coming. From the bushes near the house came a low voice. "Is that you, Paul?"

Paul walked toward the sound of the voice. "No. Do not come here! We may be watched. But tonight go to the abandoned mill beside the creek on the western side of the city. Those of us who are left meet there."

They went to the mill, expecting to find only a handful of survivors. But more than a score of people awaited them. "There are still more of us," they told Paul. "But many are afraid to come. At least a dozen were killed with Jason by the Roman soldiers. They are still looking for the rest of us."

"God bless you all for coming," Paul told them. "The peace of our Lord Jesus be with you and protect you."

"You are not safe here," a man said, and Paul recognized the voice that had spoken to him from the bushes at Jason's house. "You especially are wanted by the Romans. There is even a price on your head."

Paul smiled but there was little warmth in it. "Brother," he said, "neither you nor I shall die a moment sooner than the will of God allows. Yet I know my own time is very short. Now listen to me and tell the others what I say."

Paul proceeded to tell them what he had told the faithful at Philippi. He also broke bread and served the men and women of Thessalonica Communion with bread and wine. "Now I must go," he told them, "not because I am afraid of Nero's soldiers, but because I must finish my work. You will not see me again in this life, but remember what I have told you. And be of good cheer, for I do not leave you alone. The Holy Spirit will always be with you, even unto death."

A month later Paul and Luke reached Corinth, after visiting the other churches in Europe. They had stayed only briefly at each, giving the members instructions on how to deal with the persecution they were now facing daily. And after he had ministered to the congregation at Corinth, Paul turned to Luke. "I did not have time to go further west in Greece. Now, although I know my time is running out, I want to preach at Nicopolis."

Luke nodded his head, for it would be useless to argue with him. The aging apostle would do what he wanted anyway. And perhaps it would even be safer in Nicopolis where he had never been before. At least the chance of his being recognized would be less there.

A few days later they boarded a ship in the harbor of Corinth. Up the western coast of Greece they sailed. The weather had improved and the balmy air seemed to give Paul a restored vigor. As they passed the mouth of a bay, Paul pointed and asked him, "Do you know what happened there, Luke? A very important event happened in the Bay of Ambracia."

Luke smiled. "That's where Augustus, when he was still

Octavian, destroyed the Egyptian fleet of Antony and Cleopatra."

Paul made a face. "I can never ask you a question concerning history, but you have the answer at your fingertips! You are correct, as usual."

They entered the harbor of Nicopolis and took their bags ashore. As they walked up the quay a Roman officer stared at them. I know that man from somewhere, he thought. His face is very familiar.

And as Paul and Luke secured rooms at a nearby inn, the Roman followed, trying to place in his mind who the elderly man was and upset with himself that he could not remember.

When they had gone to their rooms, he approached the innkeeper.

"Those men," he asked, "who were they?"

The innkeeper consulted his records. "One is named Luke," he told the officer. "He is a physician. The other is named Paul. I don't know what he does."

The Roman's eyes lit up. "Paul? Of course! Paul of Tarsus!"

His hand went to his mouth and his heart raced. Paul of Tarsus! What a catch! Here was the most wanted man in the empire. What a stroke of luck! This could make his career. He would arrest Paul of Tarsus and send him gift wrapped to Nero in Rome. Caesar would certainly reward him greatly for this.

Early the next morning Paul and Luke left the inn. They walked through the streets, Paul looking for a place to preach to the passersby. When they entered the public square and he saw a crowd of people, Paul knew he had found the place. He went to a low stone wall and climbed on top of it.

"Men of Nicopolis," he began. "Listen to me! God, the Father of all men, has provided a means through which your sins may be forgiven and you may attain the reward of eternal life and salvation."

The men who idled in the public square were used to orations, and many of them looked up at Paul as he stood on the low stone wall, curious as to what this particular man could tell them that they had not heard before.

"God so loved the world that He had created that He sent His own Son into the world to teach men how to live."

A number of the men's interest had been aroused. They were intrigued with Paul's message of this God who had a Son on earth. A few even walked closer so that they could hear more clearly what Paul was saying.

"Now this man God sent was the only begotten Son of the Father, and He was taken by men who preferred darkness rather than light, and they crucified Him and He was buried. But on the third day in the grave, God raised Him up from the dead and He was seen by many."

At this some of the men laughed. "A dead man came back to life?" one man taunted. "Is this God of yours the father of ghosts?"

From the sides of the square came Roman soldiers who quickly surrounded Paul. The Roman officer faced him. "Tell me, are you Paul from the city of Tarsus? Are you the leader of the Christians?"

For a moment Paul stared at the officer. He knew his time had come, that he would no longer be able to preach the Word of the risen Lord. His eyes transfixed the Roman as he answered.

"I am Paul of Tarsus, a servant of Jesus Christ, the Son of God."

The officer motioned to the soldiers. "Seize him," he ordered. A soldier grabbed Paul by the arm, another forced his hands behind his back, locking the iron shackles on his wrists.

Luke had rushed to Paul's side. One of the soldiers looked at the doctor. "What about this man?" he asked the officer.

The Roman looked briefly at Luke. "I do not know him," he

said. "We have the man we want. Don't bother with the other one."

Paul was forced down the street between the soldiers while Luke followed a short distance behind, unwilling to let Paul out of his sight.

Several of the men jeered as Paul was led off. "Perhaps your God of ghosts will save you!" one man shouted as the crowd roared with laughter.

Several weeks later Paul was cast into a fetid cell in the prison at Rome. He had been brought by ship from Nicopolis, guarded by three soldiers and chained hand and foot. Along with Paul came a letter from the Roman officer addressed to Nero himself.

Luke had followed on the next ship and had found Paul in the cell beneath the ground with only a small iron grate in the ceiling for light and air. Luke had also found one of Paul's disciples, a young man named Tychicus.

"Bring me writing materials," Paul requested of Luke. "I must write a letter to Timothy at Ephesus. Tychicus shall bear it there for me."

When the writing materials had been brought, Paul dictated his last letter. "To Timothy, my beloved son . . . ."

He strove to include in this, his last letter, all the things Timothy should know in guiding the church at Ephesus. But there was a longing in Paul's heart to see Timothy again, for what he knew would be the last time. And there were things Paul desired to have with him in Rome, for he did not know how long he would wait upon Nero to hear his case again, for Paul had once more appealed to Caesar.

"Only Luke is with me now," Paul wrote. "Take Mark and bring him with you. The cloak I left at Troas with Carpus, bring this also, and the books, and especially the parchments."

He warned Timothy about the man who hated him and could also be a danger to Timothy. The letter ended with a salutation to his friends and co-workers at the church at Ephesus, especially Aquila and Priscilla and his dear friends of the Onesiphorus family.

He asked Timothy to make every attempt to get to Rome before winter set in. Tychicus left with the letter to journey to Ephesus. Now only Luke remained to visit Paul in the dank and filthy cell. But this did not last for long. A few days later Luke came to the prison as usual to see the apostle and found the cell empty.

"Where have you taken him?" he demanded of the jailer.

"Soldiers came this morning for him. He is being executed."

"But he has not had a hearing before Nero!" Luke protested.

"Nero did not want to see him. He condemned him to death."

Early in the morning they had taken Paul from the cell. The soldiers marched him out of the jail and down the avenues of Rome and out of the city limits. Here was where Roman citizens were executed. Prisoners condemned to death who were not Roman citizens were crucified, but citizens were beheaded, a quicker and more merciful death.

Paul was forced to kneel before the block and his head was placed in the groove, worn smooth by many other heads. A soldier raised his sword.

"Lord Jesus," Paul prayed, "receive my soul—"

The sword flashed in the morning light. The next instant Paul was standing before Jesus.

— Chapter Twenty —

When Luke got there the executions were all over. He found Paul's body lying with the other Roman citizens who had been beheaded that morning. He and two other courageous Christians carried it to a grove of trees and buried his remains there in a spot that could be found later.

"Now you had better go," Luke advised the two men. "Get out of Rome if you can. Hide until this blood bath is over. But keep the faith and encourage others to do likewise."

After they had left, Luke began the long trek to the coast, hoping to find a ship leaving Italy. He felt he must take the word of Paul's death to the churches of Europe and Asia Minor, perhaps even get news to the mother church in Jerusalem. With sadness in his heart and his eyes brimming with tears, Luke started out, first to Ephesus, for that is where the ship took him.

Timothy was just about to leave for Troas to get the things Paul had asked for when Luke arrived. Luke spoke to the congregation, describing Paul's death and giving them the apostle's last words to them. He talked with Aquila and Priscilla, Tychicus and the others. It was hard for them to accept the fact of his death. But now they must remember everything he had told them, to hold onto the simple truths of the risen Christ and to continue to spread the word of the Kingdom of God among all the nations of the earth.

A day later Luke left Ephesus, bound for Philippi.

The ship stopped briefly at Troas and Luke sat in Carpus's house. The old man held Paul's cloak tightly as he wept.

"His last words to the churches were to prepare for a time of great tribulation," Luke told him. "Do not lose that which Paul has given to you. It is up to all of us to continue the work he died for."

Carpus looked at Luke through tear-stained eyes. "Yes," he agreed, "we must, all of us, finish the work Paul began. This will be his monument, the marker of his grave. The work must continue."

PHILIPPI, SPRING, A.D. 65

Luke sat among Lydia's household as he told them of Paul's death. "And Peter is also gone," he said. "Some say he was killed on the same day as Paul was. I know he was in Rome and that is where it happened. Few of the original apostles are left now. The burden of the work now rests on our shoulders, those of us who are yet alive."

Lydia stared straight ahead. She did not cry, for no tears would come. She was conscious of the pain in her heart, the terrible empty feeling inside. Never to see his face again! Never to hear his voice, to touch his hand. She wanted to cry, to scream, to vent the anguish she felt inside, but she could not.

Clement said to Luke, "What worries me is that those who knew the Lord are going fast. Those who actually saw Him, heard Him, knew Him during His ministry. What will happen when they are all gone? Someone should write down what actually happened, someone who really knows. This should all be put into writing so that those who come after us may know."

"This has concerned me also," Luke replied. "I understand that Mark has already written down what he knows. Perhaps some of the others have, as well. And I have committed to parchment what happened after the Lord was taken up into heaven, the works, the acts of the apostles of Jesus Christ. I have finished it up to the point where Paul was in prison in Rome, awaiting a hearing before Nero. Now I must write the portion to cover his death. Someday I shall."

"I should like to read this," said Clement.

"And I as well, " Epaphroditus added.

Luke went to his traveling bag and brought out two scrolls. "Here they are. I shall leave them with you until I return. Tomorrow I must go to Thessalonica, then on to Berea, Athens and Corinth. I want to visit all of the churches. I think Paul would have wanted me to do this."

Clement unrolled one of the parchment scrolls and read the beginning. "Forasmuch as many have taken in hand to set forth a declaration of those things which are most surely believed among us, even as they delivered unto us which from the beginning were eyewitnesses, and ministers of the word; it seemed good to me also, having had perfect understanding of all things from the very first, to write unto you, in order, most excellent Theophilus, that you might know the certainty of those things wherein you have been instructed."

Clement looked up. "Who is Theophilus?"

Luke smiled. "He is a man in which I have great hope. His family is high in the Roman order. He heard Paul speak in Rome and desired to know more of Jesus. And on hearing, he believed. And so within Caesar's very household are those who call our Lord their Lord, and consider us their brothers in Christ."

Clement nodded. "There will come a day when the whole world will acknowledge Christ as Lord and Savior. The seeds are being planted and the Lord, himself, through the Holy Spirit, will water them and tend them until the harvest is made."

Luke handed him the other scroll. "And this is a copy of the letter I sent to Theophilus. It contains the essentials of the life and death of the Lord. Take care of it, Clement. I have no other copy. I shall get both of these from you when I return. Farewell, my friends."

On Nero's order the persecution was extended throughout the empire. Orders were sent to the governor of each province to appoint a trusted man who would carry out the eradication of the sect called Christians.

The governor of Macedonia received his order and pondered the question of whom he would appoint. He must be very careful in the appointment, for the man would have extraordinary power. In the hands of the wrong man, a vengeful and malicious man, many innocent people could lose their lives. He must find a man above reproach in his personal life and entirely loyal to Rome. Then to the governor's mind came the name of just such a man. Lucius Marcellus was the man he would appoint to carry out the emperor's orders.

He read them over again. "You are to arrest any person accused of being a member of the sect called Christians and have him stand trial before a suitable magistrate. Any person who refuses to sacrifice to Roman gods will be put to death."

Marcellus was surprised when the governor sent for him to come to Thessalonica right away. He had no idea what the Roman proconsul wanted but he had to obey. With a squad of soldiers he set off for the provincial capital, and the governor wasted no time in seeing him when he arrived.

"Ah, tribune, come in," the governor greeted him. Marcellus always wondered whether the governor was always so glad to see him or whether the fact that Marcellus came from a very prominent and rich Roman family flavored the welcome.

"Excellency. It is good to see you as well."

Present in the governor's reception room was also a Roman captain, and the governor indicated this man as he introduced the tribune.

"Marcellus, this is Captain Gallus. He will be your aide in the mission you have been assigned."

"Mission? I do not understand, Excellency!"

The proconsul smiled. "But of course, you have not yet heard. The emperor has ordered that I select one man in the province for a special and most important duty. I have selected you, Marcellus."

"I am honored, Excellency. What is this special duty?"

The governor reclined on a couch and indicated that Marcellus do the same. He offered the tribune a goblet of wine, which Marcellus accepted hesitantly. "As you know, there exist within the empire some radical and dangerous groups. These groups are dedicated to the overthrow of the existing government, enemies of the emperor."

"I know of no such group powerful enough to threaten Rome."

"Then let me enlighten you, Marcellus. But I agree with you, privately of course. There are no groups powerful enough to threaten the might of Rome. But it is sufficient that they exist in the emperor's mind, my boy. And if he deems them enemies of the state, then they are our enemies as well as his. Do you understand," the governor winked.

"I understand. The emperor must be obeyed. It is our sworn duty."

The governor got to his feet. "I knew you would. I knew I could count on you."

"And what is this group, sir, which has become my enemy by decree of Caesar?"

The proconsul smiled at him. "Well put, Marcellus." He turned his back and examined a tapestry. "Have you ever heard of a particular religious sect called Christians?"

Marcellus choked on the wine. He wiped his mouth and coughed. "Christians? Why—why, yes. I—I believe I have heard the name."

They are your enemies, Marcellus, as you so aptly put it, by decree of Caesar. And Nero has ordered them wiped from the face of the earth. And in Macedonia, Marcellus, it will be your assignment to see that this is done."

He sat in his magnificently appointed room in the palace at Thessalonica with his head in his hands. His mind raced. What was he to do? At first he considered going back to the governor and refusing the assignment. But what reason would he give? How could he do this and not implicate Lydia and the others—and himself, as well? He was trapped.

Lydia! Oh, Lydia, how am I going to make you understand? I can't help this situation. I had no choice.

For an instant he summoned enough courage to go and tell the governor he refused this mission, that he could not carry the assignment out. But thoughts of the consequences of this action came swirling into his mind, and he again held his head in his hands and anguished over it.

No! He could not refuse. His mind pictured his daughter. Tia was now married to a man from a fine Roman family, a distinguished family. She was expecting a child, his first grandchild. To refuse would bring down disgrace upon all of them. He would be branded a Christian sympathizer, worse perhaps. Maybe he would be accused of being one of the sect himself. No, a refusal would bring destruction upon his whole family.

Then the thought came to his tortured mind that perhaps it was for the best that he was the man chosen. He would certainly be fair. Perhaps he could even shield some of them, many of them, from the wrath of Rome. He would find a way, some way, to help them. At least he could save Lydia and her family. As far as he knew, the governor did not even suspect that a group of Christians existed in Philippi.

With the problem rationalized in his mind, he breathed easier. But still within his heart was an ache that would not go away.

Flavius Gallus was an ambitious man. He had worked hard to achieve his present rank of captain and was very anxious to impress his superiors of his worth to gain another promotion. He knocked on the tribune's door and saluted smartly when Marcellus opened it.

"Hail, Excellency. I await your orders."

"Oh, yes. Orders. Frankly, captain, this assignment has taken me unaware. I have had no time to make plans as yet."

"Then may I be so bold as to suggest an initial course of action, sir. There are known Christians in this city. Do I have your permission to arrest them? I am sure they will implicate others, with the proper persuasion, of course."

Marcellus glared at the man. To fail to act would lead to suspicion. "Very well, captain. Arrest the known Christians. But there will be no torture. We are Romans, not barbarians!"

The captain smiled as he saluted. "Of course, sir. As you ordered, sir." He left and Marcellus poured some wine from a decanter.

It has begun, he thought. There is no turning back now. The die is cast.

He drained the goblet and poured another. Perhaps the wine would ease the persistent pain in his chest. At least he hoped it would.

Luke had arrived the day before and found the leader of the church at Thessalonica. He was anxious to speak to the members, to warn them of the coming persecution and to give them Paul's last instructions. Quickly the word was passed among the Christians. They were to meet at the abandoned mill after dark on the following evening.

Captain Gallus had wasted no time. His soldiers struck quickly at the homes of those known to belong to the outlawed Christian sect. At one such home Gallus led the arrest himself, breaking in the door and taking the occupants by surprise.

"Are you part of the Christian conspiracy?" he demanded.

"I know of no conspiracy," the man replied.

"Do you deny you are Christians?"

The man looked at his wife. "I—I cannot deny Christ," he answered.

Gallus looked at the child, clinging to his mother's skirts. He reached down and seized the child by the arm and drew his sword, placing the blade firmly against the toddler's neck. "Tell me," he demanded, "who else belongs to this sect?"

The man wrenched forward but he was forcibly restrained by the soldiers. "Leave my son alone," he cried. "He knows nothing!"

"But you do. Tell me quickly or he dies."

The man strained against the grasp of the soldiers. "You beast! Leave him alone!"

The child's mother screamed. "Don't kill my son! Please don't harm him!"

"Then you tell me, woman. Who are they and where are they to be found? You have until I count to three or your son will die before your eyes."

"No!" the man shouted. "Don't tell him anything! We can't betray our brothers and sisters in the Lord!"

Gallus began to count. "One . . . two—"

"Stop! I'll tell you!" the woman screamed. "I'll tell you whatever you want to know!"

Gallus had returned to the tribune's room to inform him of the arrest of several families of Christians and the information he had obtained concerning where the rest of them would be gathering that evening. He would not tell him, however, how that information had been forced from the mother of one of the children by threat of his death.

He knocked on the tribune's door with no answer. When he tried the door he found it unlocked and quietly entered. There, in a deep sleep, was the tribune, an empty wine bottle beside him. Gallus sneered in contempt. "Decadent Roman aristocracy," he said to himself. He left the tribune in his drunken stupor and resolved to carry out his plan without the consent of his superior.

Later that night, when Gallus was certain the Christians had assembled at the old mill, he led his soldiers quietly through the woods and dispersed them around the ramshakled structure. From within he could hear the sound of muffled voices and estimated there were at least a hundred people inside.

He raised his hand to signal his men, and the soldiers with the battering ram ran toward the bolted door of the mill.

Luke had just finished telling the congregation the events of Paul's death and his last instruction to the churches. "Be of good cheer," he told them. "You must preserve the Word of our Lord and take the good news of salvation to all men everywhere."

The crack of bursting timbers came as a sudden sound of thunder to the startled people in the mill. As the door gave way, soldiers poured into the room.

Gallus, sword drawn, faced them. "Under order of the emperor, you are all under arrest!"

The banging at the door was loud and insistent. Lydia sat up in her bed, not certain whether she had been dreaming or it was real. Then she heard Clement stir and open the door, and she pulled her robe about herself and went to see who could be banging on the door at this hour.

"Dear God!" she heard Clement exclaim. "What has happened to you, man?"

In the dim light of the lamp she could see the figure of a man, holding onto Clement, about to collapse.

"Soldiers," the man gasped. "They burst in on us. Many were arrested. Only a few of us escaped."

"Where? Where did this happen?"

"Thessalonica. I was lucky to get away. I've been traveling three nights to get here to warn you. They are arresting all Christians. Nero's orders."

Lydia took hold of the man's arm. "Let's get him into bed. He's exhausted. I'll get him something to eat." They half carried the man to a bed and helped him lie down. Lydia went to get food. Then she heard Clement ask him, "Was Luke there? He was going to Thessalonica from here."

"Yes. He was speaking when they came."

"Was he taken prisoner?"

"I don't know. Probably. Only a few got away. I don't know if he was one of them."

Lydia brought a cup of wine and some food. "Here. Drink this. You must rest."

"Rest? I must flee. And you also. The soldiers may come here at any moment. I came to warn you."

"But first you must rest. Besides, we should be safe enough here. There are only a few Christians in Philippi. The Romans don't even know we exist."

As the man drifted into an exhausted sleep, Clement and Lydia exchanged glances. "How safe are we?" questioned Clement. "He may be right. We had better warn the others."

"All right," Lydia agreed. "But I am certain we are safe here. And with Marcellus as tribune of justice, he would not let anything happen to us."

Captain Gallus saluted the governor of Macedonia smartly. "Hail, Excellency."

The governor glanced at the man who was with the captain, wondering where he had seen him before. "Yes, Gallus? You said it was urgent that you speak with me."

"And so it is, sir. This man has information of great value. I thought you should hear it for yourself."

"And to what does this information pertain?"

"Christians, Excellency. This man has information about Christians in Philippi."

"Philippi! Then we should summon Tribune Marcellus. As he is a resident of Philippi, this should be of great interest to him."

"No, your Excellency. I do not think the tribune should hear this."

The governor frowned. "No? And why not?"

"This man, Vestus, claims that one of the leaders of the Christians in Philippi is a woman. She is the Tribune Marcellus's mistress."

Marcellus entered the barracks where the Roman soldiers under Captain Gallus were quartered. A sergeant saluted as he entered.

"Where is your captain?" inquired the tribune.

"He is not here, sir."

"And where is he then?"

"He rode off last night, sir, with a detachment of troops."

"And where was he going?"

"To Philippi, sir, to arrest the Christians there."

Marcellus, shaken and with trembling hands, left the barracks and went to the stables. He mounted his horse and spurred it on, forcing every ounce of energy from the animal as he sped northward on the Egnation Way toward Philippi. At last he reined up, fearing his mount would collapse from the tremendous exertion he had demanded of her. In his mind was but one thought. Lydia! He must warn her before it was too late!

Impatiently he rested his horse, and when he thought she could again ride, he flung himself into the saddle and urged her on again. "Lydia! Lydia!" he cried. "Nothing must happen to Lydia!"

Vestus led Gallus and the soldiers to the house on the river. "Are you certain this is the right place?" the captain asked.

"I am positive. Look! There are the vats behind the house. I told you she was a dyer of cloth."

As they watched from the hill overlooking the house, a man emerged and went around to the rear with the vats and began to work. "Quietly now," cautioned Gallus to his men. "You, there. Sergeant, take a squad to the back. Stay hidden in the trees until I give you the signal. We want none of them to escape."

When the men were in position, Gallus and another squad approached from the front. They had almost reached the door when a woman came out. She saw the soldiers and screamed.

"Lydia! Clement! Run! Soldiers are here!"

One of the Roman soldiers rushed at her. Euodia screamed again and beat at him with her fists. "Let me go! Lydia, run for your life!"

The soldiers' sword thrust forward and Euodia grunted in pain as the blade went through her. "Oh, God!" she moaned, "Dear Jesus! Dear Je—"

Clement had heard her cries and had run around from the rear of the house just in time to see his wife die. "Euodia!"

He threw himself at the soldier and another lowered his spear, impaling him as he ran forward. He slumped, dying, to the ground beside his wife.

"May . . . may God . . . forgive you . . . ." he managed to mutter with his last gasp of life, a widening pool of blood growing in the dirt around his still body.

Three soldiers entered the house. In a moment they came out with Lydia, her arms pinned behind her back, struggling with them. "What have you done?" she screamed at them. "You've killed them! You've killed them!"

Gallus looked at Vestus. "Is this the woman?"

Vestus walked closer to Lydia as she wrestled with the guards who held her. He put his face close to hers and asked, "Do you remember me?"

She saw his face through tear-filled eyes. "Yes! You were the one who burned my vats!"

He laughed. "You do remember! Good. Then you also should remember I swore to repay you for the trouble you caused me. Do you remember that?"

"Bring her along," Gallus ordered, "and search the house well. There may be more of them hiding inside."

The soldiers dragged Lydia up the hill and onto the road to Philippi. As she passed the bodies of Euodia and Clement, she thanked God that Epaphroditus, Syntyche and Paula had been away when the soldiers came.

Epaphroditus held the reins of the donkey that pulled the cart as he, Syntyche and their daughter walked along the road beside the river. They had gone to get a fresh supply of the white rock that was the secret ingredient used to dye the purple silk. Paula and Syntyche had been singing, the day warm and pleasant, and they had filled the cart with the white rocks from the hidden spot near the river. The rocks would be ground to powder to treat the silk and prepare it for the purple dye.

Epaphroditus smiled with pleasure as he looked at his wife and daughter, now almost fourteen and the image of her mother, with long, blonde hair and sparkling blue eyes and gentle disposition. The Lord had been good to him, thought Epaphroditus.

They turned the curve in the road, and the stone house came into view. But suddenly, out of the trees, came a voice. "Stop! Don't go any further."

"Who is there?" demanded Epaphroditus.

"Orcas," came the reply. "Quickly! Come into the trees with me. Get the cart out of sight. Soldiers have been to the house. They are arresting Christians everywhere."

He led the donkey quickly off the road and into the cover of the thick trees. "What has happened at the house?" he asked the woodcutter. "My mother, my father? What has happened to them?"

There were tears in Orcas's eyes as he told them. "Your mother and father are dead. Lydia, I don't know about. I think she was taken with them to Philippi under arrest. I am sorry, Papie! I am so sorry!"

Epaphroditus did not believe what he had heard. "My mother and father dead? That can't be true! Oh, God, don't let it be true!"

"It is true. And you must take your family away before you all are also arrested. We have taken the bodies of Euodia and Clement away and buried them. There is nothing more you can do here. Take Syntyche and Paula and do as I say."

"But where can we go?"

"Go back down the river road the way you have come. Do you know the trail that leads into the mountains?"

"Yes. I know the one."

"Take that trail. Follow it until you reach a wide creek. Follow the creek into the mountains. We have seen the possibility of just such a thing as this. There is a camp already stocked with food. Others have already gone there. We shall hide in the mountains were the Romans cannot find us. The forest will provide all we shall need until it is safe for us again."

Epaphroditus hesitated. "We shall do as you say. But there is something I must get from the house first. I hope the Romans have not found them."

"Then make it quick," Orcas said. "They may be back at any time."

He ran quickly to the house. As he entered the door he saw the pool of blood, soaked into he ground now, and his fists tightened as he realized it was the blood of his parents. He went to his father's room and found what he had come for. "Thank God they are still here."

He clutched them tightly in his arms as he ran from the house toward the trees. He placed them in a leather bag which he strapped beneath his tunic. "We can go now," he said and led the donkey down the river road. He had also thought to bring heavy cloaks for them all, two sharp knives and an ax, remembering the winter he had spent at the gold mine.

"What was so important that you had to go back to the house?" Orcas asked him.

"Books," Epaphroditus told him. "Luke's books. I could not let anything happen to them."

They reached the trail off the river road, and the young man, his wife and daughter started up into the mountains. Strapped securely to Papie were the manuscripts of what the world would come to know as the Gospel of Luke and the Acts of the Apostles.

As Marcellus crossed the bridge on the Egnation Way he stopped first at the house by the river. He rode down the hill shouting. "Lydia! Lydia!"

He reined to a halt at the entrance and leaped from his horse, his eyes wide with horror as he saw the brown spots of blood in the earth before the door. Hurriedly he searched the house. Finding it deserted he leaped again into the saddle and spurred the mount up the hill toward the city.

"You there!" he shouted to a soldier in the square. "Where is Captain Gallus?"

"He is at the jail, sir, with the Christian prisoners."

Marcellus was off hurriedly, and a few moments later dismounted in front of the stone building that served as the jail.

"Gallus!" he shouted. "Come out here!"

A moment later the captain appeared. With him was Vestus. Marcellus recognized the man and glared at him, knowing instantly it had been Vestus who had led the soldiers to Lydia's house.

"Gallus," Marcellus demanded, "who gave the orders to come here? Why was I not informed of this?"

The captain made a mock salute. "But, sir, I was only obeying the orders of the emperor. And of the governor."

"The lady, Lydia," Marcellus demanded through clenched teeth, "is she here?"

Captain Gallus grinned at him. "She is here, sir, with the other Christian prisoners. They are to be taken to Neapolis and from there by ship to Rome, sir. To serve as sport against the gladiators in the arenas."

"Gallus, bring out the woman. I want to see her."

The captain nodded to a guard and Lydia was brought out of the building. "Marcellus," she cried, "they have killed Euodia and Clement!"

"Release her," the tribune ordered. "I will take custody of her."

Captain Gallus pursed his mouth, "I cannot do that, sir."

"Captain, that is an order! Obey it!"

The captain wiped his chin with the back of his hand. "I'm afraid I must refuse that order, sir. You see, the governor has given me strict orders to ship all the Christians directly to Rome. Now you wouldn't want me to disobey the governor, would you, sir?"

Marcellus strode forward. "I am countermanding that order, captain." He look Lydia by the hand. "She will come with me."

Captain Gallus stepped in front of the tribune. "But the lady will not deny she is a Christian, sir. Unless she does that, I can't release her."

"Lydia, tell him you are not a Christian!"

Her eyes met his. "I—I can't do that, Marcellus. I can't deny my Lord."

"Lydia, in the name of common sense, tell him you are not a Christian! Prove it by making a sacrifice to the gods of Rome. Or to Caesar. Lydia, don't you realize it means your life?"

She shook her head. "My life would not be worth living if I did that. I can't deny my Lord Jesus. Those who deny Him on earth, He will deny before the Father in heaven."

"Stop that dribble! Lydia, they will kill you!"

Her eyes were steady as she answered him. "They may kill my body, Marcellus, but they cannot kill my soul."

"But, Lydia!"

Gallus turned to the tribune. "You outrank me, sir. If you are willing to take complete responsibility, then I will release her into your custody."

"No!" shouted Vestus. "I won't let her get away! He will let her escape!" He seized a sword from the soldier next to him and ran toward Lydia. "I won't let her get away again!"

"Stop that man!" Marcellus shouted, lunging toward him. But he was an instant too late. The blade entered Lydia's chest just beneath her heart. Her eyes were wide as she moaned. "Marcellus! Marcell—" She slumped to the earth at the feet of the tribune.

He tried to catch her as she fell but managed only to cradle her head in his arms as she lay, still and unbreathing on the street.

"Lydia! No! You can't die, Lydia! You can't!" Her eyes were still open, locked with his in death. A low cry started from deep within him, gaining in pitch and volume as it issued from his throat. He looked up from her face into the crowd of men about him. From Vestus's face, Marcellus's eyes turned to Captain Gallus. There was almost a smirk on the Roman's countenance, a look denoting his thoughts, and Marcellus realized that this man, this petty little man, was typical of the officers of the army of Imperial Rome. To them killing was a way of life. A human being had no value, no worth at all. And suddenly his heart was filled with revulsion. Rome was a sickness, a terrible disease with which he had also been infected.

He held Lydia's inert body close and looked again into her glassy, staring eyes. And he could see through them into the terrifying void of his eternity.

Lydia opened her eyes. She was running through the soft, green grass. In the branches of the trees birds were singing and the breeze was cool on her face. Effortlessly she ran toward a stream of sparkling water. Her legs were not tired at all. In fact her whole body seemed young again, and fresh, and strong.

Then she was at the edge of the water and on the other side she could see someone standing, His arms outstretched to her, a man who seemed to shine with a brilliance and radiance from within. His face was so familiar, a face full of love and compassion. And next to him stood other familiar figures. There was Doronius. And there were Euodia and Clement. And standing next to them was Paul, his hair once again the reddish-brown she had known from the early years.

From across the water she heard the voice of her son. "Mother, come over to us."

Her feet splashed in the crystal water as she ran across the shallow stream. And as she ran she heard His voice, saying to her, "Well done, Lydia, good and faithful servant. Enter into your reward."

And the next instant she was enveloped in His loving arms.

THE END

MEADOWBROOK CHRISTIAN CHURCH
2741 Walton Blvd.
Rochester Hills, MI 48309